The SEA
PEOPLES

N. K. Sandars

The SEA PEOPLES

Warriors of the ancient Mediterranean 1250-1150 BC

WITH 140 ILLUSTRATIONS

Revised Edition

THAMES AND HUDSON

To Sheila and John Campbell,
who taught me to love the mountains of Greece
and to see a fragment of the Bronze Age living

THIS IS VOLUME EIGHTY-NINE IN THE SERIES
Ancient Peoples and Places
GENERAL EDITOR : GLYN DANIEL

Frontispiece
Around 1186 BC Pharaoh Ramesses III beat off an attack by a combined force of Sea Peoples and other northern enemies. There was a fierce naval battle, probably not far from the Nile Delta, and many of the enemy were killed, others enslaved, others settled in Palestine. An Egyptian boat (left) is seen successfully grappling one of the Sea Peoples' boats. Cf. 80 and 83.

First published in Great Britain in 1978
Revised paperback edition 1985
Reprinted 1987

Printed and bound in the German Democratic Republic

Contents

Preface to the revised edition

In archaeology there is no standing still, and in the last eight years much has happened in the East Mediterranean and the Aegean. There has been new work in Cyprus, in Sardinia, on the Greek mainland and in Israel. In Cyprus excavations under Dr Vassos Karageorghis at Maa-Palaeokastro and Pyla-Kokkinokremos have led to a reassessment of the last decades of Bronze Age Enkomi, along with the date and nature of the introduction of ashlar masonry (see chapter 6). New work on the late Hittite texts, and a lucky discovery from Ugarit, have given body to some of the confused events of the thirteenth and early twelfth centuries in western Anatolia, and provide a startling confirmation of the Egyptian account of the Sea Peoples (chapter 5). In Sardinia recent large finds of Mycenaean pottery reinforce the tenuous evidence of relations, apparently peaceful enough, between the nuragic people of that island and the Mycenaean east. Above all there has been a flood of information and interest in handmade pottery from late Mycenaean sites, the so-called 'barbarian wares'. Finds now occur from Euboea to Patras, Tiryns, Mycenae, Sparta (the Meneleion) and even in Crete, notably at Khania. The search for explanations has led some, with Dr Kilian, to Italy and the Adriatic, while Professor Wardle's work at Assiros in Macedonia, and that of Dr Th. Papadopoulos in Epirus has also looked to the Balkans. Here great problems remain, as they do at Troy. The history of excavation, and the chronological ordering of the material in Palestine, has received welcome treatment in Dr Trude Dothan's monograph on the Philistines, and the last volumes of Professor Schachermeyr's study of the early Aegean which have appeared recently are teeming with ideas. Many of these exciting developments can only be briefly indicated here and there in the text and notes. But on the whole they tend to amplify rather than alter the story told in these chapters, while all too many of the same problems still await a solution.

N. K. SANDARS, *March 1985*

Introduction

For modern Famagusta read ancient Enkomi and you have the setting for a vital part of this history. The subject, the Peoples of the Sea, is perhaps something of an odd man out among the Peoples and Places of this series. They are not a single people, nor did they inhabit *one* particular place; but they certainly are to be counted among peoples of the ancient world, and they did occupy certain distinct places. Time is less of a problem, for it is fixed within limits by Egyptian historical inscriptions. The places are also easily indicated as the East Mediterranean and adjoining lands, from Egypt in the south to the northern frontiers of Greece, with sympathetic tremors recognizable as far west as Sardinia and even Corsica. When, however, it comes to naming the *people*, we face an enormous question-mark.

It was the Egyptians who invented the Peoples of the Sea. If it were not for certain Egyptian texts of the 13th and 12th centuries BC* their existence might have been guessed at, but certainly never known by that name. Only five years after Merneptah's accession as Pharaoh in about 1224 he was faced by a major crisis: attack from the western desert by Libyans and their allies, 'northerners coming from all lands'. A generation after this, about 1186, when Ramesses III was Pharaoh, the events took place which now go by the name of 'the Great Sea and Land Raids'. Again it is the Egyptian monuments – the 13th- and 12th-century inscriptions and carvings at Karnak and Luxor – that are the sources for our knowledge.

*All dates given in this book are BC unless otherwise indicated

1 After the defeat of the Sea Peoples in a naval battle around 1186, prisoners were presented to Pharaoh Ramesses III. They were branded on the shoulder, listed and enrolled in gangs for forced labour. Manacled prisoners wearing their distinctive headdress and led by an Egyptian official are seen here in a relief at Medinet Habu.

> The foreign countries . . . made a conspiracy in their islands. All at once the lands were on the move, scattered in war. No country could stand before their arms . . . . Their league was Peleset, Tjeker, Shekelesh, Denyen and Weshesh . . .[1]

A great deal more will be heard of these names in later chapters. There have been many guesses as to who these peoples were, but they are only guesses. Something *is* known about where they went to later on, but the Egyptian texts give no sort of explanation for the centuries of recession, the long Dark Age of the Aegean and of Anatolia that set in soon after 1200.

Confusion has been increased by throwing together all sorts of widely differing events. The wars of Merneptah and Ramesses III on the borders of Egypt, the fall of the Hittite Empire in Anatolia and the disasters that overtook the Mycenaean palaces on the Greek mainland, the 'fall of Troy' and the rise of the Philistines: all these are attributed to the 'Sea Peoples'. Whoever or whatever they were, the trouble-makers were not 'a people', and only to a limited extent were they 'of the sea'.

Raids and piracy had been intermittent all through the 2nd millennium, border wars too; but this was not just a particularly virulent bout of raids and rivalries. It was something more, and something different. It is the purpose of this book to try and discover what that something was.

Very broadly speaking throughout history, and for that matter prehistory too, periods of thrust and bustle are superseded by periods of depression, of decline and fall. What is perhaps odd is the fascination that the latter have always exerted over historians, from Gibbon's English classic to the hectic vision of a Spengler. Perhaps it is the unknown quantity, the inexplicable, that attracts us.

How does it come about that so much order and prosperity, with their obvious advantages, are obliterated in a very few years? Sometimes the causes are clear, but it is always tempting to go back one stage further to the cause behind the cause. The Dark Age of the Roman Empire, or the collapse of the Maya; China's Age of Disunion or of Warring States: the deep decline that set in in the East Mediterranean was no less strange and calamitous.

An epoch of prosperity and comparative stability throughout the East Mediterranean and the Near East had depended upon an equilibrium that held between the two major powers, Egypt and Hittite Anatolia; and it virtually ended with the death of Pharaoh Ramesses II around 1224, and of Tudhaliyas IV, the last really powerful Hittite king, a few years later. The years from around 1220 to 1150 saw the collapse of Egyptian influence in the Levant, the total ruin of the Hittite Empire in Anatolia, with the abandonment of their capital Hattusas (modern Boğazköy), and widespread destruction of cities in the Levant, Cyprus and mainland Greece. A long period of absolute decline and comparative isolation, whose ferocity is hard to explain, had set in. In the Aegean the Dark Age lasted till the end of the 9th century, and in Anatolia very nearly as long. Egypt, though enfeebled, maintained a semblance of civilization. In the Levant the eclipse was less prolonged but none the less real, while Israelites, Philistines and Aramaeans were fighting for the old Canaanite strongholds. The evidence is easy to see in sacked cities, tumbled walls, broken communications, depopulation and deprivation.

Why did this happen? Many explanations have been tried and few have stood. Unparalleled series of earthquakes, widespread crop-failures and famine, massive invasion from the steppe, the Danube, the desert – all may have played some part; but they are not enough. Catastrophes punctuate human history but they are generally survived without too much loss. They are often followed by a much greater effort leading to greater success. After an earthquake the city is rebuilt, whether it is San Francisco, Lima, Ugarit or Knossos. After a series of crop-failures growth is stronger than before. The enemy raiders sweep down and pass on. Before searching the horizons for the bearers of catastrophe it will be worth while to look at the shape of society itself, within the total environment, to see how well it is constructed to last.

The speculative and controversial nature of much of the matter to be used in this short history make it necessary to present it backside first as it were. It would have been pleasanter, and easier for the reader, if a narrative of events in sequence could have been given, with the sources discreetly clothed; but in fact this would have been cheating. We must start with the sources so that the reader can gauge to some extent their quality and reliability: to see where the ground is firm, where it begins to quake, and where the horrible abyss opens in front; for only then can the faint outlines of a consecutive story be seen as just emerging.

In assessing the sequence of events we will have to employ different systems of chronology of varying degrees of soundness. In Egypt the reigns of Pharaohs are counted in calendar years, with some accuracy, though there is considerable latitude as to when we begin certain key reigns, such as that of Ramesses II.[2] Dates in the Levant depend on the one hand on Egyptian, and on the other hand Babylonian and Assyrian records and king-lists. The ample Hittite archives provide further cross-reference to individual rulers and events, as well as a record of local affairs in Anatolia. There is only one possible fault, though that is a rather large one, in the sequence of Hittite rulers.[3] The smaller Levantine states such as Ugarit and Alalakh can be related to others through the correspondence of their princes with the great powers.

When we turn to Cyprus the difficulties are much greater and texts of far less help; but here archaeology provides cross-checks with Egypt, the Levant and the Aegean. The years with which we will be concerned fall entirely within that part of the Late Bronze Age that is known to archaeologists as late Cypriot or LC II–III.[4] In the Aegean the corresponding periods are those of the changes in Mycenaean pottery styles as set out by Arne Furumark in 1940–41, but with Egyptian correlations and real dates somewhat modified following other authorities. So for the Late Bronze Age of peninsular Greece – the Hellas of the Greeks – we follow the usual subdivisions into Late Helladic periods, subdivided LH I, II, IIIA, IIIB and IIIC; and in Crete into the corresponding Late Minoan periods LM I–III.[5] Our study starts with early LH IIIB in the first half of the 13th century, and ends during the later phases of LH IIIC, and the corresponding LM IIIB–C, towards the end of the 12th century. For the sake of consistency, but without any claim to its use as a definitive date, the end of LH IIIB is taken as lying soon after 1200. As far as possible I have attempted to avoid the circular argument which dates events in the Levant by the pottery styles of the Aegean, themselves dated from Egypt and the Levant.[6]

Where more distant regions are visited – the Balkans, the Middle Danube, Italy and Sicily – much can be learnt of the local cultures through their archaeology, but their chronological correlations with the literate East Mediterranean can only be extremely tentative. In fact the further we travel from Egypt the less confident we must be, and the less clear the contours; and where Egypt is a broken reed we are hard put to know where better to turn for help. The narrow limits of the period make

Table I

Table III

Table IV

radiocarbon dating, with its wide margins of error, of no avail, so in general for this whole region we must rely on a combination of historical and archaeological methods.[7]

It will be obvious that the field of study is very wide indeed, touching on many different, though related, departments: Egyptology, the history of the Near East and of the Hittite Empire, Mycenaean and European studies. Where so much is to be encompassed accusations of superficiality may be all too justified. To know all equally well is impossible; my hope is that by standing back and contemplating these strangely patterned surfaces we may become aware of some currents, some conformations, some structures that are missed in the detailed view – as in a photograph taken from an earth satellite that makes plain features too large or too complex to be appreciated on the ground.

2 A general map of the East and Central Mediterranean, the Balkans and Danubian lands in the 13th and 12th centuries BC, showing some important sites mentioned in the text, diagnostic cultural features in Europe (flat graves, nuraghi etc.) and political entities in the East Mediterranean (Hittites, Amurru etc.) Of Europe's many cultural groupings only those of direct interest to the subject are named, e.g. Noua, Coslogeni etc.

Arrows indicating land movements are to be taken only as lines of general drift in Europe, but in the Levant also for probable historical events, such as the movement of Libyans to Egypt, and Hittites to northern Syria.

Seaways are those for which there is evidence of use during some or most of the period. In reality they could probably extend further west from Italy and along the North African coast.

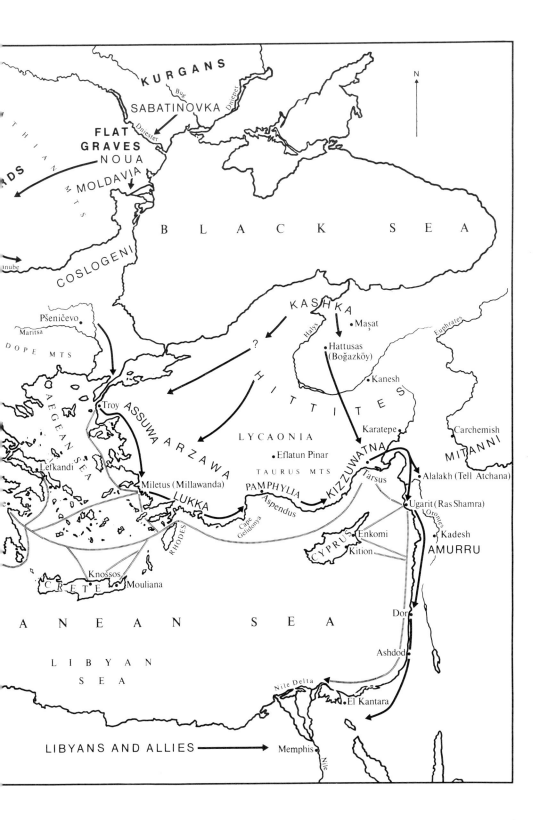

KURGANS

SABATINOVKA

Bug

Dnieper

FLAT
GRAVES
NOUA

Dniester

MOLDAVIA

C A R P A T H I A N   M T S

WARDS

Danube

COSLOGENI

B L A C K   S E A

N

Pšeničevo

Maritsa

RODOPE   MTS

KASHKA

Halys

Maşat

?

Hattusas
(Boğazköy)

Euphrates

H I T T I T E S

Kanesh

Troy

ASSUWA

AEGEAN SEA

Lefkandi

ARZAWA

LYCAONIA

Eflatun Pinar

Karatepe

Carchemish

MITANNI

Miletus (Millawanda)

LUKKA

PAMPHYLIA

Aspendus

TAURUS   MTS

KIZZUWATNA

Tarsus

Alalakh (Tell Atchana)

Ugarit (Ras Shamra)

Orontes

RHODES

Cape
Gelidonya

CYPRUS

Enkomi

Kition

Kadesh

AMURRU

Knossos

C R E T E

Mouliana

A N E A N   S E A

Dor

L I B Y A N
S E A

Ashdod

Nile Delta

El Kantara

LIBYANS AND ALLIES

Memphis

Nile

1
The lie of the land

When, at the end of the last century, George Adam Smith wrote his *Historical Geography of the Holy Land*, he spoke of the need to 'hear the sound of running history' and to discover 'from the lie of the land, why history took certain lines'. He set himself, quite deliberately, the task of finding out what geography had to contribute to questions of biblical criticism. In 1896 this was new territory; it is no longer so. Nevertheless I hope to keep similar aims in mind throughout the essay that follows, not of course as concerning biblical criticism, but in the almost equally complicated study of Near Eastern and Aegean records, literary and archaeological.

We will begin with the 'lie of the land'; at the same time it does not do to forget the warning of a contemporary explorer in this territory who writes that 'history is not made by geographical features, but by the men who control and discover them'.[1] In order to 'hear the course of running history' we must put our ears to the ground; but we must also be ready to stand back, at times, and listen from some isolated height even when,

> . . . whoso hearkened right
> Could only hear the plunging
> Of the nations in the night.[2]

Some parts of the globe have altered so much in the last 3000 years that they hardly seem to belong to the same planet, now as then: the plains and the forests of the United States, for instance, and the great northern European plain that was once as deeply forested as North America. But other regions, and the Mediterranean is one, have changed comparatively little, or had until a few years ago. The same Citheron, the same Olympos, Ida, Lebanon stand over the same coasts, less wooded perhaps, but easily recognized. As a small boat plods round the shores and islands of the Aegean everything must look remarkably unchanged. The thousand-foot promontory is rounded and a tiny sheltered strand, with a few houses beside it, reveal the

3   In Greece the soil is shallow and the rock is near the surface; the sea is never far away and when at sea one is seldom out of sight of land, whether it be islands, as in this view of the Aegean island of Ios, or the mainland.

4–6 The shores and hinterland of the East Mediterranean change from north to south. The Anatolian coast is mountainous, like the Greek, but on a larger scale. From the west coast the land rises in giant steps to the central plateau, while in the south the coastal range reaches over 2,000 m in places (*above*). In Cyprus (*right*) the landscape is gentler from the more mountainous north coast to the fertile south where Bronze Age sites are clustered along the shore plain. In southern Palestine the shoreline is low with coastal dunes, while in the Nile Delta flatness is total (*opposite*).

'skala' or harbour of some isolated community; while above on the mountainside the half-fortified village or little town shows white against the rocks and olives. One great island, Crete, reproduces the features of the mainland in a smaller compass, while the Anatolian coastland does so on a great one. Here and there a coastal plain opens out, but it is not very large, nor seemingly much exploited. Travelling south the aspect changes. Mountains are not so much individual heights as ranges. The outline of Cyprus, the other great island, is smooth, even to its central massif, a foretaste of the long flat coast of Palestine with its sandbanks, its dunes, its thin groves of palm, and the even flatter Nile Delta.

The best way, I think, to come to a just estimate of the truly exceptional nature of the centuries of regression after 1200 BC, and in particular to come to conclusions as to how far what happened was a *political* event, or series of events, is by first taking account of the permanent factors in the situation.

In the lands surrounding the Mediterranean there have *always* been earthquakes, famines, droughts and floods, and in fact dark ages of a sort are recurrent. Sir John Myres in his

Frazer lecture for 1943 meditated on why the Greek city-states, like medieval Italian cities, did not do better in the struggle to survive; but each 'throve like an artificial growth for a short time over the cultural roots out of which they emerged and into which their people have relapsed again and again'.[3] The cultural root is subsistence farming based on the ancient trinity of wheat, olives and wine, with a little fishing and herding thrown in.

The typical Mediterranean climate is the climate of a coastal fringe subject to two great alternating forces: the Sahara and the Atlantic. These act differently on mountains, foothills, plains and the sea, but they dominate all. Climate has of course changed over the years, but at present there is still not enough information to draw any conclusions about past patterns of change. Theories of catastrophic drought towards the end of the 2nd millennium, for instance, do not stand up to investigation. Equally plausible arguments have been put forward in favour of much greater wetness at that time. Climatic specialists have not yet found it possible to link phases in the Mediterranean with those of northern Europe, or even to link the East Mediterranean at the time of the Mycenaean recession with climatic events at the western end.[4] Much more information is needed before we can start talking about widespread changes. On the other hand there are permanent and recurrent features of Mediterranean climate and geography that must be taken into account.

The Mediterranean is a very deep sea formed by geological collapse, with no continental shelf, such as in the Atlantic supports a rich maritime life. Most of this inland sea is over 200 m deep and much of it more than 2000. The Aegean and the Levantine coastal waters are generally between 200 and 2000 m deep. The water is old and biologically exhausted. Perhaps this was less marked in the 2nd millennium BC, but for as far back as history takes us the sea was never rich enough to feed the coastal population. It is argued that the scarcity of fish explains the scarcity of sailors. It has always been difficult to find ship-builders and crews for the navies of would-be aggressive powers, and in the 16th century AD there were not enough sailors to man the boats then afloat in the Mediterranean:

Fernand Braudel, in his great *History of the Mediterranean World in the Age of Philip II*,[5] shows how prosperity in the Mediterranean has always contained the seeds of decline. Rises and falls in the maritime population occur not only for external reasons, but also because of an inbuilt factor. When the population is low and labour is scarce men work hard and acquire wealth, thus creating prosperity and generating a rise in population; but wealth brings corruption in its train, and since corruption leads to decay the population eventually declines once more. Braudel calls this a natural law determining the life-cycle of the sea, and reminds us of a Venetian saying that 'the seaman is like a fish, he cannot stay long out of water without going rotten'. At the other extreme, however, the fisherman who is also a farmer living on the coast can support life at a frugal level which is almost indestructible.

The Mediterranean is not so much one sea as several seas, joined by narrow waters between islands and promontories, often not easy to distinguish one from another. The Ionian Sea III and the West Mediterranean basin were for a long time maritime deserts, avoided by shipping as late as the 16th century AD. Most traffic was coastwise, but certain regular winds and currents made the crossing to North Africa from Rhodes or Crete possible even in the 2nd millennium. The east-west passage, from Syria to Cyprus, Crete and Sicily, is probably also very ancient.

Sailing was seasonal in the late 8th century BC when Hesiod lived and wrote, and until much later too. Even in the days of the Byzantine emperors there was no sailing between 25 October, the feast of St Dimitri, and 5 May, St George's day. Hesiod was able to fit his advice on sailing into the pattern of the farmer's year; but then it was not the main occupation. Among communities more heavily dependent on the sea there was real want during the winter months.

In the 2nd millennium 'sailing' can only be used very loosely to mean oars supported by sail-power with a following wind. This was all that the square rig of boats, like those of the Egyptians and Sea Peoples, could compass. The sail simply 80–4, II acted as a great bag to catch the wind when the boat was running before it, and no tacking was possible.[6]

A northern European arriving in the Mediterranean for the first time is struck by the appearance of fruitfulness and plenty. It is difficult to appreciate the desperate poverty that prevails and 7 the precariousness of life around these shores. Though drought is the scourge of the Mediterranean, Braudel rightly reminds us that 'there is not a plain in the Mediterranean today, from Portugal to Lebanon, that is not threatened by danger of floods'. When forests are cleared too quickly from the hills the danger becomes worse. If the farmer's care of the land and his work is relaxed at all, it quickly reverts to nature; so that malaria may be as much a consequence as a cause of depopulation.

7–9 The Mediterranean lands are subject to periodic drought and endemic want; livestock is small and the herdsman and labourer suffers like his beasts and like the stranger, probably a Libyan, depicted in a late-3rd-millennium Egyptian tomb at Meir (*above*). In Greece and the Balkans shepherds and their flocks migrated seasonally from upland summer pastures to winter grazing in coastal lowland regions like these (*opposite, above*) near Mycenae (vertical transhumance). In the Levant the seasonal movement is between the inland desert (*right*, in Judea) and the more fertile coastland (horizontal transhumance).

1 Leros in the Dodecanese supports some agriculture along with fishing. The steep island coasts, like many on the mainland, are terraced for cultivation.

Mediterranean livestock is small and poor compared to herds in the Danube lands and farther north. In 1900 only 46 per cent of the whole of Italy was cultivated land, and still more recently less than half of Rhodes, a large and comparatively fertile island. Some decrease in fertility and the acreage sown since 1200 BC is quite possible, but there have been gains as well as losses. The thin soil and biennial crop-rotation, which was, and still to a great extent is, the common practice, rule out the creation of large surpluses, or any surpluses at all unless under strong and well-organized direction, which may stimulate a change to a single-crop economy with its immediate advantages and long-term dangers.

All round the Mediterranean, a precarious living is won by painful labour. If a south wind blows just before harvest the wheat shrivels before it is ripe; or if it is already ripe it falls from the ear and is lost. Winter sowing is obstructed by floods, and frost attacks a crop sown too early. So life is frugal. A handful of olives and a little cheese may be all that a labourer has to keep him going through the long day.

This is the constant, the norm against which to set the luxury of court and castle: a Thebes, Pylos, or Mycenae. It is no exaggeration to say that in the past the Mediterranean was always on the verge of famine, but that equally – despite the total lack of records to prove it – there was a sort of very simple existence that could continue through any Dark Age, any set of disasters, however prolonged. It is against this background that the artificial growths of city and city-state, empire and confederacy, stand out.

The normal climatic and ecological pattern is one of *local* shortages, not of widespread famine. When corn was short in Cilicia there was plenty in ancient Mukish, not far away on the Orontes; and ships at Ugarit could carry it where it was needed. Such local famines might be caused by war as well as weather. Hattusilis III, the 13th-century Hittite ruler, estimated that in a land ravaged by war it was not possible to sow corn for ten years; such ravages were fairly commonplace, but the land did normally recover. Local shortages only became serious when the machinery of transportation and commerce failed, and there was no organization and no authority to see that relief was sent. Then even a local shortage became a major disaster. These two things, organization and transportation, are essential for the survival of the sort of life for which there is evidence in the Near East and in the Aegean in the second half of the 2nd millennium.

In Greece the best land for supporting life lies in the foothills between 200 and 400 m. This is where one finds a truly mixed cultivation. The plains have too many problems, chief among them the perennial floods which create stretches of stagnant water and fine breeding grounds for disease. The mountains have seldom been an insurmountable barrier for determined individuals or armies, but they do impose a pattern on day-to-day life. This is as true of the Balkan and Rhodope ranges as it is of the mountains of peninsular Greece, of Anatolia and the Levant. Nor are mountains necessarily the poorest region, although they do easily become over-populated, when the overflow spills down into the valleys and coasts.

Transhumance, the seasonal moving of livestock from one region to another, plays a large part in the economy of the Mediterranean. In some places the autumn descent of the shepherds and flocks from their summer grazing in the mountains is like an invasion. Doors are locked against the strangers and there is much relief when they have passed on. In the Levant the movement is horizontal rather than vertical. During the spring the inland winter pastures dry up and revert to desert, so flocks are moved towards the coasts. There is usually a measure of interdependence between farmers and migrating herdsmen. Wheat, fruit, oil and wine are exchanged for wool, skins and cheese. It is even arguable that the usual Mediterranean practice of ploughing and reploughing the same ground leads to greater exhaustion of the soil than grazing by sheep and goats; so when periodically the land falls into the hands of the nomads it is a way of resting it. Conversely if something goes wrong, if the seasonal movement is interrupted or the numbers are too great, then there is friction.

History records the rapid and violent shifts of population, it does not record slower movements, as when, for instance, a people used to mountain living and transhumance give this up for life in the plains and valleys. Braudel states that as a general rule it takes between 100 and 200 years for the plains to absorb as many waves of immigrants from the mountains as it can use. This is one of 'history's slowest processes' and it brings us back to our problem: the Sea Peoples and the great recession that began at the end of the 13th century BC.

11 One type of Aegean boat did not alter much between the early 16th and the 12th century. Among the pleasure boats of the 16th-century Theran wall-paintings there is one square-rigged ship with a large sail that could only be used for running before the wind. The boats of the 12th-century Egyptians and Sea Peoples were no better equipped (80–4). Note the two steering oars (rudders) on the same side of the stern.

8

9

Progress to disaster

The 13th-century equilibrium in the East Mediterranean

In the course of a few years not only Greece, but Anatolia, Egypt and the whole of the Levant fell into total disarray. The nature of this collapse is our subject. In this chapter we will look at the kind of world it was that came to an end around 1200 BC. In order to do this something must be understood of the Hittites and Egyptians, the cities and peoples of the Levant and Cyprus, as well as the part they played in the years leading up to the crisis and in the crisis itself.

It would be quite impossible in a short chapter to give even a brief general summary of the 13th-century political background in the East Mediterranean. Yet as a controlling factor in the collapse that followed political circumstances cannot be ignored. All that is attempted here, therefore, is a jackdaw-like selection of objects, events and situations that have a special bearing on what was coming. The selection may seem haphazard, yet the pieces in the puzzle do, I believe, combine together to make a pattern and impose a certain result.

The equilibrium that had held for centuries between the two great powers, Egypt and Hittite Anatolia, was a delicate one, and when it failed the repercussions were felt far beyond the confines of the East Mediterranean. Yet disaster, when it came, cannot have been entirely unexpected. The late annals of the Hittite Empire give an all-too-plausible picture of internal disintegration, the revolt of more-or-less independent border states and the return of old enemies such as the Kashka on the north and the Assyrians on the east.

The Hittites and their allies: the battle of Kadesh

We must go back a little in time, go back in fact to the battle of Kadesh on the River Orontes fought in about 1286/5[1] between

10   The battle of Kadesh on the Orontes, *c.* 1286/5, depicted on the walls of the Ramesseum, Thebes. On the left the Egyptian chariots are attacking in line of battle, each with two men, one shooting the bow, the other holding a shield; the reins are fastened to the chariots. On the right the Hittite force is in disarray; horses and men are falling wounded by Egyptian arrows. The Hittites usually rode three in a chariot with an extra man to hold the reins, as can be seen in the two chariots following each other near the top of the picture.

11 The battle of Kadesh, relief at Abydos. Egyptian foot-soldiers are facing Hittite chariots; to the right a Shardana (foreign mercenary) of Ramesses II's troops, armed with a shield and short pointed dirk is severing the hand of a fallen enemy in a long robe (the Shardana helmet here is the earliest form of simple rounded cap with a disc or ball between the horns: see ch. 5 and cf. 66, 67). The Abydos reliefs were made shortly after the battle itself.

12 In the first year of his campaign against the Hittites a contingent of Ramesses II's foreign troops, probably Shardana, are storming the fortress Deper in Amurru. They wield long swords and wear tasselled kilts and the horned Shardana helmet without a disc. Note that the round shields appear to have bossed decoration, and contrary to the usual Egyptian convention the helmets are shown in true profile. Compare the physiognomy of the right hand man with 67, time of Ramesses III.

the young Pharaoh Ramesses II and the Hittite ruler Muwatallis, because it brings on to the scene many groups of people who were to be actors in the later drama. Kadesh has to be counted as one of the great battles of the world, not because it was decisive – it was not – but because this was the last time that Egypt and Hatti (the Land of the Hittites), which had dominated the Near East for 300 or 400 years, faced each other in an open

trial of strength, each ruler in the full panoply of war at the head
of his army. After Kadesh nothing was ever the same again.

For Egypt the war was the culmination of an immense effort 12
aimed at regaining the commanding position she had enjoyed in
the 15th century, when Syria had been reduced to an Egyptian
province. All the strategic gains of this period had been lost by
the later 18th-dynasty kings in the course of the 14th century.
The power of Hatti had increased as that of Egypt diminished,
till the Great King of Hatti, Suppiluliumas I (1375–1335),
could claim that he had made Lebanon his frontier.

It has been said of Ramesses II, who may have become
Pharaoh in 1290 and did not die until 1224, that the length of his
reign and his sheer assertiveness made him appear more
formidable than is justified by his actual achievements. The
battle of Kadesh is known from the Egyptian side alone, but in 10, 11
spite of the brag and bluster of the account, the hard fact is that
the Hittites were left in possession of the field; there is no doubt
as to who had the real advantage. The battle was fought with
chariots. A surprise attack by the Hittite chariotry on the second
Egyptian division, when it was at a disadvantage crossing the

Orontes, nearly carried the day. The first division was set upon while attempting to make camp, but though it too was taken by surprise it held on till the lagging third division caught up and attacked the Hittites in the rear. This belated assault saved the Egyptians from disaster, giving Pharaoh the chance to reform and make an orderly retreat and a face-saving explanation. It was a battle fought according to accepted rules between forces that understood each other. It was therefore quite unlike the fighting at the end of the century when the Land and Sea Raiders were active. The scene of the battle is portrayed on the walls at Luxor and Abydos in a realistic style that is unique among 2nd-millennium Egyptian monuments.

The power of Egypt was exhausted by this effort. Although desultory warfare continued for some years, a peace treaty was at last agreed around 1269, by which the Egyptians confined their interest to southern Syria (Palestine), and an understanding was entered into under the terms of which each would help the other if attacked by a third party, and would extradite political undesirables. This firm peace was followed some thirteen years later by a marriage between the now ageing Ramesses and the daughter of Hattusilis III, the new king of Hatti. Henceforward Egypt was under repeated attack from land and sea, but not from the Hittites.

III   The strength of Hatti was a great source of stability in the East Mediterranean and the Near East. It will be part of my argument that the disappearance of this power around 1200 was a major cause of the long Dark Age that followed. The Hittite army was itself a stabilizing factor. An army dependent on its chariotry had to be a professional army, for the rearing of horses and maintaining of the great areas of land needed to feed them was a full-time occupation. It is assumed that the king was ultimately responsible by making grants of land in return for services rendered. The infantry too probably formed a permanent standing army used to garrison the difficult long frontiers. There was also a royal bodyguard which was maintained on a feudal basis, service to the king being rewarded by gifts of land.[2] The army with its Roman virtues even to the ceremony of the oath of allegiance taken by the individual soldiers, the system of roads and frontier posts, defended and patrolled, the great administrative machine, the network of allies bound by treaty – all this ran a long course apparently confident and commanding, then suddenly it collapsed almost at a touch. This is how it seems now, but the late texts are particularly defective and controversial.

However, between the battle of Kadesh in 1286 and the fading out of the last Hittite king a century later we have a number of pointers to what was in fact happening.[3]

Muwatallis, the victor of Kadesh, died around 1282; he had no legitimate heir, and was followed, after a few years, by his brother Hattusilis III who reigned till 1250. Hattusilis was a successful general who had fought at Kadesh. He seized the throne from Muwatallis' illegitimate son, sending him into exile, either in Cyprus, or more probably, Egypt. On the whole he held on to the position and possessions that his brother had enjoyed. There are hints of insecurity in Syria which made him all the readier to conclude an alliance with Ramesses II. But a more ominous threat lay in the growing power of Assyria on his south-eastern flank. Here too for a time Hattusilis checked the danger, concluding a treaty with the Cassite King of Babylon. He also, and at the expense of Egypt, made an ally of Amurru (the Land of the Amorites), a comparatively new power in northern Syria, and married a daughter to the King of Amurru.

Hattusilis was followed by his son Tudhaliyas IV, who succeeded in maintaining the power of Hatti, but more precariously and under relentless pressure. He fought major wars with Assyria and the neighbouring western state of Arzawa, and there were always the Kashka on the north to be watched. At one time he was strong enough to make a foray against Alashiya (Cyprus), and even claimed to have conquered the whole of it, taking the king prisoner (see chapter 6).[4] Under his son Arnuwandas IV, who followed him c. 1220, the Empire really began to fall apart. With Egypt relations remained good, but this was as much a sign of mutual weakness as anything else. The last Hittite ruler that we hear of is a Suppiluliumas, probably a brother of Arnuwandas, who held a semblance of authority around 1190, or a little later. He was troubled by other claimants to the throne, and complained of the fickleness of the people of Hatti. His name, like that of the last Roman emperor Romulinus, is an unhappy reminder of the past, for the first Suppiluliumas had been a strong ruler who had greatly extended the frontiers of the Empire in the course of the 14th century. As the documents begin to fail, our view of these times becomes more oblique, with only a little help coming from Syria and the Egyptian records.

The basis of Hittite power in northern Syria had rested on the control of two strong cities – Carchemish in the east and Alalakh of Mukish, known to archaeology as Tell Atchana, in the west – and on treaties with Ugarit, north of Latakia on the coast, and

with Amurru, south of the Orontes. Tudhaliyas IV still dominated Carchemish and Ugarit and held the Assyrians on the Euphrates; but it was he also who probably strengthened the Hittite capital Hattusas by completing the formidable inner
33 fortress, the Büyükkale, an undertaking which must have been in response to some very intimate threat. The Büyükkale is built with massive irregular masonry over a chasm on a craggy height. It is hard to think of anything less like the tell-cities of Mesopotamia and the Levant, with their neat brick walls, surrounded by plains or in river valleys. Oddly enough it is to the west we have to look for anything comparable, as we shall see in a later chapter.

34

13-15 Representatives of the chief Hittite allies at the battle of Kadesh are lined up on the relief of the battle at Luxor (*left*). There are 12 allies and they should come from among the 19 listed in the Kadesh inscription of Ramesses II. Here they are not named, but an interesting comparison can be made with some of the allies and enemies of Ramesses III 100 years later, such as the troops on parade with a trumpeter following a campaign in Syria-Palestine (*opposite*) or the group of prisoners returning after Ramesses III's second Libyan war in year 11 of his reign (1183) (*left, below*). Three allies on the Luxor relief carry the usual Hittite shield, most have short broad dirks, three wear short kilts, the rest the long Syrian robe. The 2nd man from the right has the Amorite hairstyle, the 6th might perhaps be compared with the Teresh of 68, and the leader and 7th to the Tjeker, or even more to the Peleset of 113; for the wild-haired rear figure see 90.

The Hittite Empire was always under threat from north and west, as well as from the east. The enormous reserves of power, which had carried it through the alternations of strong and weak rulers and successive wars and reverses, eventually seem to have run out. This is one reason why the names of the Hittite allies at the battle of Kadesh in 1286 make such interesting reading: many of them will reappear during the later troubles, and in a few cases actually among the so-called 'Peoples of the Sea'.

The full list of names, not all of which can be identified, is a long one. It comes in an inscription of Ramesses II at Luxor for which there is no Hittite equivalent.[5] The names of most concern to this history begin with Nahrin or Mitanni, a once powerful

13

14, 15

state lying east of the Euphrates and at this time reaching west to Aleppo, but which was shortly to be engulfed by Assyria. Then Arzawa is named, south-west of Hatti and in constant political contact both with the Hittites and with coastal states such as Millawanda (almost certainly Miletus) and the Lukka Lands. The frontier with Arzawa was strongly defended by strings of guard-posts. It was regularly patrolled, at any rate under a strong ruler such as Muwatallis. Trouble in Arzawa was an element in the decline of Hittite power.

The Dardany (Drdny) are a new name to history and of great interest, if as is likely, they are the same as the Dardanoi, Homer's name for the people of Troy; they should in any case be located in north-western Anatolia. Next on the list come the Kashka or Keshkesh. It is likely that the Kashka, although apparently among the allies at Kadesh, played a sinister role in the final dissipation of the Hittite state. They were already menacing the northern border of Hatti in the early 16th century, and their seizure of the Pontic regions may have been a direct cause of the fortification of Hattusas. This long northern frontier was highly vulnerable to attack, in spite of a system of defensive guard-posts, fortified towns and regular patrols. In a prayer of Arnuwandas IV memories are called up of earlier troubles when the terrible Kashka carried off all sorts of treasure: gold, bronze and textiles, goats and fat oxen. They plundered temples and bore away priests, musicians and labourers as slaves, as well as annexing the tribute of much farmland. The abject Arnuwandas can only propose a manner of 'danegeld', buying the Kashka off with presents, and asking them on oath not to seize the tribute of the gods. From the texts it does not sound as though the Kashka were a wholly barbarous people. They got a bad press from the Hittites, but they owned chariots and were able themselves to garrison frontier towns. They were also skilled craftsmen in demand as far away as the Egyptian Empire in the 15th century, when Kashka prisoners were used for forced labour in Palestine. Unfortunately we do not know what their particular craft was. The Kashka occupation of a part of Anatolia rich in iron is another factor that may have had repercussions even in the Balkans. There is no doubt that they plundered and terrorized deep into Hittite lands whenever there was weakness there. Although they fought as allies of Muwatallis at Kadesh, this did not prevent them from sacking Hattusas during one of his absences in the south.

None of the allies mentioned so far appear among the Land

and Sea Raiders of a few generations later on the Egyptian monuments, although they certainly played no small part in the background of events leading up to those raids (Arzawa, for instance, is named as having been overrun by a part of the enemy that descended on Syria and eventually reached the borders of Egypt *c.* 1186). After one or two names of less importance on the Kadesh inscription we come to the Lukka, pirates famous in the East Mediterranean for centuries. Scholars disagree as to where they should be located in Anatolia: in the north-west, inland in Lycaonia or in the south-west in coastal Caria. The latter is most likely to have been their homeland, and in the 13th century in particular their exploits agree best with a situation in or close to the Caria and Lycia of later geography, facing the sea which took their name, *mare lycium*.[6] Their last appearance was as allies of the Libyans in the wars of Merneptah (see chapter 5). Some Hittite texts seem to refer to Lukka along with Kashka, perhaps because both had a reputation as raiders.

As we would expect, the people of Kizzuwatna, or Cilicia, formed part of the Hittite army, for with them Hittite relations were particularly close. The fertile coastal plain below the Taurus and Amanus mountains made theirs a prosperous country, with thriving merchant cities: Tarsus, Mersin, Adana, Ura. A large part of the population spoke Luwian, an Indo-European dialect related to Hittite, and used in parts of western Anatolia, including Arzawa. Overlying this Luwian population there was an eastern element brought by the Hurrians, a people of uncertain origins who had spread from the Middle Euphrates over much of the Near East in the first half of the 2nd millennium BC. At Hattusas there are a number of texts written in the Hurrian language. In the 13th century the Luwian part of the population was the strongest but, judging by the variety of names in the texts, men from Mitanni and the Lukka Lands were included also. The importance of Cilicia to the Hittites was economic as well as political, for the whole busy trade between the Anatolian plateau, Syria and Egypt passed this way, and there are many texts concerned with the regulation of this trade (see below).

Continuing south and east we reach Carchemish, a neighbour of Kizzuwatna and for some time a direct Hittite dependency ruled by Hittite nominees. Carchemish, like Arzawa and Kizzuwatna, is named in the overthrow of nations in the reign of Ramesses III. Other northern Syrian cities listed among the Hittite allies at the battle of Kadesh are Ugarit, Khaleb (Aleppo)

VI

96

and Kadesh itself. Ugarit is the most important of these and requires its own section.

Ugarit

101   While the world became steadily more chilly and unfriendly for the Hittites, the King of Ugarit seems to have continued to enjoy a measure of prosperity at least for a little longer. During the 13th century Ugarit (modern Ras Shamra) was a busy, highly

17   literate cosmopolitan city. Its ruler was a prince-merchant, almost a Renaissance type of banker-prince, better able to supply his friends and allies with gold than with men, with ships than with corn. Under the king there was a corps of writers, and there were libraries consisting of many thousands of clay tablets for the various languages spoken in the city. These included, as well as West Semitic (Canaanite), Hittite, Hurrian, Egyptian and Babylonian (Akkadian), but not, on the available evidence, any Aegean language, a curious and important omission. In the city there were many races, and many different artisan quarters. Ugarit was an earlier Antioch or Alexandria. Other harbour-cities down the coast, Byblos and Tyre, were in the same mould, but states such as Amurru immediately to the south and Mukish to the north were more war-like, more dependent on manpower and less on merchandise.

However, when it came to fighting, the King of Ugarit, or the crown prince, would probably be found at the head of his troops, like other Near Eastern rulers. The marvellous and unique Ugaritic archives can be used in order to form some idea of how other states operated as well. Directly under the royal commander there was the corps of chariots, an aristocratic élite that owned its own, immensely valuable, horses. The Egyptians called such fighting men *maryannu*, which means, literally, 'young hero'. They were often foreign in origin and Indo-European in connections; and they were superior to the usual type of mercenary. At one time the King of Ugarit could call on 2000 of the best horses. The field-commanders had the status of feudal vassals, and ranked equal with the priests and members of the royal family. They were specialists in chariot fighting appointed directly by the king himself and from him received their grants of land in perpetuity. Besides feudal retainers, a large part of the infantry was made up of mercenaries, and from the 14th century non-Semitic names are in the majority in the palace and general administration.[7]

16 The lid of an ivory box found in a 13th-century tomb at Minet el Beida, on the coast near Ugarit, is carved with a seated goddess in a mixed Aegean-oriental style. The face and dress derive from the Minoan-Mycenaean world, but the seated position, the grouping and gesture of the goddess are oriental. Ht 15 cm.

Important as the army was – and in matters of status and prestige it was probably supreme – for a mercantile state such as Ugarit the navy would have been even more vital. Ugarit itself did not possess a harbour, but there was a sheltered anchorage at Minet el Beida, a few miles distant, which could be used when the south winds made the Ras Shamra and Latakia shore unsafe. At one time the Ugarit navy numbered as many as 150 ships some of which had an estimated displacement of 500 tonnes.

These vessels had the range of all the major Levantine ports: Byblos, Sidon, Tyre, Acre and the Nile Delta. Northwards they rounded the capes to the Lukka Lands, for they were there when Sea Raiders threatened the mother-city after the outbreak of the troubles. There is at least a strong probability that they rowed on to Crete and into the Aegean, but the writings are silent on this point, apart from one mention at Ugarit, in the early 13th century, when the prince Amishtamru granted a certain Sinaranu complete exemption from taxes, and names one of his ships returning from a land which can only be read as Kabturi, that is Caphtor (probably Crete).[8] But the closest relations were with the harbour cities of Cyprus some 100 miles away to the west (Latakia to Famagusta). This silence of the Ugaritic archives with regard to Crete and to Greek lands is a strong argument for Cyprus having been the centre of exchange where goods were off-loaded from Levantine, and possibly Egyptian, merchantmen on to Cypriot or Aegean boats, and vice versa.

Amongst the more valuable goods that travelled to the Aegean in this way was lapis lazuli and the cache of seals, originally carved in Cassite Babylon, Hittite Anatolia and in Syria, that were found in Boeotian Thebes, and which must have been lost when the palace was destroyed perhaps in the 14th century. Ivories carved in the international Levantine style may have come this way too. In the other direction large quantities of 14th- and early 13th-century Mycenaean pottery were conveyed from Greek mainland centres to be dispersed all over the Levant, together with whatever commodity they held.

Cyprus

Alashiya (Cyprus) is not named in the Kadesh inscription and must have remained aloof from the fighting; but it appears constantly under this name in Egyptian and Levantine, especially Ugaritic, correspondence, and again in the later Hittite annals. Its equivocal position between Asia, Europe and Africa is, for the archaeologist and ancient historian, uniquely important. Unfortunately, notwithstanding the literacy of a few, there is no Cypriot literature in the 2nd millennium, and the texts that have been found are still unread. What we know of Cyprus, apart from its archaeological sites, comes from Egyptian, Hittite and Asiatic archives.

With its two mountain ranges, its many trees, its copper ores and its great plain for growing corn, Cyprus was in a happy situation. Communications across the island were easy, with good access to the copper-mining districts in the foothills of the

17, 18 The links between the kings of Ugarit and the rulers of Cyprus were very close, in art and in commerce. These merchant princes employed the finest craftsmen to furnish their palaces and temples. A 14th-century gold dish from Ugarit (*above*) shows a charioteer, probably the king himself, hunting wild cattle and goats with a pack of hounds. A 12th-century ivory gaming-box from a tomb at Enkomi, Cyprus (*below*) has a more realistic version of the same scene. Hunting with the chariot, like fighting, had special rules and probably a symbolic significance (single charioteer and four-spoked wheel). The Enkomi box shows two men on foot very like some of the Sea Peoples attacking Ramesses III (cf. 131 and 68). Dish, diam. 18 cm; box, l. 29 cm.

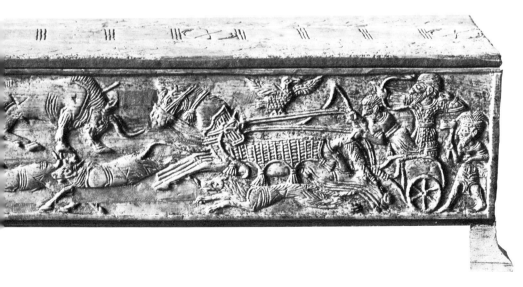

19–21 In the 13th century international trade in
luxury goods – faience, ivory and seals – and in raw
materials flourished; amongst the latter copper was of
the greatest importance for Cyprus. A conical rhyton of
a well-known Aegean shape, but made of faience, is
possibly the most precious object found at Kition (*right*,
Late Cypriot II). Faience-working had spread from
Egypt through the Levant and to Greece. In brilliant
colours a man in a kilt with a well-known type of
headdress (cf. 91 and 103) is catching bulls. Ht 27 cm.

Another pointed rhyton is carried by a 15th-century
ambassador to Egypt (*below right*), painted on the walls
of the tomb of Rekhmire at Egyptian Thebes. He wears
Aegean dress and carries on his shoulder an 'ox-hide'
ingot of copper. Such ingots have been found from Iraq
to Sardinia; many are thought to have orginated in
Cyprus. The examples *below left* are from Cyprus
(upper) and S. Antioco di Bisarcio, Sardinia (lower);
max.l. 66 cm.

Egyptian fashions are also seen in seals and lasted into
the 12th century. An impression from a haematite
cylinder seal with men and monkeys (*opposite, above*)
comes from tomb 9 at Kition, probably Late Cypriot
III; ht 2.4 cm.

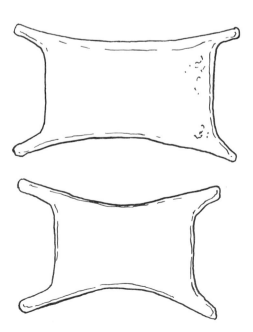

mountains. In the first half of the 2nd millennium the plain was densely populated, but wealth was concentrated in the outward-looking coastal cities. From the 16th century, in the late Cypriot period, the south coast in particular increased in importance. Enkomi, which is now a mile from the sea, was then near the mouth of a navigable river; Kition, now high and dry, once had a good harbour; and the salt lakes, with Hala Sultan Tekké, another Bronze Age city, perhaps as large as any, were then open to the sea. In addition there were many small anchorages that are now unusable. After the 12th century BC, however, when the harbours silted up, the life of many Bronze Age cities ceased, although some transferred to other sites nearer the new shoreline: Enkomi, for instance, moved to Salamis.

The political history of Cyprus, unlike that of Ugarit, has to be constructed almost wholly from the archaeology of its sites. Excavations at Enkomi and Kition have shown that the 13th century (Late Cypriot II) was a prosperous time.[9] Later in this century, however, a fortification wall was built at Enkomi (Late Cypriot IIC), the occasion for which may have been the aftermath of the expedition of Tudhaliyas IV, or it might have been due to the familiar Lukka raids or, but this is highly speculative, to the unrest that went with the Libyan attack on Merneptah. The wall did not stand for long but was destroyed with other buildings, and this destruction marks the end of an epoch. Thirteenth-century Cypriot buildings are inferior to those of Ugarit in point of masonry, though this would be reversed later. Where stone *was* used it was rough rubble work; even the fortification wall was not of ashlar. Much mud-brick was employed, with lime facing, so the buildings may have had quite a well-finished appearance. The wealthy dead were buried

19
18
21

beneath the courtyards of their own houses like their counter-parts at Ugarit. They took with them into the next world faience, ivory, alabaster and gold-work, earrings, finger-rings and fine worked seals, as well as a large number of bronze objects and Mycenaean vases, since the native Cypriot pottery was monotonous, dull stuff.

20

Temples were built on the oriental plan with gardens and an inner 'holy of holies'. Copper-working was carried on as part of the life of the temple, as in other Near Eastern cities. Crucibles and much slag and ash from the smelting of the sulphide ores have been found. Kition and Enkomi were the Sheffields and Hamburgs of their day.

Two sets of objects, both found in the temple precincts, show the twin sources of Cypriot prosperity: large numbers of stone anchors evidently dedicated to the gods; and copper ingots of the so-called 'ox-hide' shape, that has in fact nothing to do with an ox or a hide, but is a rectangle with ends drawn out for easy handling.

Archaeology confirms the close links between Cyprus and Ugarit. It also points occasionally to Egypt. But of the Hittites it has nothing to show. Early references to Alashiya in the Hittite archives have to be treated with circumspection; but the claim of Tudhaliyas IV in the 13th century to have taken Alashiya and carried off its king is probably historical fact.

22 Stone anchors found at Ugarit and dedicated to the gods in the temples at Kition are evidence for the importance of mar-itime trade. The holes on this Cypriot example are for a hawser and two stakes to dig into the sea-bed. Ht 64 cm.

His wives, his sons, his servants, all his wealth in gold and silver, copper and a great spoil of people I collected together and carried to Hattusas. I made the whole land of Alashiya subject to me and liable to pay tribute.[10]

Copper was a large part of the tribute. Rather than outright conquest this may have been no more than a successful foray, since the Hittites returned home with booty but never gained a lasting overlord-ship of the island.

The Hittite rulers may occasionally have deported political exiles to the island, as was certainly done by the King of Ugarit. Such banishings of awkward relations, or too powerful subjects, was a custom of the times, and it was the duty of the 'hosts' to keep watch on their 'guests'. 'This man guard, and if you hear evil for the land of Hatti . . . from the country of another prince, do not keep it to yourself.'

This comparatively civilized way of dealing with difficult characters may be faintly remembered in stories such as that of Homer's Bellerophon who was exiled to Lycia. The predicament of the local ruler would have been much the same as that of the King of Lycia, and his actions as ambiguous as those of Iobates.

Syria, Palestine and Egypt

We know more about the Cypriot and northern Syrian bazaar cities, but all down the coast there were others, equally illustrious. Byblos was richer and more influential than Ugarit at one time, and would become so again. Sidon, Tyre, Tell Abu Hawam, Ashdod, Tell Mor and Acre were all trading centres and places of importance. Inland too the Canaanite cities stand thick together. Megiddo and Taanach are four miles apart; Beth Shan (Beisan), Tell es Saidiyeh and Deir Alla lie within a few miles of each other. The north seems sparser than the south, but this is partly due to the accidents of excavation which have left gaps in our knowledge. If the capital of the important Amorite state were known, and if we possessed Amorite archives, our picture would be infinitely fuller.

Already by the end of the 15th century the Amorites had formed a political state with a king, and during the 14th and 13th centuries they occupied the country north of Byblos, straddling the hills and reaching to the coast, though they were never a maritime power. In the early 14th century (that is the Amarna period), they were within the Hittite sphere. But Ramesses II in his march north to Kadesh swept up the Amorite king and his people. Around 1200 the Amorites ceased to exist, overrun in the same series of land campaigns that brought down Hatti, Arzawa, Ugarit, Mukish and other Near Eastern states (chapters 6 and 7).

The peace treaty that followed Kadesh had left Syria and Palestine, from the Negev in the south to the kingdom of Byblos and the northern Lebanon, including Beth Shan and Damascus, as an Egyptian province, at least nominally. Even when Egypt was at her strongest in Syria no serious attempt was made to remove the rulers of the various city-states or to set up an Egyptian administration under Egyptian officials. Highly evolved indigenous administrative systems already existed in these states. The native dynasts remained as heads of their respective governments, and although now responsible to Pharaoh, they came under only limited surveillance from higher Egyptian officials. Inspectors were appointed to estimate the yield of the harvest in Palestine, as in Egypt, and overseers collected the revenue. This tribute was what chiefly interested

23

Pharaoh, and it became the test of loyalty. The system survived periods of Egyptian eclipse and was still operating over a much restricted area in Merneptah's reign and even in the 12th century under Ramesses III.

For Syria some have drawn a distinction between the 'theocratic' Egyptian and the 'juridical' Hittite systems of administration, but in practice there was not very much difference between the two. There was also a lot of give and take between Egypt and Syria in the arts and crafts, with Egyptian influence being strongest in literature, faience, art and music, and Syrian craftsmanship in ivory-working. In religious matters the interaction was probably more apparent than real.[11]

Periodic destruction was the lot of the close-packed Canaanite cities. Ugarit and Alalakh were frequently destroyed, wholly or in part, by earthquakes or by enemies, but until the 12th century they generally rose again. After the end of the 13th century, however, many of these cities suffered total abandonment; while Hazor, one of the greatest, perhaps destroyed during the 13th century, did not rise again until the time of Solomon.

Commerce

Our knowledge of the correspondence between heads of states is now complete enough for an economic history of the Near East in the 2nd millennium to be a practical proposition, since much of this correspondence is concerned with commerce. The ambassadors of Egypt to Cyprus and other states were also merchants. In the 14th-century Amarna correspondence Pharaoh writes to the King of Alashiya: 'My brother, return my messenger quickly, so that I may hear your greetings. These men are merchants.' These two rulers address each other as 'brother', whereas kings of weaker states address Pharaoh as 'father'. It was probably the commercial strength of Cyprus, as well as its more secure position as an island, that permitted the familiarity. Diplomatic correspondence refers to trade in copper, elephant's ivory, box-wood (these last two commodities probably originating in Syria), timber and perfumed oil. With characteristic hyperbole a text of Ramesses II speaks of 'endless quantities of copper'. The King of Alashiya writes to Pharaoh: 'Dear brother, do not take it to heart that there is so little copper, since in my country plague has killed all the people, and there is nobody left to smelt the copper.' The dangerous conditions under which primitive smelting was carried out may have caused this

23 A wall-painting from the Tombs of the Nobles at Thebes (no. 69, Tomb of Menna) shows an Egyptian official measuring corn. Similar officials were probably employed in Palestine to oversee the assessing and delivery of tribute during periods of Egyptian domination.

shortfall, rather than a common epidemic. Another interesting point is that the King of Alashiya is commissioned to build ships for Egypt.[12]

In exchange, from Egypt Cyprus imported fine furniture, chariots, horses, linen, ebony, oil, silver, ivory and gold. Some commodities – ivory, oil and horses – could be provided by either country. Teams of horses were frequently exchanged between rulers, probably because these were the gifts most prized, and so highest rated, in the competitive game of giving for glory.

In the reign of Ramesses II, between *c.* 1290 and 1224, Egypt was importing from Babylon silver and precious stones, teams of horses and various scents and unguents. A king of Hatti requested from Babylon lapis lazuli, horses and a stone carver. Much of the Babylonian material wealth came from farther east, while a Cypriot (or Aegean) ox-hide ingot reached Dur Kurigalzu, the Cassite capital founded in 1370 in Mesopotamia. Cassite seals reached Amman as well as Thebes in Boeotia.

It is these fine luxury articles that appear most often in royal correspondence, besides the marriage treaties and alliances; but the bulk of ancient trade was no doubt in more basic materials. The question of how far the Aegean played a part in this oriental commerce must wait till the next chapter. Opinion does not now favour the existence of a Mycenaean enclave in Ugarit, or Mycenaean colonists in Cyprus before about 1200 BC.[13] The lack of Aegean names in the Ugaritic archives where Hurrian, Hittite and Egyptian names are found has been already mentioned. Occasional visits by Aegean boats to Levantine ports is another matter, but this too depends on whether there was a Cypriot monopoly on all trade, and on the controversial question of the identity of the boat wrecked off Cape Gelidonya (see chapter 4). Although great quantities of Mycenaean LH IIIB pottery are found all over the Levant, even larger amounts of Cypriot pottery generally accompany them so that the trade, whatever it was, may have been channelled through the great Cypriot emporia like Enkomi, Hala Sultan Tekké and Kition.

As long as either the Hittites or the Egyptians dominated Syria and Palestine there was a reasonable degree of order: conditions were good for business, men grew rich and perhaps soft. Babylon, the other great player in the diplomatic game, was a source of beneficial trade, some of it very long distance, with lapis lazuli coming from Afghanistan and tin perhaps also from somewhere to the east (but see ch. 3). Apart from an occasional raid Babylon was not a territorial menace. It was Assyria which

43

in the 13th century became the King of Hatti's most dangerous enemy, preventing him from taking advantage of Egyptian weakness to press his interests in Syria, as in the great days of his forbear, the first Suppiluliumas, in the 14th century.

What I wish to stress here is that the advanced commerce of the Near East was itself a danger point, since its complexity absolutely demanded conditions of reasonable security. The careful provision made by the King of Ugarit to protect the movements of merchants shows how well this was recognized. Lawlessness on the roads, the robbing and murder of merchants, meant loss of merchandise. When this happened within the borders of a friendly state great care was taken to prevent matters degenerating into vendetta. Occasionally a very powerful ruler, such as the King of Hatti, took a strong line to impose agreement between, for instance, Ura in Cilicia and Ugarit. Much correspondence is also concerned with regulating the seasonal journeys of pastoral tribes transhuming between the Mediterranean coasts and the Anatolian plateau through the passes of the Taurus; and parallel movements took place in Syria and on the borders with Egypt where again they might well be potential flashpoints.

A different sort of danger came from the great vassals appointed by the Hittite rulers in northern Syria. When control from the centre faltered they struck out for themselves as sovereigns in their own right. But this independence left them vulnerable to attack and infiltration by their displaced neighbours when the great troubles started. The situation is a commonplace of history. Southern Syria, however, was partly cushioned from the worst dangers by distance and (in the Jordan valley) isolation, and some cities survived them, like Beth Shan and Megiddo, holding out, with or without their Egyptian garrisons, against Israelites and Philistines until the late 12th or even into the 10th century. In them the Dark Age was almost bridged over.

Mercenaries and outlaws

One cause of Egyptian weakness was dependence on foreign mercenaries for her army, which was quite as damaging as the Hittite system of feudal service with its over-powerful barons. City-states such as Byblos and Ugarit seem to have used both systems on a small scale, and so were subject to the advantages and dangers of both.

III The Hittite capital
Hattusas in central
Anatolia, built on a
rugged site among hills
and ravines, is seen here
from the citadel looking
west down to the lower
town and the ruins of one
of the temples (temple I).

The term 'mercenary' is a vague one, since in the later 2nd millennium it can cover a variety of classes from the aristocratic *maryannu*, barely distinguishable from feudal vassals, down to unruly bands of nomads. In the 14th century Egyptian garrison-commanders stationed on the strategic passes through the Carmel range near Taanach and Megiddo, on the approaches to Acre and between Galilee and the Shephelah plain, had foreign (Indo-European) names. The practice of employing foreigners persisted to the end of the 13th century, by which time the pressure of new populations on the move had exposed the weakness of the system.

11, 12
66

Some of the best troops employed by the Egyptians were the Sherden or Shardana, whose origins are obscure and about whom there will be more to say in chapter 5. Shardana raiders had attacked the Nile Delta some time before Ramesses II's northern campaign. A very fragmentary inscription on a stela from Tanis describes 'Shardana, rebellious of heart . . . [and their] battle-ships in the midst of the sea'. Ramesses 'destroyed warriors of the Great Green [the Mediterranean], and lower Egypt spends the night sleeping peacefully'.[14] From this time on Shardana troops formed part of the army. They fought at Kadesh and their special status, recorded in many later texts,

14, 74

shows a potentially dangerous Egyptian dependence on the foreigner.

Among the mercenaries employed by the various Near Eastern states we hear of wandering bands called *hubshu*, who were equally troublesome to friend and foe in time of war: always ready to plunder, always on the look out for food or booty. Some came from the semi-nomadic tribes on the edges of the settled

9

lands where migrant shepherds and their flocks lived a life constantly at risk from sudden changes in climate and the supply of natural resources. These *hubshu*, and other bands, often travelled only short distances. They might raise a crop to supplement their food supply before moving on, and so avoided being entirely dependent on their stock. Sometimes they formed mixed groups of cultivators and herdsmen. They were a constant, if fluctuating, reservoir of manpower.

Ramesses II had trouble with certain *ḥapiru* or *'apiru* (the cuneiform version of the name written *'prw* by the Egyptians). This is one of those elusive designations that seems to have meant very different things at different times. It is probably Hurrian in origin and was at first specifically connected with the Hurrian people. In Egyptian texts the 'land of the *ḥapiru*' is a

land without political unity. The name is known in Egypt from the 15th century, and much earlier in Mesopotamia. As a military aristocracy the *ḥapiru* sometimes joined with the *maryannu*, perhaps as foot-soldiers to the others' chariotry; but at other times they were simply a marauding rabble, feared and distrusted. They were already south of Jerusalem in the early 14th century. The Hittites knew them, and so did the people of Ugarit. They acted sometimes as mercenaries and sometimes as condottieri. Occasionally they settled down, for we hear of a 'town of the *ḥapiru*'. Their connection with those other wandering pastoralists, the Israelites, has given rise to a great deal of speculation and controversy. The Israelites did not refer to themselves as *ḥapiru*, though they were apparently conscious of a common interest with these people; but the name was used by the Egyptians for Asiatic foreigners amongst whom Israelites were included. This is the sense in which it appears at Beth Shan in Palestine, on a stela of Pharaoh Seti I around 1300, commemorating a successful campaign against marauders from east of the Jordan. By the 1st millennium the *ḥapiru* are no longer heard of. The Israelites are referred to once only by name in Egyptian texts, on a stela of the time of Merneptah, written after the Libyan campaign of *c.* 1220. There the name is given without the determinative for 'country', so it would appear that at that time the Israelites were still wanderers without a permanent home.

Such people as the *ḥapiru*, landless, outside regular society, roaming between cities and sometimes banding together to attack the townsfolk, are not likely to be discerned archaeologically, and this is also true of the Israelites until they came out of the stony hills and began to take over the Canaanite cities.

Yet one more enemy was preparing to edge into the fertile Levant. The Aramaeans from the north-east were on the move in the later 12th century, although in the 13th they were only one of the more distant sources of unrest, like Moab and Edom, east of Jordan. There is a suggestion that after Kadesh a Hittite expedition into Transjordan upset the balance there and started fresh movements among Israelite and other pastoral tribes.

By the death of Ramesses II in 1224 all these forces of disruption and danger were waiting to press in, already showing their muscle: Assyrians, *ḥapiru*, Kashka, Lukka, Israelites and many more, Sea Peoples and Land Peoples. Far away to the north still other actors were waiting for their cue, and to them we must turn in the next chapter.

IV The citadel of Mycenae looking west over the Argive plain. The massive fortification walls still ring the central acropolis, much of which was once occupied by a great palace.

62

The Aegean in the 13th century

The nature of the evidence

In the last chapter we were able to look back at the Near East to a time of comparative calm that lasted into the beginning of the 13th century. We saw the seeds of the troubles to come, multiplying in the course of that century. In the Aegean too the late 14th and early 13th century was a time of relative calm and prosperity. Yet here the situation was in fact very different, and so are the tools of our investigation.

Stated crudely it is necessary to substitute guesswork for history. We leave behind us the written documents and dated events (however controversial), the dynastic sequences of kings and their reigns which, though imperfect, are still a very solid scaffolding compared with what we find in the Aegean. As we saw in the Introduction, the chronological framework of the Greek Late Bronze Age (Late Helladic (LH) I, II, IIIA–C) is based on the stratigraphy of sites which is itself based on nothing more than fashions in pot-making and the skills, idiosyncrasies and innate conservatism of the pot-makers; and that is truly a very odd way of counting the passing of time and fixing dates. The linear B documents (tablets inscribed with an early form of Greek), though absorbingly interesting, are virtually valueless for establishing actual dates. Again the contrast with the Near East is absolute. Even in the Near East we had to some extent to extrapolate forwards into the 13th century, for the best documents came from earlier. In Greece, outside Crete, we have to do the opposite, since the most important mainland linear B tablets, those from Pylos in the south-western Peloponnese, belong to the last years of the existence of that palace, probably in the later 13th century.[1] They are the spoils of destruction and the relics of catastrophe. On Crete itself the documents from Knossos also show us the situation at the fall of a palace some two centuries earlier. Between these wholly

Table III

24 Hunting and religious ceremony took up much of the time of the ruling class in Greece, as in Western Asia and the Levant. Wall-paintings in the 13th-century palace at Pylos depict a procession with the huge mastiff-type dogs used in the hunt (17 and 18) and tripods for ceremonial use. Greaves (leggings) of leather or cloth would be needed for the hunt, but it is curious to find them worn by the tripod-bearers.

25 A linear B tablet from Pylos. Routine administrative matters and accounts were recorded on unbaked clay tablets for immediate use, but the flames of the disaster that destroyed the 13th-century palace at Pylos have baked and so preserved these records of its last days. L. 25 cm.

isolated points chronologically we are much at a loss, almost entirely dependent on the accident of Aegean pots occasionally turning up in Egypt in a context in which they can be given Egyptian dates. But we do know that the main centres were still literate after the fall of Knossos, judging from inscribed jars found at Thebes in Boeotia and other tablets, including a few from Crete itself. If records were kept elsewhere it was on some less durable material.

The linear B tablets cannot have been intended as permanent records, nor as part of a state archive, or they would hardly have been written on unbaked clay. They may have been destroyed each year, and only a baking in the ruins of their respective palaces has preserved these records of the last days of Knossos and Pylos. It is as though nothing had survived from Ugarit except the latest tablets describing the final disaster (for which see chapter 6).

Another great contrast between the Levant, Cyprus and Egypt on the one hand, and mainland Greece and the islands on the other, is the extent and density of settlement. There are no more packed cities standing as close as Taanach and Megiddo. Where sites *are* clustered close together, as in the Argolid, we see a castle IV, 30 or a palace with not much more than a village outside the walls. Some beginnings of merchants' and artisans' quarters might be inferred at Mycenae, and the town at Pylos (modern Ano Englianos) was a more substantial beginning, but that was exceptional. The old 'village fashion' of settlement may mask real power, as Thucydides says of Sparta, but it is something very different from the urban, cosmopolitan centres of the Levant. Crete stands aside in a special position that was rather closer to the orientals.

The Cretan lesson

At Knossos around 1380 there do not appear to have been any premonitions of disaster, no signs of want or unrest. There had been other destructions, but this one was different, for Knossos did not rise again as it had done after the change of dynasty around

1450 when Greeks from the mainland had swept through the island, leaving a pattern of selective destruction and introducing new martial values. What happened in Crete in the early 14th century was almost a dress-rehearsal for the disasters that ruined mainland sites at the end of the 13th century; it is, therefore, of some interest to this history.

The wealth and splendour of palatial Knossos could only be supported through the production of large surpluses and the employment of a large workforce. The tablets give evidence for both.[2] Olive oil may have been exported to Egypt where the olive does not grow easily, but of grain there is not likely to have been a surplus. The tablets name exotic merchandise that must have come from the Levant. Sesame and cumin, gold and purple dye, are known by their Semitic names. The lists of craftsmen include many working in the textile industry such as spinners and fullers. An interesting comparison has been made between sheep-raising organized from the palace at Knossos and the great English sheep raising manors of the later Middle Ages. The flocks of Knossos were larger but the organization was similar. The wool-tablets show a very sophisticated system depending on many overseers, much record-keeping and good communications. Surpluses were essential to feed the workers in the palace factories, as was access to markets where the finished products could be disposed of in exchange for other goods. It may be relevant that in Egypt textiles rated next after gold in value as a commodity of exchange.

The change of dynasty and of ruling class around 1450 did not upset these commercial activities for very long, nor the wealth of the palace and its grandees. Nevertheless the concentration of authority in one place brought increased dependence on communications and the efficiency of the bureaucracy. When such a society breaks down it quickly reverts to the standards of small-scale subsistence farming. The individual farmer is thrown back on his own holding where he can survive indefinitely after a fashion, weathering periodic scarcities and local disasters. The Cretan countryside is not well suited to the sort of mixed farming that is combined with intensive shepherding. Too many men would have to move up to the mountains in the summer with the flocks. Perhaps it is significant that there is no word in the Knossos tablets for 'farmer' in the sense of cultivator of the land pure and simple. But when the small independent shepherd takes to the mountains, he combines the care of his reduced flocks with small-scale cultivation, or exchange of products with his farming neighbours, trading skins and cheese for grains, fruit and oil. Life goes on but the era of the palace, with its large workforce, great resources, and its need for economic surpluses is over. This seems to be what happened over most of Crete in the 14th century.

There is no question of barbarians from far places bringing havoc. Different causes have been canvassed: earthquake, great raids of Lukki from south-western Anatolia or other corsairs, an expeditionary force from mainland Greece aimed at ending the commercial dominance of Knossos and breaking into the markets in the south. This last, though certainly not the entire answer, has much to commend it. An ambassador in Cretan dress shown on the walls of the 15th-century tomb of Rekhmire in Egypt is overpainted by one wearing a mainland kilt, and this seems to show that the mainlanders were successful. For a time Cretan exports to the Levant, to judge from the pottery found there, continued alongside Mycenaean ones, and there are still Egyptian imports in late-15th-century warrior graves at Knossos; but a significant increase in the amount of mainland pottery in the Levant follows the fall of Knossos in the early 14th century. The ruin of these years left Knossos in a backwater, bypassed by the international shipping routes. But the mainland and the islands were not troubled, and may even have benefited. There was no general regression. As Knossos sank Mycenae and the other Mycenaean centres prospered.

Palaces and castles

In the Near East the battle of Kadesh gave us a convenient vantage point from which to begin a rapid review of the state of affairs in the 13th century. The appearance of the style of pottery known as LH IIIB may do the same for the Aegean. Real dates have to come from Egypt and are not too reliable, because Egyptian dates are still subject to readjustment (and see Introduction note 2). In this chapter we will be considering the seventy-odd years from the accession of Ramesses II in *c.* 1290 to the Libyan war of Merneptah *c.* 1220, in which northern allies from over the sea took part.

A little historical information may be squeezed from the excavation of Mycenaean sites such as Tiryns and the reinterpretation of other sites such as Mycenae which help to fill the 13th century. It is possible that somewhere around the beginning of the century the last of the great ashlar chamber tombs at Mycenae, the Treasury of Atreus, was completed. This is probably the finest example of ashlar stonework on the mainland, where there is in fact not very much of it at all, and the source of the workmanship is uncertain. The carved ceiling of the side-chamber to the so-called Treasury of Minyas at Orchomenos in Boeotia shows refinement of taste. But it is in Messenia, at Pylos, the 'Palace of Pylian Nestor', that we find the most humane and spacious of mainland buildings. Its painted walls, its great hall, its stores and archives show plainly that the men who lived there had learnt soft manners and were aspiring to Egyptian and Levantine standards of comfort. All its refinements notwithstanding, the palace at Pylos was not an ashlar building like the palace of Ugarit. Finely dressed stone was used only for thresholds and footings; the walls above were of rough stone covered with plaster like the contemporary buildings in Cyprus (see chapter 6). The palace was enlarged in the 13th

26 Entrance to the Treasury of Atreus at Mycenae. Here is perhaps the finest use of true ashlar in Mycenaean Greece. Either late 14th or very early 13th century, it must be the tomb of a king of Mycenae. But for the loss of its contents in antiquity our knowledge of life in the palaces would have been far richer.

27, 28   The megaron or great hall of the palace at Ano Englianos, Pylos as it appeared when excavated (*below*) and in a reconstruction drawing by Piet de Jong (*right*). Unlike Mycenae Pylos was never fortified. The walls of the palace were decorated with gaily coloured wall-paintings, evidence for the comfort and luxury of daily life. The megaron, with its central hearth and four pillars, was the heart of the building, surrounded by store rooms, archives, and private apartments.

century, probably by a new dynasty, but it was never in fact fortified.

There is no ashlar in the town and citadel at Mycenae;[3] instead large roughly dressed stones were used. The area within 29   the walls is not large, some 30,000 m². Even taking account of the

greater size of the palace as it has been established recently, it is still a fortress, the castle of an unquiet state. The massive fortifications here and at Tiryns have a beleaguered look. The 13th-century additions would have taken quite a long time to build. They were not put up against a sudden and unexpected

30, 31

29 A sketch plan of the
citadel of Mycenae. Fresh
excavation has recently
extended the area of the
palace towards the east
further than is shown
here. Within the massive
defensive wall of the
citadel there were a
number of private houses,
workshops and stores in
addition to the palace
itself. Cf. IV.

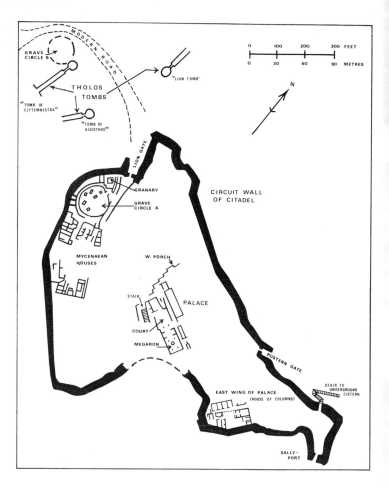

Opposite
30, 31 An aerial view of
Tiryns from the south-
west (*above*) shows the
massive wall surrounding
the citadel. The main
entrance is on the far side,
to the left of the bulge,
and the covered gallery
(35) runs inside the
casemate wall to the right
of the entrance. The
megaron is visible in the
middle between the
entrance and the curved
western bastion with a
postern gate at the bottom
of this view. The massive
blocks in the
neighbourhood of the
eastern entrance (*below*)
show well the strength of
the late 13th-century
defences here, as at
Mycenae 10 miles away. In
both sites ashlar was used
only for thresholds and
some footings.

enemy; nor were the fortifications of Gla in Boeotia, although
never finished. Gla was planned on a grandiose scale by men who
had not lost confidence in their capacity to rule.

The lack of fortification at Pylos stands in total contrast to this.
Pylos was not, it appears, threatened when the lords of Mycenae
found it necessary to strengthen their defences, in the middle of
the 13th century, which suggests that during this century the
areas of danger were local and selective: internal warfare and
feuding rather than external invasion.

But there is one other site that *is* like Mycenae and Tiryns,
though on a vastly grander scale. At the Hittite hill-top capital in
central Anatolia, Hattusas (Boğazköy), there are the same huge
boulders, the so-called cyclopean masonry, the same craggy hills
only larger. The defences of the inner fortress, Büyükkale, are
perhaps the most impressive of any in the ancient world; they too
were reconstructed during the 13th century, under threat of

32–4   On the Anatolian plateau the Hittite capital Hattusas
was not unlike Mycenae but larger, rockier and more heavily
fortified. The reconstruction (*right*) shows the bridge over a
chasm that defended the approach to the central citadel,
Büyükkale. One of the entrances through the tremendous main
fortifications at Hattusas is guarded by lions carved in a
typically heavy style (*above*). The rough-hewn blocks are
reminiscent of the Lion Gate and rampart at Mycenae (*opposite*). The Mycenaean gate is shown as it was before a recent
reconstruction of the walls. The two lions or sphinxes flanking
a column are an Aegean subject but carried out in an un-
characteristically heavy style, perhaps learnt from Anatolian
masons.

enemy attack. The corbelled 'gallery' at Tiryns is well matched 35
by the much longer gallery under the fortifications and the sally 36
port on the hill slope outside the walls at Hattusas. The
sculpture of the Lion Gate at Mycenae is in the monumental 34
Hittite style of the guardian of the gate at Hattusas and the 32
sphinxes of Alaca, north of Hattusas.

By repute the walls of Tiryns were built by Lycians, and
perhaps those of Mycenae too. 'Lycians', if a memory from
Mycenaean times, can be either the seafaring Lukka, who were
well within the Hittite ambience, or the inland Lycaonians on
the Anatolian plateau, still nearer to the Hittite homeland. This
was a time when Mycenaeans at Miletus were in touch with both
Hittites and Lukka, and there were other Mycenaeans round the
Anatolian coasts at Colophon and Tarsus. Even at Maşat on the
plateau some 75 miles south of Samsun, and north of

Previous two pages
35, 36 A covered gallery
with a corbelled roof of
large blocks runs inside
the south-east casemate
fortification wall at Tiryns
(*left*, cf. 30). Its purpose is
uncertain but the con-
struction, though fairly
basic, is another link with
Hattusas: here a long
passage and tunnel (*right*)
pass under the exposed
southern rampart (where
it is at its strongest on the
crest of the hill) to emerge
in a sally-port some
distance down the slope
outside the walls. The
strength of these Hittite
fortifications is so great
that only treachery and
connivance are likely to
have caused the downfall
of Hattusas, where the last
stage of 13th-century
fortification was probably
completed at about the
same time as the last
fortification at Mycenae
and Tiryns.

Hattusas, LH IIIB pottery has been found in a Hittite building. This does not imply more than trading activities, but trade does mean some sort of contact. Even if the controversial document known after the name of a rebellious Hittite subject as the Maduwattas Indictment,[4] with its many references to the Mycenaean world, is to be dated in the 15th and not the 13th century, there are other Hittite texts referring to Ahhiyawa (identified with the Homeric Achaeans who came from Greece to attack Troy), that do fall within the 13th century. They include the intriguing Tawagalawas Letter, addressed to an unnamed Hittite king, probably Muwatallis, which refers to Lukka pirates, Millawanda (Miletus) and the practice of chariotry, as well as to Ahhiyawa (see chapter 6).

It has been objected that virtually nothing specifically Hittite has been found on Mycenaean sites at this time, but the same can be said of Cyprus in the 13th century when, according to the Hittite documents, the island, or a part of it, was actually conquered by Tudhaliyas IV (chapter 2). Moreover Hittite suzerainty in northern Syria, which is a fact well documented, has very little to show for itself by way of archaeological material. This was no longer the case when disaster drove the Hittites down from the plateau to establish new little kingdoms at Karatepe and Carchemish. Then they took their styles of building and carving and their hieroglyphic writings with them. So the links between Mycenaean and Hittite architecture may be stronger in reality than the lack of more superficial evidence suggests.

The wall-paintings of Pylos, Tiryns and Mycenae, many of which are of 13th-century date, show peaceful occupations, 24   religious processions, hunting and a very few scenes of combat and violence. These cannot have anything to do with the final catastrophe. They come from confident years when the threat to palace life was still a long way off. There is nothing in the paintings at all like the oriental and Egyptian portrayals of martial triumph. The fighting has a haphazard look: local 37   skirmishes, or even perhaps gladiatorial displays. The 'enemy' is dressed in skins, poorly armed and wild-haired. These are not serious enemies, nor are such men likely to have been lurking on the slopes of the Haghia range in the 13th century; this is the dress of the Old Stone Age many millennia before. Skins were still occasionally used in sacred rituals, for we see them in Cretan ceremonies; or, even more plausibly, these may be adaptations of Egyptian paintings of wild men from Nubia.

At Mycenae paintings in the Citadel House are conventional, the figures rather in the style of the sarcophagus from Aghia Triadha in Crete and a still older Minoan tradition. They look like the work of people who planned to go on living where they were in reasonable comfort for years to come. We know from other sites that the Mycenaeans were not caught unawares by the troubles when they broke. It is hardly likely that these elegant paintings were commissioned by men immediately threatened by an enemy.

The strange ceramic figures from the shrine in the Citadel House are in a quite different convention. This shrine has been compared to a temple in Palestine (Tell Qasile) and the mask-like faces are oddly reminiscent of certain Phoenician grotesques of much later times. Fragments of gold leaf, ivory and a sensitive small ivory head are again materials from a larger, more peaceful world of taste and commerce.[5] The palace workshops were still producing these fine objects till at least the end of the 13th century (LH IIIB–C). The rulers of Mycenae kept large stores of oil and employed master-potters and other craftsmen. The palace at Thebes that was destroyed at or before the beginning of the century (early LH IIIB) has already been referred to. As well as the cache of oriental cylinder seals and the fragments of worked lapis lazuli, there is the naming of the god of a place known to be near Ugarit. It is an example of cosmopolitan, especially northern Syrian, contacts which may have come by way of Crete. The people who lived in these palaces were surrounded with wealth and comfort. A second palace at Thebes may have been destroyed later in the 13th century or in the early 12th century (developed LH IIIB pottery). Though few tablets have been found outside Pylos, all these were literate Mycenaean centres, each one the hub of an administrative network, with Pylos probably the most literate and the most prosperous. Pylos commanded the best harbour on the western sea-board of the Peloponnese and its comparative isolation from other centres made it less vulnerable to outside aggression.

Mycenae was the home of violent men: that is how it was remembered, and in this case it is probably a just memory. The old stories all concern family and dynastic revolts, while the geography and planning of the site are eloquent of external dangers. Mycenae is distant enough from the sea to be safe from sea-marauders, and yet not too far for access to a tributary port or harbour. It dominates a plain like the castles of German robber-barons in the Odenwald and Black Forest which look down on

40

IV

37–40 The type of the Mycenaean lord – proud, aggressive, sensual – is expressed in the small ivory head from a chamber-tomb of around 1300 outside the walls at Mycenae (*opposite, below*). This man is bearded and wears a boar's tusk helmet like the fighters and huntsmen of Pylos (37, 39). Ht 8.5 cm.

The wall-paintings of the palaces at Pylos, Tiryns and Mycenae show the typical aristocratic pursuits of their 13th-century rulers: fighting (*above*) and driving out to the hunt (*opposite, above*) (both from Pylos; cf. 24). The identity of the 'enemy' in the skirmish is a problem, for these sort of skin-covered savages

are unlikely to have been lurking in the mountains of the Peloponnese at this time. The scene of action appears to be a river boundary, but the subject might be traditional or even religious.

Chariots in Mycenaean representations are slow-moving or stationary, unlike the galloping chariots of the orientals (10, 17, 18, but see 123 from Lefkandi). The chariot from Pylos (*above*) is part of a hunting scene as may also be the two figures with female features but dressed as men driving out between stylized trees pictured at Tiryns (*opposite, below*). Note in both the fragile build of the chariot with four-spoked wheels.

the Rhine valley. The plain ensured grazing for horses, though this may well have been a source of friction. For Mycenae had a great many neighbours – Argos, Tiryns, Prosymna, Dendra, Asine – and, even though all were not occupied all the time, there was never very much elbow-room in the Argolid. The horse is an economic liability, and the pressure on the limited areas of productive land must at times have been extreme.

There is no reason to think that the Mycenaeans drank mare's milk or ate horseflesh. The horse was a weapon and a symbol. The chariot and mystique of horse-owning, and the status of charioteer, were quite as important here as in the Near East to judge by the paintings, seals and documents. But chariot warfare, as carried on by Levantine powers, was a very specialized, even stylized affair. It could only take place on well-chosen, not too hilly terrain free of rocks and watercourses – not, that is to say, the usual terrain of Greece and the Levant.

The defeat of the Canaanite chariotry at Mount Tabor, probably sometime in the 13th or 12th century, by Deborah, Barak and the Israelite infantry, is a good example of the ease with which a clever enemy, who did not 'stick to the rules', could out-manoeuvre an army whose strength lay in its chariots, and which fought according to the conventions of chariot warfare established between the great powers. The Canaanites were drawn into the hills and routed by a watercourse. It is very rare in the wall-paintings and on painted pots for a Mycenaean chariot actually to be engaged in combat, or to be moving at more than a sedate walk; more often it is quite stationary.[6] If its importance was greater as symbol than as weapon, it did nonetheless play its part in the decline of the Mycenaean economy.

Materials and commerce

It is sometimes said that the whole of the 13th century was a progressive dégringolade, with objects of value growing scarcer, metals harder to come by, and life more drab and more dangerous. Up to a point this may be so, particularly towards the end of the century, but the statement needs qualification. The commissioning and subject-matter of the wall-paintings, many of which belong to this period, has already been referred to. Many of our judgments concerning earlier centuries are based on the shaft graves at Mycenae or tholos tombs in Messenia; our view of the richness or penury of the princely gear of the 13th century might therefore be very different if we had seen the

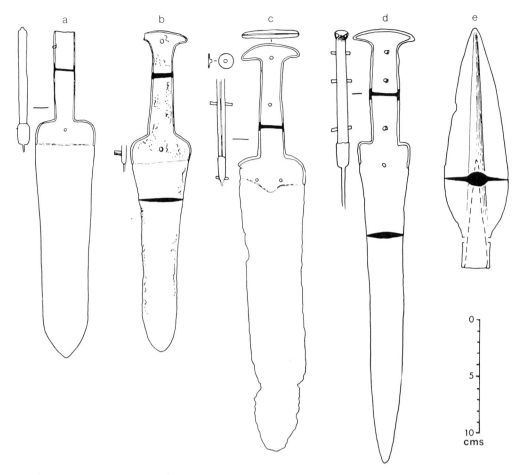

contents of the Treasury of Atreus, given that it too is of this century and that its contents had been on a level with the grandeur of the architecture. Negative evidence is unreliable, but in this case it must be kept in mind.

The disappearance of the gold-, niello- and lapis-lazuli-decorated weapons of an earlier age is given as evidence for impoverishment, but the waste from the workshop area at Mycenae proves that these luxury materials were obtained and worked into the 12th century. The rapiers of the 14th century had disappeared, but dirks derived from the cruciform sword (known as type Dii) were probably still in use during the first half of the 13th century and are shown in the Pylos painting. Towards the end of the century there was a multiplication of swords and daggers, some of them very eccentric. What really happened, rather than any shortage of metal, was a change in fighting tactics, with the long spear now the principal weapon,

41   In the later 14th and throughout the 13th century the normal weapons of the Mycenaeans were a long spear and a short dirk, used both in warfare and in the hunt (37). The bronze dirks and spearhead illustrated here are from a, Olympia; c, Corinth?; b, Mavrospelio and d, Zapher Papoura Knossos (both in Crete); the short spearhead e, of 'northern' type, is from the Mycenae acropolis hoard found in 1890.

and the dagger (types E and F) a supporting weapon. War was a much more bloody and pitiless business than the elegant rapier duels of earlier days. Before the end of the century new foreign weapons had appeared about which there will be more to say in chapter 4.

The linear B tablets give a lot of information about metal-working and supply. Greece is poor in minerals and had to import most of what it used. The source of metals – copper and tin ores for the armament industry – is very difficult to assess. The Aegean had of course to import tin, but how much copper it needed to obtain from elsewhere has been much debated. Supplies from the Greek mainland have proved illusory, nor is there much evidence for ancient copper-mining in Crete. If Crete is eliminated the chief sources are the sulphide ores of Cyprus which would have been imported in the form of 'ox-hide' ingots (see chapter 2), though there is another possible source in eastern Turkey, where ores from the area around Ergani Maden had been worked from early times.[7]

Much depends on how we interpret the remarkable collection of bronze, copper and a few tin ingots found in a boat wrecked off Cape Gelidonya in south-western Turkey. As well as a large number of ingots the boat had carried a metal-worker and his tool-kit, and a merchant's weights for conducting his business. Whether the boat was Cypriot or Aegean or native to Syria or Anatolia, whether the ores came from Cyprus or Turkey, whether the wreck occurred before the outbreak of troubles or whether it was a casualty of those years – these are all unanswered questions. Some of the tools look Cypriot rather than Aegean while analysis of an ingot, probably from this source, suggests Anatolia rather than Cyprus, but nothing is conclusive.[8] The date of the fatal voyage does not greatly matter, for we may take both ship and cargo as being fairly typical of the Aegean-Levantine trade at the end of the 13th century. The question of the tin supply is at present wide open, with possible sources in the Near or Far East (still unidentified), in the Erzgebirge (the nearest and most direct), in the far west on Europe's Atlantic coast, and in Egypt (the most recently identified).[9]

If metals were probably the largest Aegean import, pottery was the largest export, though we have to remember that gaps in the evidence are enormous. The accidental durability of potsherds may have distorted the record, by how much we will never know. LH IIIB pottery is a very professional, rather monotonous product that was in huge demand outside Greece – for what it contained as much as for itself – as well as on the home market. Much was produced in the Argolid for export and in some other parts of Greece. In Cyprus large quantities of Mycenaean pottery have been found in the coastal emporia – more in fact than in the whole of the Levant – and there have been doubts as to whether some of it was not produced in Cyprus itself by Mycenaean colonists; but on the whole clay analysis and other arguments do not support the colonial case for the 13th century.[10]

42, 43

In the last chapter we saw how IIIB pottery was usually found with even greater quantities of the (inferior) Cypriot ware. In the Levant most of it comes from the coastal cities, but it also found its way across the Jordan to Amman, Deir Alla and Tell es Saidiyeh. It would be good to know what commodities the pots contained. Some perhaps held resins, animal fats and olive oil, used in preparing food, for paints and in cleaning. The large stores of olive oil in the House of the Oil Merchant at Mycenae may have been for export.

If we use the Mycenaean pottery found overseas as a criterion of the level of trade, always remembering that we only have that part of the trade that travelled in durable containers, then we find that Egypt imported goods from Greek lands in the early 14th century (Amarna period), but that the trade fell off sharply after this.[11] At the same time Cypriot pottery disappears almost · completely from Egypt, though the texts give no indication of a break in Cypriot-Egyptian relations. In the Levant Mycenaean imports reached a peak in the later 14th century (LH IIIA2) with finds from 90 sites between the Orontes and Nubia; but there was a falling off to 75 sites in the first half of the 13th century (LH IIIB1). In Cyprus, however, Mycenaean imports in the same period increased to 61 sites (LH IIIB1) as against 47 with LH IIIA2 pottery. This trade is reflected also on the Anatolian coasts, at sites such as Miletus, and in the Dodecanese, where population increased to such an extent that it has been argued that colonies on Cos and Rhodes may have been cutting out the mainlanders in the trade with Cyprus and the Levant, though hardly before the end of the 13th century. The contents of tombs on Cos and Rhodes show that the people there were well supplied with bronze weapons, ornaments and utensils, with perhaps some evidence for a levelling of the social grades.

What this seems to mean is that after breaking through the (hypothetical) Cretan monopoly at the beginning of the 14th

century, the mainland Mycenaeans enjoyed the trade with Egypt for a short spell. They were very active in the Levant immediately after the Amarna period, but in the 13th century, though still operating in Cyprus, they may have been diverted from the Levant by the Cypriots, who insisted on controlling the trade themselves. So it is probably from Cyprus that copper came and through Cyprus luxury goods: ivories and jewels, perhaps skills too.

Indeed Cyprus became more than ever important as middle-man between the Aegean and not only the Levant, but all that lay beyond in Transjordan and even Mesopotamia. This system was, I believe, vital to the survival of the princely houses, the whole order of society, and the economy of the palaces and castles of mainland Greece. We shall have soon to look at various attempts made by the Mycenaeans to widen the base of their commerce, and to find new markets north and west, as well as in the old south-east Mediterranean bazaars.

Economic danger-points

There was a large increase in population in Messenia from 50 sites during the Middle Helladic period (early 2nd millennium) to 137 in the Late Helladic period.[12] A peak was reached in the later 13th century just before the troubles, with an estimated population of 50,000 in Messenia alone which was probably the most highly populated district on the mainland. Even higher figures have been proposed. This led to the use of marginal land instead of good land and to reclamation work like the drainage of Lake Copais in Boeotia. Some of the new Late Helladic sites in Messenia are on very poor land indeed. This must have been followed by the division of estates into ever-smaller lots. The tablets tell of the diminutive size of many holdings and quarrels over ownership. It is a process that still goes on wherever inherited land is divided equally between heirs.

An interesting analogy has been drawn between the wealthy medieval abbey estate after the crusades and the kingdom of Pylos.[13] Pylos, like the medieval abbey, was a unit of indirect consumption. A large part of the agrarian population had left the fields to produce artifacts which could be exchanged for profit, luxury goods, imported materials and extra food. The flax, grain and wool tablets from Pylos show that this actually happened.

In medieval Europe an unsatisfactory ratio of arable land to population had disastrous results. In the 14th century AD, with

42, 43 Pictorial style pots from Cyprus. A chariot crater (mixing-bowl) for wine comes from Maroni, Cyprus (*above*, LH IIIA2, late 14th to early 13th century). These handsome pots were made in the Peloponnese and were enormously popular in the Levant, above all in Cyprus, where they are found in tombs. On the mainland they were also used but seldom placed in tombs, so they survive only as broken sherds. Compare the potter's rendering of this favourite subject with that of the palace wall-painter (38). A crater in a slightly later Levanto-Mycenaean pictorial style (*below*) comes from Enkomi (mature LH IIIB, 13th century). The decorative treatment of the bull and bird already foreshadows the 'rude style' (see ch. 6) and contrasts with the more naturalistic style of the Maroni crater, where the pair of horses have not yet fused into one as they were to do later. Hts: *above*, 42 cm; *below*, 27 cm.

the prevalent low crop-yields, less than one third of the land was available for cereal growing. When the marginal land lost its fertility it was no longer possible to feed the increased population. As well as providing staple food Mycenaean agriculture was a source of many other commodities, some to be stored, some exported, so that a large percentage of the population was supported directly and indirectly by the economic network based on the palaces. From here went out the organization of pasturage and animal products. There were too many people for much dependence on game. Hunting had probably already become an aristocratic prerogative. The seasonal migration of some sorts of fish might have led fishermen to distant islands, but there is no documentary evidence for this.

We find in Mycenaean Greece a dangerous concentration on a single crop, grain in Messenia, flocks and wool in Crete. A recent Greek writer has put it that 'the long period of prosperity and stability seems to have encouraged the production of high-yield crops like wheat, barley and the raising . . . of sheep. Mycenaean industry used raw materials that had to be carefully raised, or that were imported from abroad'.[14] Government was highly centralized, depending on a network of roads connecting with distant and peripheral areas which were essential to its survival. Strict accounting was also essential so that records could be kept of surpluses in one area to be set against deficits in another. The tablets are this accounting system.

In a good season Messenia would have been able to export surplus grain, but a population of the size estimated would be extremely vulnerable if faced by a series of bad years with crop failures. Local shortages, however, only become tragic when the machinery of transportation and commerce fail, and there is no organization and no authority to see that relief is sent. Then even a local shortage becomes a major disaster. These two things, organization and transportation, are essential for the survival of the sort of life for which there is evidence in the Near East and in the Aegean in the second half of the 2nd millennium.

In the correspondence of the great powers, Egyptian, Hittite and oriental, and to some extent in the linear B palace archives, trade and war are the most important and time-consuming topics. Both require large surpluses, especially war as it was carried on between the 'civilized' peoples of the East Mediterranean: for if war is to be more than mere piracy and reiving it depends upon a leisured class, the feudal aristocracy and the professional fighting-man, feudal subject or mercenary soldier.

The prosperity of the Levant, and I believe also of the Aegean, was commercial. It depended on the existence of markets for surplus products. The world revealed by the linear B tablets from Pylos, though it is in its last days, still shows, in full operation, an advanced system of accountancy dealing with surpluses and deficits, and the support of the central authority.

The rulers of Pylos and Mycenae lived in a luxury that is a reflection of the greater luxury of Memphis and Hattusas, of Ugarit and Enkomi. Such wealth renders the possessor highly vulnerable, particularly when it depends on foreign relations and the availability of certain rare raw materials such as tin and gold; for with it there goes also the down-grading of the producer of basic commodities, the farmer and fisherman. But in the event he has the last word for, 'The masters come and go, the rest remain'.

The princes of Mycenae, Thebes and Pylos did, and could, only exist because of the organization for amassing produce and disposing of the surpluses: the flocks of Minos, the oil of Mycenae, the grain of Messenia, were exchanged for raw materials such as the tin needed for their weapons. It was this organization which gave them the leisure to fight as well as feast.

The fact is that the Mycenaean kingdoms were over-specialized, over-dependent on central bureaucracies. Three danger-points were to become acutely sensitive as the years of the 13th century ran out: the high population, dependence on the palace and the over-specialized economy. If this is set beside the permanent features of the Mediterranean world outlined in chapter 1 there will be less surprise at the changes that were coming.

OTOMANI

WIETENBERG
• Wietenberg

CARPATHIAN MTS

MONTEORU   NOUA

BANAT

• Sărata-Monteoru

VOJVODINA
Drava

Sava

R O M A N I A

DOBROGEA

Babadag
•

Vattina
Peracin
•

Danube

BLACK   SEA

• Gîrla Mare

• Cîrna

COSLOGENI

S E R B I A

Moravia

• Mediana

Gabarevo
•

B U L G A R I A

Struma

Maritsa

• Pšeničevo

Vardar

T H R A C E

R H O D O P E   MTS

ALBANIA
Mati

Pažok
•

M A C E D O N I A

• Kilindir

Vardaroftsa
• Saratsé

Verghina
•

EPIRUS

PINDUS   MTS

THESSALY

A E G E A N

Troy
•

TROAD

Pergamon
•

CORFU

Parga
•

Iolkos
•

LESBOS

• Ilias

EUBOEA

SKYROS

CHIOS

L Y D I A

Thermon •

PHOCIS
Orchomenos • • Gla
BOEOTIA • Lefkandi
• Thebes
ATTICA
Athens
•

Colophon
•

Teikhos Dymaion •

ACHAEA

PELOPONNESE

• Perati

C A R I A

Miletus
(Millawanda)

S E A

CYCLADES

DODECANESE

COS

LACONIA

NAXOS

Korakou •
Corinth •

MESSENIA
Vapheio
•

Pylos

• Zygouries

Mycenae •
Prosymna •
Argos •

• Berbati

• Tiryns

Lerna •

Asine
•

THERA

Ialysos
•

Siana

RHODES

0   200 Kms

0   120 Mls

0   25 Kms

0   20 Mls

Knossos
•

C R E T E

• Mouliana

Aghia Triadha •

4

High barbary

A case of misconceptions

Of three directions from which danger threatened the old civilizations of the Near East and the Aegean, two have been glanced at so far: the hills and desert to the east and south, and the highlands of Anatolia to the Caucasus. There remains Europe: the western Mediterranean lands and, most important of all, since it has sometimes been credited with the principal role in toppling the whole fabric of Aegean civilization, the Danube and the people of the Balkans.

We may start with these last, but first some misconceptions have to be cleared away about what we mean by 'barbarian societies'. In central and eastern Europe the Middle Bronze Age, that is the middle of the 2nd millennium BC, has been called 'High Barbarian Europe'. 'High' because of the grandeur of the artifacts and the great technical expertise that went into the making of the gear and weaponry of the chieftains, their families and followers: what they chose to have buried with them and what was hidden in merchants' hoards near their settlements. In his study of ancient Europe, Stuart Piggott has written of an heroic world.

> Archaeologically we find it represented over much of Europe at this time in the form of graves which with their lavish profusion for the dead warrior and his women-folk, show us that we are dealing with a stratified society, with an aristocracy at once patrons of the arts and crafts, and the potential cause of their disruption by internecine wars.[1]

These barbarians lived in undisturbed occupation of their settlements for many years, even centuries, in tells such as Tószeg on the Hungarian plain, or on hill-tops where many occupation levels can be separated out, as at Monteoru in Moldavia. They drove their horses in spoke-wheeled carts or

44 A map of the Aegean and the Balkans, showing principal areas and sites mentioned in the text.

chariots, they ate and drank from fine pottery cups and bowls and, if one may judge from certain small clay figures, their clothes were rich and ornate. They were successful cultivators and ranchers. Above all they had large supplies of minerals: gold, copper and tin from the Erzgebirge and the Carpathians. Only silver was rare at this time.

There is a sense in which literacy actually distorts the archaeological record, for while it illuminates the centres of civilization, it makes the darkness surrounding even darker. This is the case in the last centuries of the 2nd millennium BC where it has led to two fundamental misconceptions. One is the ready interpretation by Mycenaean experts of the wild-haired, skin-covered gladiators of the Pylos wall-paintings as 'northern invaders'; another is the uncritical assumption that the coarse hand-made pots found in many late Mycenaean sites (see chapter 8) are also evidence of northern strangers. 'Hand-made' applied to pottery can be very misleading, especially if it is taken as synonymous with 'ill-made'. Although they were ignorant of the potter's wheel, the potters of Middle to Late Bronze Age Europe were craftsmen of a high order of competence. Their wares are often beautiful in shape and carry a burnish that gives an almost metallic sheen, while the decoration is studied and harmonious. They can hold their own with all but the very best Aegean work, are superior to the run-of-the-mill Cypriot wares and have nothing in common with the squalid 'hand-made pots' of late Mycenaean sites.

Wild northerners, coarse pottery, a new sort of sword and other bronze weapons and ornaments were all once taken as adjuncts of the great barbarian invasion that swept down from the Danube to overrun Mycenae and many other cities and even, throwing probability to the winds, took ship to arrive on the borders of Egypt as those mysterious 'Sea Peoples' who so terrified Ramesses III. There are as many objections to this scenario on the European, as on the Mediterranean side. It is not easy to bring large numbers of new people south from the Danube. There is too much continuity in these, and in intervening, lands. There are signs of over-population within the Carpathian ring; but the Transylvanian bronze industry flourished, and there is no disruption in the trade routes to and from the sources of ores in the Erzgebirge, the Carpathians and, probably to a lesser extent, in the Rhodope.

In Hungary Füzesabony (Tószeg) and Otomani, in Transylvania Otomani and Wietenberg, in south Moldavia Monteoru,

45, 46 (*Above*) A view of the Carpathians in Slovakia. Running in a great arc from the Iron Gates on the Middle Danube (Transylvanian Alps), the mountains stretch east, then north and finally west into Slovakia. They effectively separate the Black Sea and its hinterland of steppe and coastal plain, the Ukraine and Moldavia, from Transylvania. They are rich in ores which were exploited by the peoples living near the Danube, and indeed much farther afield. One of the richest and most successful Bronze Age civilizations of the Carpathian regions was the Otomani of Slovakia, Hungary and Transylvania. Gold was worn and used extensively, like the collection of neck-rings, earrings and other finery from Barca in Slovakia (*below*).

2

46–8

these names spell 'High Barbarian Europe'. Wealthy and long-established in their homelands, they shared to some extent a great inheritance in metal-working, with interconnected workshop traditions that specialized in the technique of casting bronze, and in fine ornamentation with the tracer. At the same time the traditions in potting were very different, one from the other, though all were very accomplished. Otomani and Wietenberg both lasted through the final phases of the Middle Bronze Age into the changed world of the Late Bronze Age (till Reinecke Bronze D and Hallstatt A1 in central European terms). There is no complete agreement among scholars on the extent of this survival. On the other hand Tószeg to the west, and Monteoru to the east, came to an abrupt end.

Table IV

Continuity and change in the Balkans

Moldavia, by reason of its geography, lying outside the Carpathian ring, is a back-door open to the South Russian steppe and the Ukraine. When the Middle Bronze Age was well advanced, after the middle of the 2nd millennium, a change began to come over Moldavia which had significant repercussions farther south. Hill-top sites such as Sărata-Monteoru were first heavily fortified and then abandoned. A more pastoral way of life was adopted in the eastern parts, spreading thence over the Carpathians into Transylvania and across the lower Danube into north-eastern Bulgaria. This is the phenomenon that goes by the name of Noua (Noa).[2]

The Noua of Romania is allied to the Sabatinovka of South Russia. Between them they extended from the Dnieper and the Bug to the Danube. The Noua people were tolerant of a very varied sort of environment: steppe, forest, mountain, river-valley and plain. The sites are always open, with slight and fragile remains of temporary dwellings in place of the deep deposits and permanent agricultural settlements that they supplanted. They are recognized by patches of ash known as *zolniki* in which hearths, wattle and daub, clay flooring and great quantities of animal bone are found. The animals are mostly domestic with 50 per cent cattle and 10 per cent horse bones, but there are not yet enough recorded sites for general inferences. What does emerge is a well-defined change from cultivation to stock-breeding, perhaps combined with a partly nomadic pastoralism. In Romania people were buried in the crouched position in flat graves, but farther east the related Sabatinovka people buried their dead under barrows or *kurgans*. The Dniester was the western limit of these *kurgans*.

There is a dramatic debasement in the standard of potting, with ugly little rough cups and mugs in place of the ornamental Monteoru and Cîrna wares of Middle Bronze Age Romania. There are also large and very characteristic 'sack pots' that have a cordon below the rim. Some of these pots hark back to an old Early Bronze Age style. After a time the standard of potting improves again, and even some of the Monteoru tricks and ornaments are readopted, but coarsened and dulled. Bone-work has a new importance for tools, with a corresponding falling off in the bronze industry; apart from a few knives and sickles, the metal-work has a curiously archaic look, like the pots. 49

With this one exception of Moldavia there is little sign of change in Danubian lands at the end of the Middle Bronze Age, no dramatic shifts of population. The old Middle Bronze Age societies continued in the Banat and Vojvodina, producing their fine dark-faced flamboyant pots. Here and in northern Serbia and Croatia people were buried in cremation cemeteries (urnfields: Vattina, Dubovac-Žuto Brdo and Bjelo Brdo groups). Much of the pottery is impressed or incised with 'embroidery' designs; while further north-west, in the region of the Middle Danube urnfields, a superb sleek undecorated style of potting is found which gradually extended southwards from Slovakia and Lower Austria (Baierdorf-Velatice group). This style is perhaps at its finest in Slovakia where we find princely graves with bronze weapons that continue the Middle Bronze tradition. A style of fluted pottery, at home in the Hungarian urnfields (Gava: see chapter 8), spread gradually eastwards down the Danube and south down the Morava to Mediana near Niš. On the Glasinac plateau in Slavonia and Herzogovina the earlier rite of burial in small graves grouped under barrows continued, and something similar appeared in Albania. In border districts, between groups, there was a certain amount of mixing, with cremations under barrows, but the overall picture is one of continuity. Urnfields continued between the Sava and Drava, while nearer Greece's northern frontiers the local Bronze Age of the Morava valley (Perácin and Mediana) persisted into the Iron Age. 47

50

There have been attempts to trace the tumulus graves of Bronze Age Albania and northern Greece back to the Danube, and even to the *kurgans* (barrows) of South Russia; but neither time nor the detailed archaeology of settlements supports this

47–9 Craftsmen in the barbarian cultures of the mid-2nd millennium were fine potters as well as metal-workers. An Otomani culture pot from Barca (*below*, cf. 46) is well-fired and decorated with a bossed motif that has a long history in the Danubian lands. Over the Carpathians to the east in Moldavia, the largely contemporary Monteoru culture flourished. An ornate pot (*above*), with ram's heads surmounting the two handles, comes from the hill-site of Sărata-Monteoru which was destroyed at the beginning of the Late Bronze Age by people from the north-east, bringing a drab, coarse style of potting. This 'Noua' pottery (*opposite, above*) is practically indistinguishable from the coarse pottery of many other regions and periods. Noua pots from Trusesti inhumation cemetery and from a *zolniki* (area of burnt earth with occupation debris); not to scale.

Below
50 A new, technically superior style of potting evolved in the earliest Late Bronze Age in central Europe from lower Austria through Czechoslovakia and south into Hungary. The pots of this Baierdorf-Velatice style are highly burnished, dark-faced and copy metal shapes (56). They are found at their best in a 'Royal Grave' at Očkov in Slovakia which belongs to the same group as the Čaka burial (51, 52). Scales various; cup above, diam. *c.* 13 cm.

interpretation of events. Whatever is masked under the term 'Kurgan cultures', implying a great barrow-burying movement out of Russia, was finished by the beginning of the 2nd millennium as far as the Balkans were concerned. It belongs to times too remote to concern this history. The numbers and variousness of the groups throughout eastern Europe are a warning against simplistic conclusions. The patterns of settlement and of cultural groupings throughout the Balkans and on the lower Danube are of the utmost complexity.

Noua is the exception to this pattern of a variety of small, tenacious groups. It is so unlike what went before, and has so many links with lands farther east, even as far as the Volga, that we must, I think, in this case accept a sizeable westward shift of population. These people then mingled with local groups which were not liquidated but managed a degree of revival in the following centuries. How far the changes represented by Noua made their way into Bulgaria is questionable. They certainly crossed the lower Danube, for the Coslogeni of north-eastern Bulgaria is virtually an extension of Noua. The Coslogeni, and certain Urnfield groups from eastern Hungary which moved into north-western Bulgaria, were important elements in the make-up of the Thracian Late Bronze Age.

Over the Carpathians in Transylvania there is a little Noua pottery, but it is very scattered. Here older settlements survived, either as small well-defended sites with shallow occupation or as larger sites with deeper occupation and without defences.

A sudden multiplication in the number of large hoards of hidden and abandoned bronzes at the start of the Late Bronze Age in Transylvania and in Hungary speaks strongly of trouble. The old tribal groups held their own, but the times were bad and the hoards of bronzes show it.

Bronze workshops of Transylvania and Hungary

The continuity of the bronze industry which flourished in Transylvania and Hungary at the beginning of the local Late Bronze Age, probably to be equated with the 13th to 12th centuries, is even more striking than the continuity in potting. Several chronological horizons have been identified in which new types of artifact gradually supplant the old; but there is no major disruption. The divisions of the Hungarian hoards do not exactly coincide with those of Transylvania, but slightly overlap.[3] Objects characteristic of the Middle Bronze Age, such as shaft-hole battle-axes, were still current in the earliest of the Late Bronze Age hoards of Transylvania, but had disappeared in the second horizon which is called Cincu-Suseni after two important Romanian hoards. This is the horizon in which flange-hilted swords came to predominate: not the earliest such swords, but those sometimes known as 'Nenzingen', more exactly type IIa; these swords reached the Aegean and Cyprus as 54c we shall see.

In this same horizon are the so-called Peschiera (two-edged) knives or daggers, named after the site in northern Italy, that are also found in the Aegean. There are amber and blue glass beads probably from the far north and the Mediterranean south respectively, and miners' and metal-workers' hammers. The hammers are extremely significant, for what astonishes in these hoards is the sheer quantity of metal: 4000 kg from 5 of the 70 Transylvanian hoards alone is surprising enough, but that they also held 300 kg of 'pure' tin is really startling. There was certainly no problem here in acquiring metal ores. The bronze was of good quality with 17–25 per cent tin alloy. This is at a time of suspected scarcity in the supply of metals to the Aegean. There are also hammered bronze cups and buckets, fragments of 56 helmets and other sheet-bronze work.

The great strength of the Danubian workshops had always been in the technology of casting from moulds: these workshops were foundries not smithies. So the second cause for astonishment is the sudden and wholly revolutionary appearance of forging as a production technique. In the earlier hoards there had been very little use of sheet-metal, and most of it was goldsmiths' work. The conservatism of workshop practice is notorious. Failing some radical stimulus for change the old methods will persist almost indefinitely. Just that revolutionary stimulus must have been experienced in the workshops at a given moment. We know pretty well when this was in the relative chronology of the European Bronze Age – a little after the beginning of the Late Bronze Age (Bronze D/Hallstatt A1) – but the more important question is, how are we to link this relative chronology with the dates ascertained for the Aegean? Imperfect as the Aegean chronology is, it is much better than any applied farther north. At present the only way is to make use of so-called 'northern bronzes' found on Aegean sites, since Aegean objects from northern sites are both exceedingly rare and exceedingly hard to place. In order to assess the little evidence there is it is necessary to go behind the artifacts and see, if possible, what they mean in human terms.

A sheet-bronze corselet found in a rich chieftain's or warrior's grave at Čaka in Slovakia is an early example of bronze forging in central Europe. The man's other possessions are of the expected local sort: spearhead, axe, safety-pin and the good-quality local pottery. The corselet is evidently native work too, not imported from the Mediterranean, nor is it isolated: fragments of at least two more-or-less contemporary corselets have come to light.[4] To account for their presence it is not enough to suppose that some enterprising chieftain, on a visit to the Aegean, saw and envied an armour-plated warrior (if such existed) or welcomed such a one in his own country, and then persuaded the local workshops to copy the exotic panoply for his own use. It was not possible to think of forging body-armour before there was an active school of bronzesmiths at home, who were familiar with the new technology required. The know-how must have come from the Mediterranean where forging had had a long and distinguished history. Mycenaean swords were forged when northern swords were cast: the expertise was available but only south of the Pindus.

Almost as revolutionary as was the introduction of forging to European workshops was the introduction of the IIa flange-hilted slashing sword from central Europe to the Aegean and East Mediterranean. The flange-hilted sword was the culmi-

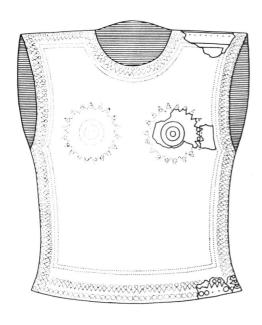
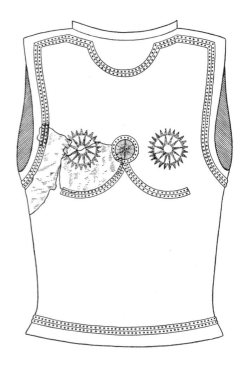

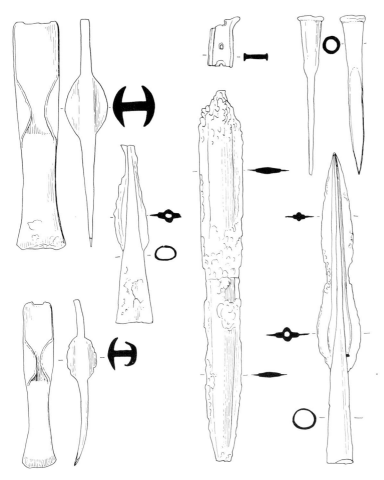

51, 52 At the beginning of the Late Bronze Age (late 2nd millennium) a revolution took place in central European work-shop tradition, with large-scale forging of bronzes in place of casting. Corselets (*opposite*) and cups (56) were hammered and embossed with fine decoration. Recon-structions are shown here of two corselets from Slovakia, one from a hoard at Ducové (*opposite, right*, ht *c.* 44 cm), the other found in a princely burial under a tumulus at Čaka (ht *c.* 36 cm). In the ashes of the pyre was found pottery of Baierdorf-Velatice type (50) and bronze tools and weapons (*left*). The damaged sword (centre) is one of the new flange-hilted IIa type and, like the short spearhead and the median-winged axes, it was to have considerable influence on Aegean metal-work. Sword-blade l. 18.3 cm.

nation of a long period of trial and improvement on earlier thrusting weapons. In its homeland it had to make its way against thoroughly viable alternatives, such as solid-hilted slashing swords and simple tanged swords, neither of which required any change in combat practice.[5] It was an altogether different matter south of the Pindus.

108 centre

'Northern bronzes' in the Aegean

With the flange-hilted swords we are pitched full into the problem of the much-discussed 'northern bronzes' and their appearance in the East Mediterranean.[6] The swords arrived a little before LH IIIB had given way to LH IIIC some-time before 1200 and before the worst outbreak of des-truction on the Greek mainland. A good, and probably early, example was found at Mycenae itself (group I according to the

53

system set up by Dr Hector Catling), but unfortunately in an undated context. Another, this time from a grave and with a spearhead that may also be a northern type, was discovered on the island of Cos with late IIIB pottery (Langada tomb 21). Others have been found on Naxos and Cyprus with pottery of the IIIC style that followed IIIB

The abandonment of Mycenaean sites at, or near, the end of LH IIIB has for the past twenty years been seen as 'the occasion for a mass-immigration, and permanent settlement in Greece of non-Mycenaean peoples, with the prime basis for this conclusion the occurrence of new metal types in Greece.' One authority on the problem, Professor A. M. Snodgrass, however, has been able to demolish this evidence apparently convincingly. According to his argument the flange-hilted sword would have come by normal trading and the 'natural adoption' of a superior weapon, in the same way that the 'northern' violin-bow fibula spread rapidly in Greece and the Balkans because of its practical merits.[7] This explanation would be entirely satisfactory if the problem were no more than that of accounting for a sword and spear in Cos, or at Mycenae or Enkomi. But this is not the real problem. The problem is to explain an exceptional situation, the onset of a period of deep recession, more romantically a 'Dark Age', that lasted several centuries. It is here that the minimal explanation fails. The economic and social argument for collapse outlined in the previous chapter takes us a certain distance but not the whole way.

In the Aegean of the 13th century the spear was the fighting and hunting weapon *par excellence*, although the bow may have seen some use as well. Swords had been getting shorter and shorter. However, the extraordinary blades that began to appear towards the end of the period of Mycenaean ascendancy (classes F and G) were not so much experiments as despairing attempts to counter a new form of attack introduced with the flange-hilted sword. But just as one corseleted warrior striding into Slovakia could not have initiated a school of body-armourers, so one, or a very few, northern swordsmen could not have revolutionized methods of fighting all over the East Mediterranean. The superiority of the new weapon must have been demonstrated in grievous action before such a lesson was learnt by the lords of Mycenae and the noble families of Cyprus. The fact that the northerner could back up his new weaponry with almost unlimited supplies of copper and tin would have been another powerful reason to respect him.

37

55a, d

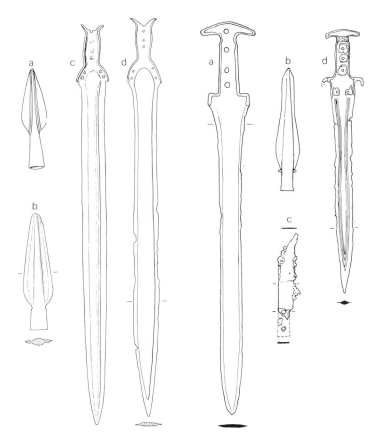

A new type of
sword from central
Europe transformed
combat tactics in the
Aegean at the end of the
13th century. One of the
first generation of these
type IIa swords found
south of the Balkans came
from a house inside the
walls at Mycenae (*op-
posite*). Not many of the
swords come from graves
and can be dated, but a
sword and spearhead were
discovered together in
Cos, Langada tomb 21,
with later LH IIIB
pottery (*far left, b, d*).
They stem ultimately
from the early type
IIa sword e.g. from a
hoard at Aranyos, Hun-
gary (*far left, c*). The Cos
spear is broadly of the
same family as Čaka (52
left) and Páncéleseh,
Szolnok-Doboka, Hun-
gary (*far left, a*) (Opalyi
hoards, table IV).

To counter the new
tactics Aegean sword-
smiths lengthened the
native dirk (41) during the
12th century into hybrid
weapons (*left, a* from a
late tomb at Mouliana,
Crete and *d*, from the
largely LH IIIC cemetery
at Perati, Attica). The
spearhead (*left, b*) also
from Mouliana is derived
from a European type.
During the 12th century
iron appears in small
knife-blades such as (*left,
c*) from Perati. 53, l.
60 cm; 54a, l. 14.6 cm; b,
17.5 cm; c, 62 cm; d,
59.5 cm; 55c, l. 15.2 cm;
d, 57.5 cm (all approxi-
mate).

The long life of the IIa sword in Europe, particularly in
eastern Europe where it was not overtaken to the same extent as
in the west by other developments, is one of the difficulties in
correlating northern periods with Aegean chronologies, let alone
real dates. There is also the question of Italian contacts (see
below). Albania does not enter the argument since apart from
one sword found at Scutari, which could be Italian or Greek, all
the IIa swords from Albania are untypical and probably very
late.

The distribution of the different groups of IIa flange-hilted
swords in the East Mediterranean does not support a north-to-
south progress, as of an invading force. The most characteristic
of the early swords (group I) come from Mycenae, Cos and
Cyprus, and if they indicate anything it is small, mobile, well-
scattered bands. A more attractive explanation is that the
Mycenaean princes employed barbarian mercenaries and
adventurers from the north. Dr Catling writes of 'military
necessity' driving the Mycenaeans to 'hire warriors from outside

Greece. These warriors brought their own armouries with them
... greatly admired by their employers, who set their own
swordsmiths to copy and adapt them.'[8]

We saw in chapter 2 to what extent oriental states depended on
mercenary troops for their fighting power. Crete too, at an earlier
date, probably employed foreign soldiers; but in Greece the
texts are silent. No word for 'mercenary' has been found. If
anything, systems of military service were more akin to the
feudal arrangements of the Hittites than to those of Pharaoh or
the King of Ugarit. I think nevertheless that these 'northern
bronzes' – the flange-hilted swords, a type of rather short leaf-
shaped spear with a whole-cast socket (both in the Langada tomb
21 on Cos), and possibly the two-edged Peschiera knives – are
sufficient evidence for the presence of northern adventurers as
individuals or in small war-bands. The scattered distribution of
these objects, combined with their startling impact on native
workshops, support the argument.[9] The spread to Cyprus is
easily understandable, for that great island was still rich, the hub
of trade and nexus of many lines of communication, a natural
magnet. So if the Mycenaean ruling class were on the look out for
support in their feudings it would have been natural to scan the
north for manpower and metals, where both abounded.

On the Danube the situation was ripe for dispatching younger
sons and disinherited chieftains to richer lands. Pressures at
home were mounting. But there was no wholesale migration:
instead, small well-organized and well-equipped bands would
have moved swiftly southwards, most likely taking with them
their own armourers, since this was the practice not only in
large armies but even for a single ship. The luckless wreck off
Cape Gelidonya had its craftsman as well as its merchant on
board. These armourers would have been keen observers of all
they saw on the tables and the backs of their hosts, and may thus
have obtained the new knowledge of sheet-metal-work that
could be applied to cups, bowls and the rest. The two revolutions
were complementary: the northern sword that surprised the
53, 54 Mediterranean, and the southern art of smithing that transformed northern workshops – these adopted the new tool-kit and
56, 52 in turn began to produce cups, bowls, buckets, body-armour and
a great new range of hammered and embossed bronzework
which had long been the stock in trade of Mycenaean workshops.

The problem before us now is two-fold: first, what sprang the
trap that started the dreadful mechanism of disaster in the
Aegean; and second, what was it that inhibited recovery? The

56 Two views of a beaten bronze cup with bossed decoration from Jenišovice, Czechoslovakia, a rather later (Hallstatt A2) version of the bronze cups that appeared almost at the beginning of the Late Bronze Age contemporary with Čaka.

northern weaponry belongs to the first part of the problem. The appearance of hand-made coarse pottery in the south belongs to the second – it must therefore wait for treatment till a later chapter, for reasons which will appear. Equally the question of Troy and the north-eastern approaches belongs to the history of the 12th rather than the 13th century (see chapter 8).

The north-western approaches

The importance of Greece's north-eastern approaches has been recognized to be crucial for as long as Greek history has been studied; but recently the north-west, Epirus and Albania, has come more into the question. The whole of Epirus and much of Albania is highland. In Greece wheat will grow up to 1500 m; but mountains are the home of shepherds, the scene of their migrations, the refuge for brigands. Although quite rich in natural resources, the mountains soon become over-populated. At such times in recent centuries highlanders from Albania have been lured down to the coasts and plains, often to raid and settle, or to hire themselves out as soldiers, as they did in the 16th century AD, going as far as Cyprus, Venice, Sicily and Naples. They were probably repeating an older pattern. The elusive Dorians, who in later Greek tradition, after the Trojan War, invaded Thessaly and Boeotia from the north-west, crossed into the Peloponnese, and finally occupied Crete and other islands, have been looked for here. Tradition as well as archaeology, hints at small populations on the move rather than invasion from farther north. There is no need to conjure up Early or Middle Bronze Age hordes from the eastern steppe, by whatever name, to explain changes in Late Bronze Age Greece.

Albania, even Epirus, were more remote from Mycenaean centres of civilization than Troy, which is farther off in actual distance, more remote even than Sicily and Apulia; but they were not entirely unexplored. Mycenaean adventuring up the Adriatic seems certain from the 15th century judging by the discovery in a tumulus at Pazok in Albania of an LH I-IIA cup of 'Vapheio' type (named after the site near Sparta). Some of the more startling finds in Albanian tumulus graves, such as Mycenaean rapiers and early daggers, must however be accounted archaic anachronisms and the majority dated not much before the 12th century. There is Mycenaean pottery at Thermon on the way to the north (LH IIA) and a tomb at Ilias near Amphilochia may have been that of a Mycenaean settler.[10] Some hundred years later, during the 14th century, Mycenaeans were farther north still in Yugoslavia, leaving LH IIIA pots at Debelo Brdo near Sarajevo.[11] At about the same time Mycenaean interest began in the Ionian islands; while we find firmer evidence for north-western contacts with a Mycenaean tholos tomb at Parga near Kiperi in Epirus, containing LH IIIA2 pottery.

A command of Mycenaean technology, which may even have extended to combat tactics, is shown by local imitations of the Mycenaean horned sword (type Ci) in Epirus, and of cruciform swords (Di) in Albanian sites, in the Mati valley and at Nënshat. The horned swords have still more eccentric counterparts in Bulgaria. These early experiments are followed in Epirus by a number of dirks and daggers of 13th- and 12th-century Mycenaean type (Fii and Fiii), found in settlements and graves. By this time Mycenaean pottery was probably produced locally in Epirus, as it was in the north-east in Macedonia. Native hand-made pottery was still used in the settlements. Some of it is not unlike the Macedonian Thracian burnished wares, but there is no sign of the typical Thracian incised ware (chapter 8). However, dating is very difficult and some of the Mycenaean pottery itself may be very much later than it appears to be if taken at face value.

Socketed axes of a sort found on both sides of the Adriatic, in Albania, southern Italy and Sicily, were produced by a native school of bronze-working. The spear was the weapon most used, as in the Mycenaean south, but here a more northern type with whole-cast socket was preferred. In north-western Greece sixty-four spearheads have been found, of different varieties, which is more than in all the rest of Greece put together. One type has a facetted butt and exaggerated 'fiddle' shape, and is peculiar to this area and possibly to Italy too. Small trinkets of twisted bronze have a northern and European, rather than Mycenaean, look. But burial in a cist-grave, which was so popular in Epirus, can no longer be seen as intrusive and alien to the Greek mainland. An interesting absentee is the flange-hilted sword, not one of which has yet been found in Epirus, and only uncharacteristic examples in Albania. It looks as if the true Mycenaean dirk used with a 'northern' spear was the counterpart here of the 'canonical' flange-hilted sword. What the increased activity of the 12th century, shown by LH IIIC pottery and Mycenaean bronzes, meant in more human terms will engage us in a later chapter.

Italy, Sicily and the central Mediterranean

The Ionian Sea has a bad name among 'maritime deserts'. One is told that it was a no-man's-land and that shipping avoided it by following the coastline from promontory to promontory; and yet one has one's doubts. Cretan and mainland navigators of the 16th century BC were visiting Apulia, Sicily and the Lipari Islands. There is Middle Helladic pottery of this time in Apulia and at Monte Sallia in south-eastern Sicily, and LH I and LM I on Filicudi and Lipari islands respectively.[12] Had the navigators only been hugging the shores, calling at anchorages a day's row apart, like the one-day stages of 16th-century-AD sailing boats, there should be more signs of their passage on the coasts of Epirus, in the Ionian Islands, in Calabria and north-eastern Sicily. By the 14th century at the latest they were up the Tyrrhenian coast as far as Luni near Viterbo in Tuscany, where LH IIIA pottery has been found in a house of the local first Apennine period. They were probably looking for copper ores.[13] There is evidence of trade, if not settlement, on Lipari, Ischia and Vivara (LH II-early III), while in Sicily at Thapsos, a little offshore island north of Syracuse, there may have been a small Mycenaean colony in the late 14th–13th century (LH IIIA–B pottery), as also in the Gulf of Taranto at Scoglio del Tonno. Thapsos and Scoglio del Tonno seem to have been part of a more serious expansion which may have been connected with the increased Mycenaean interest in Epirus and the Ionian Islands of much the same period, but which also continued into the 12th century. There were quite frequent visits to Apulia by ships of Rhodes, even possibly Cyprus, from as early as the 14th century. It is even possible that Scoglio del Tonno was engaged in the purple trade with the East Mediterranean.[14]

97

In the 13th century the ports of call were of many sorts. Those around the Gulf of Taranto lay in good agricultural country far from sources of metal. The Lipari sites were rocky, infertile but defensible. Thapsos was undefended and apparently unafraid. Up the Tyrrhenian coast Ischia was well placed for handling ores from Elba and Tuscany, perhaps Sardinia. The revolutionary potter's wheel, introduced at Taranto by the Mycenaeans, was never lost thereafter. In the 12th century all this changed, for though Apulia remained in touch with the Aegean (Torre Castelluccia, Leporano and Scoglio del Tonno) and though Salerno, Monte Novello and Ischia, even Luni, all have some LH IIIC pottery, the Aegean boats no longer visited Sicily, although the native Pantalican society was thriving.

The relationship of Italy and Sicily to the Aegean and the Levant in the Late Bronze Age is paradoxical. There was a strong independent metal industry in central and northern Italy, the inspiration for which came from over the Alps: flange-hilted swords and knives, various sorts of spear and axe and, more especially from the north-east, fibulae and the urnfields themselves. Distribution maps of flange-hilted swords and of urnfields have the same northern concentration, which is complementary to the concentration in southern Italy and Sicily of LH IIIB–C pottery and a scatter of Aegean bronze weapons and tools.[15] A T-handled dirk (type Fii) was found at Surbo near 57b Lecce in Apulia; it is of Greek workmanship and a type popular in Epirus and the Ionian island of Kephallenia; a Greek dress-pin came to light at Mottola near Taranto; while small hammers found at both Surbo and Mottola were probably part of a metal-57a worker's tool-kit. If bronze bowls from Caldare in Sicily were in fact made when Thapsos was giving way to the succeeding Pantalica, either at the end of the 13th or beginning of the 12th century (see chapter 5), they probably indicate the date of the earliest beaten bronze from either Sicily or southern Italy.

The reciprocal export of Italian bronzes to the Aegean is not confined, as might have been expected, to those types characteristic of southern Italy and Sicily: Peschiera knives which are at home in northern Italy have been found in Crete and Naxos, another sort of northern Italian stop-ridge knife is known from Corfu and yet another from Crete (Psychro). Most 57e intriguing and controversial of all is the mould for casting a variety of winged axe, which was found in the House of the Oil Merchant at Mycenae in what has been claimed to be a good 13th-century (LH IIIB) context. The mould would produce an

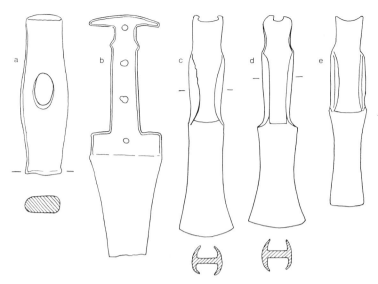

57 Evidence for contact across the Ionian Sea is shown by bronze tools and weapons in southern and central Italy. A broken Mycenaean dirk (*b*), found with other bronzes at Surbo in Apulia, is a 13th-to-12th-century development of the round-shouldered dirk of 41. Winged axes from Surbo (*c*) and Ortucchio (*d*) in the Abruzzi are European not Aegean, but they are close relatives of a mould for casting similar axes found at Mycenae (*e*). The hammer (*a*) from Surbo is a metal-worker's tool. *b*, l. 19 cm; *a* and *c* to same scale.

axe that is almost identical with an Italian axe found in a grave in the Abruzzi at Ortucchio. It is also quite like the axe in the Surbo group with its Aegean dirk. This find gives rise to a chronological problem, since the Ortucchio axe was probably associated with a fibula and knife, the latter a northern type, though sometimes found in Italy. The axe would therefore be of the so-called Protovillanovan rather than Peschiera horizon in Italy, Hallstatt A1 in the Tyrol or Bavaria, and so, according to most calculations, later than the destruction of the House of the Oil Merchant. The association of the mould with LH IIIB pottery at Mycenae is not absolutely watertight, and if it was in fact lost after the destruction of the house, the problem may resolve itself.[16] Shaft-hole axes and a few other bronzes link southern Italy with Albania and Epirus independently of Greece, as indicated above.

The question of the flange-hilted swords pinpoints a difficulty. Italy has a few examples of the early sword (the type known as Sprockhoff Ia) that in central Europe immediately precedes the IIa sword. They are found around the head of the Adriatic, in the Po valley and the Gargano peninsula; but none have been found in Greece. The IIa 'Nenzingen' swords, like other early types, are concentrated in the Veneto at the end of the Transalpine trade route, but only a very few can be reliably associated with particular sites. Those that can be include swords from Tuscany and Modena (Cetona, Treviso and Frassineto types). There are none from Sicily and southern Italy, that is to say the regions best known to the Mycenaeans.

Moreover this Italian IIa type is the 'Common Sword' to which the first authority on these swords, J. D. Cowen, has given a very long life from Bronze D to Hallstatt B in central European nomenclature (broadly speaking 12th to 8th century); so in spite of its likeness to the Aegean flange-hilted swords of Catling's group I, there are no grounds for deriving the one from the other. The later developments of these swords are more promising, and some connection between Italian swords of the 'Allerona' type and Aegean swords of Catling's group II, which is on the whole later than group I, may well exist. There are a great number of odd and individual variants in both Italy and the Aegean, most of them very late; but curiously in neither area did the parallel-edged flange-hilted sword develop a leaf-shaped blade for strong cutting action, nor a milled ricasso at the grip, both of which were highly successful in the rest of Europe.

It is difficult to know how to interpret this scatter of knives, swords, pins and late Mycenaean pottery in an historical sense. Are they later than the first fierce round of disaster in the Aegean, and are these the effects of refugees fleeing from danger? Or do they antedate the time of troubles and show the peaceful operations of friendly commerce? From how we answer this question will follow the even more crucial one as to whether or not the western navigators themselves were among the 'Sea Peoples' who played a leading and sinister role in the disasters. A long-lived settlement such as that at Scoglio del Tonno, with its plentiful 12th-century and later IIIC pottery, must have survived the onset of the troubles, but unfortunately there is no way of refining sufficiently the dates of the Italian bronzes found in the Aegean, or Aegean bronzes in Italy, to give a convincing answer.

Sardinia and Corsica

The search for 'Sea Peoples' does not stop on the eastern shore of the Tyrrhenian Sea. Across the water in Sardinia and Corsica there were vigorous and original Bronze Age cultures. The inhabitants of both islands built formidable towers of cyclopean masonry, known in Sardinia as 'nuraghi' and in Corsica as 'torre'. Sardinia has valuable copper ores, and the people who built the nuraghi were metal-workers adept at smelting and casting, so that it is surprising to find copper ingots of the East Mediterranean 'ox-hide' sort connected with some of the earlier nuraghi. A few of the ingots weigh over 30 kg, and two have

'Minoan' signs on them. Either merchants, such as the owner of the Cape Gelidonya wreck, were already exploiting Sardinian ores, and insisted on handling them in the form current in the East Mediterranean; or, less plausibly, copper-rich Sardinia was importing ingots from farther east. The Sardinian ingots might be as early as the 14th century when Mycenaeans were active in the Tyrrhenian Sea, or from the beginning of the 12th century and part of the baggage of the 'Sea Raiders' of *c.* 1186. They are more like Cypriot ingots of the 14th century than later ones. Increasingly Mycenaean pottery (LH IIIB and IIIC) is being found in Sardinia, some of it in nuraghi.[17] That from the nuraghe of Antigori appears to have affinities with Cyprus and the Levant. The Aegean (possibly Rhodian) and Cypriot trade with Taranto may have been a stage to markets farther west. An ingot of Sardinian type is reported to have been found in Crete. The nuraghi were still occupied, and indeed grew larger and more complex, during the first half of the 1st millennium BC, by which time the island had gained its name and some of its famous bronze statuettes (ill. 130).

In Sardinia 100 nuragic villages are known, and in Corsica there are as many torre. But Corsica also possesses some 70 hewn-stone blocks, roughly shaped into heads at the top, and with weapons carved on them in relief, some of which have been interpreted as Mycenaean swords and dirks (dirks with T-hilts and cruciform swords). Different interpretations are possible and the date of the torre is uncertain, although uncorrected radiocarbon dates have given an estimated age of between 1500 and 1400 BC. In one of the torre at Filitosa a hewn block has been reused in the construction, and this led the late Dr R. Grosjean, a specialist in the archaeology of the island, to believe that the Bronze Age inhabitants of Sardinia and Corsica were among the raiders defeated by Ramesses III.[18] Some connection between the raiders and the great islands of the central Mediterranean has been thought likely for a long time, and will be considered later. The harbours of both Sardinia and Corsica are superb bases for pirates, but for the moment we must leave the question as to whether seamen from these islands were among the contingents that plundered the East Mediterranean, or whether they were themselves the prey of these marauders from overseas.

Now that we have assembled all the likely *dramatis personae* we must turn to the drama itself, at the same time not forgetting that its action had to be played within the economic and environmental limitations outlined in chapter 1.

58 Copper ingots of the so-called 'ox-hide' shape found in Sardinia show commercial relations with the East Mediterranean. This example is from Serra Ilixi, one of the earliest nuraghi on the island. The shape of the ingot itself is not early in the series but is similar to ingots found in the Cape Gelidonya wreck of *c.* 1200, off the southern coast of Turkey.

59 Torralba, Sardinia. The Bronze and Early Iron Age inhabitants of Sardinia built strong towers and castles, places of
refuge known as 'nuraghi', which, though of rough-hewn stone,
are superbly executed. Many of them were still used by the
makers of the small bronze gods and warriors with horned helmets
and other accoutrements of the 8th to 6th centuries (130).

60, 61 In Corsica a number of stones carved with human figures

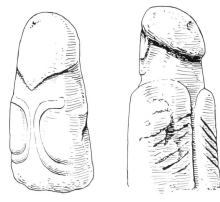

and weapons have been found. The date is not certain and may
cover a wide range of time. A likeness has been seen between
carvings from Filitosa VI (*top left*) and Scalsa Murta (*top right*)
and the body-armour of 'Sea Peoples' on the Egyptian monuments
and also the Sardinian bronze figures (cf. Filitosa VI (back view)
and 130 side; also Scalsa Murta and 88 and 89). The weapons,
especially swords like that on Filitosa V (*above*) are also hard to
date; the Mycenaean parallels are not very convincing.

The crisis in the East Mediterranean I: Egypt and the north

Merneptah's Libyan war and the northern allies

This long excursion through the years during which the troubles were building has brought us to the point when disaster was declared; but even here paradoxically we have to begin at the end, since only the last act, in the Nile Delta, is documented at all well. The wars of Merneptah and of Ramesses III against the enemy from the west and north provide the best vantage point from which to unpick the events immediately preceding. Like Theseus in the Labyrinth we begin with the crisis of the action, and from it return through ways of tortuous approach.

Some sixty to sixty-five years after the battle of Kadesh (c. 1286/5) Egypt was faced with another dangerous threat. Merneptah ascended the throne in middle-age, and in year 5 of his reign had to meet a massive attack of Libyans and their allies coming from the western desert. Inscriptions at Karnak describe the campaign. Meryry, the Libyan king, brought his entire family, his treasure and his beasts; for this was no raid after loot but an invasion with the whole purpose of settling down in what must have appeared a lotus land of luxury and security.

The Libyan attack failed, and after a hard-fought six-hour battle in the desert, about 15 April 1220, victorious Pharaoh boasted:

> The wretched chief of Libya, his heart was paralysed with fear, it shrank, he stopped and knelt down leaving his bow and quiver and sandals on the ground behind him.

The huge spoil included silver and gold, weapons and furniture, cattle and goats. The numbers of the slaughtered were counted in thousands.

With the Libyans, and their neighbours the Meshwesh, came a number of northern allies: the Sherden or Shardana and the

62 The 'Victory Stela' of Merneptah shows Pharaoh between the gods and proclaims his success against the Libyans and their allies from the north in the war of c. 1220 (year 5 of his reign). Less an historical document than a hymn of praise, it is also known as the 'Israel Stela' since it has the only mention of Israel in ancient Egyptian writings.

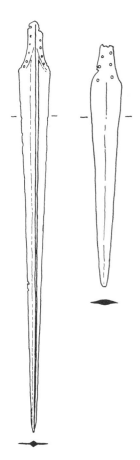

Lukka, already well known; also three new names, Ekwesh (Egyptian 'Ikwš), Teresh (Trš) and Shekelesh (Škrš).[1] The Shardana had been about in the early 14th century (chapter 2), when they are heard of at Byblos, and again in the 13th century, but without any indication of their homeland. Inscriptions at Karnak single them out as troops of especial importance in the Egyptian army where they were employed from at least the time of Ramesses II, under whom they fought at Kadesh (chapter 2). Other Levantine states also made use of them. They were swordsmen and spearmen, whereas the native Egyptian troops used the bow. Some confusion has been caused by naming a certain type of long sword with a very tapering blade and narrow triangular hilt-plate as a (or *the*) Shardana sword, and therefore as foreign to the Levant, whereas it is in fact a development of the ordinary Middle Bronze Age Levantine dagger and has only an incidental connection with the historical Shardana.

It is not surprising to find the Shardana in Merneptah's wars fighting both for, and against, Egypt. The mercenary and adventurer acts as a spy for his free relatives, like the Varangian Guard employed by Byzantine emperors in Constantinople. The name Sherden-Shardana has, since it was first recognized, been connected with Sardinia, but the nature and dates of the connection are problematic (see chapter 7). It has also, rather less convincingly, been linked with Sardis.

That the Shardana wore horned helmets is one of the few sartorial certainties in the complicated history of Egypt's friends and attackers. Until the time of Ramesses III (*c.* 1190), when worn by Egyptian bodyguards and allies the helmet was a round cap, or a cap with cheek protection, probably of leather, with curving horns, and between the horns a spike, with a disc or sphere on top of it. This must have been a form of regimental insignia. The Shardana who came as raiders, on the contrary, wore a helmet shaped to protect the back of the neck, with a curving outline and without the insignia between the horns. Since the battle of Kadesh Shardana had carried round shields.

Horned helmets were alien to the Aegean and for some time longer to Europe also, but they were indigenous in Mesopotamia, Anatolia and the Levant. Over this whole region bull's horns, worn on a tiara or helmet, were the mark of divinity. The greater the god the more horns he wore. Mortal kings had had a single pair since Naram Sin (2291–2255 BC) of Akkad in Mesopotamia was portrayed wearing what appears to be a very practical helmet with a pair of bull's horns. This particular

66
14
74

82, 89
66

64

helmet is very like that worn by a captive leader of the Shardana carved on an early-12th-century relief at Medinet Habu in Egypt. This sort of cap-helmet but without horns is very ancient indeed. It exists in metal in the Ur graves of the mid-3rd millennium BC.[2] The Shardana also wear a characteristic short kilt, and both helmet and kilt appear on a 14th-century stela of a god, probably Baal, found at Ugarit. The cap is very like the earlier Shardana cap-helmet worn by allies or mercenaries of Ramesses II's time, with the centre spike but without the disc or sphere on top. Although the faces, the clothes and the weaponry of the Shardana have been so often and clearly portrayed, the land of their origin is still quite unknown. Wherever these great fighters came from it is a fair assumption that it was not far from the northern Syrian coast, and the same might hold for the troop on the Warrior Vase from Mycenae to which we shall return in chapter 8.

68, 69

64

65

124

The Lukka, who also joined the Libyan invaders, had been allies of the Hittites at the battle of Kadesh. We have met them already as pirates from south-western Anatolia, notorious since early in the 2nd millennium. Their raids on Cyprus were a recurrent irritation. A 14th-century king of Alashiya-Cyprus wrote to Pharaoh: 'Does my brother not know that every year the Lukka people take a small town away from my land?' It is not surprising to find these Lukka pushing in once more where there was a chance of plunder. When ancient Greek historians, writing of the troubles of the distant past, refer to 'Carian pirates' it is probably the Lukka who lurk behind this name. Reasons were given in chapter 2 for placing the Lukka Lands in or near the Carian coast.[3]

Also among the Libyan allies are the Ekwesh, not heard of before this time, who are singled out as forming the largest contingent from overseas. They have been connected with the Ahhiyawa of the Hittite texts (chapter 3) and so with the Homeric Achaeans; if so, it is rather surprising that, as Indo-Europeans, they were circumcised. One inscription, the Athribis stela, says only of the Ekwesh that they are 'of the Countries of the Sea'. But in the Great Karnak Inscription, Shardana, Shekelesh and Ekwesh are all 'of the Countries of the Sea', although not curiously the Lukka.

Because of the uncertain date of some of the Hittite archives, references to Ahhiyawa have to be treated with caution. At one time the King or Prince of Ahhiyawa was of sufficient standing for the Hittite king to consider marrying into his family. In the

Opposite
63 A type of long sword with a tapering blade (*left*, from near Jaffa) has come to be known as the Shardana sword because a similarity has been seen between it and the swords carried by Egyptian Shardana troops (66 and 82, man top right wielding sword). But it is no more a newcomer to the Levant than the Shardana themselves; its ancestry can be traced from a common type of Middle Bronze Age 'Canaanite' dagger and dirk (*right*). Sword, l. 104 cm.

64–7   The history of the horned helmet worn by Ramesses II's Shardana bodyguard (*opposite, above*), and by bodyguard and enemy of Ramesses III (14 and 82), probably begins in Iraq. Metal cap-helmets were found in the Ur graves (mid-3rd millennium, *below*), while Naram Sin of Akkad (late 3rd millennium) on his victory stela wears a horned helmet (*bottom*). A spike between the horns seems to appear first at Ugarit on a stela taken to represent Baal, god of storms and vegetation (*right, c.* 14th century). Worn by Ramesses II's troops the helmet usually has a disc or sphere on the spike which may be a regimental insignia. In

Ramesses III's wars it appears in the earlier form (14), but also with a variety of different helmet shapes, some with neck- or cheek-guard (*left*, detail of 80), 74 the normal Egyptian helmet with insignia added, and 112. The larger helmet with guards is identical to that worn by the attackers in the sea battle (82), but with the insignia. An exception is the captive named as a prince of the Shardana (68, 69, cf. 79). The man attacking in the boat (*left*, not necessarily a Shardana) carries a spear and an unusually large shield; cf. 12. Baal stela, ht 1.44 m.

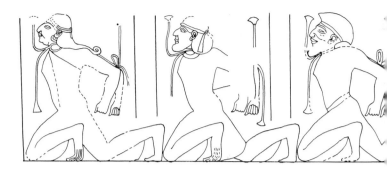

second half of the 14th century, in the reign of Mursilis II, the gods of Ahhiyawa and of Lazpa, perhaps Lesbos, were summoned to aid the ailing Hittite king. This means that their statues were carried to Hattusas, which presumes a degree of mutual understanding and respect between the royal houses. At various points the correspondence links Ahhiyawa in some way with Millawanda (Miletus). The Tawagalawas Letter, addressed to an unnamed Hittite king, probably Muwatallis (1306–1282), refers to a former Hittite subject who was now playing the corsair from a base at Millawanda and causing trouble in the Lukka Lands, which were evidently at that time a no-man's-land between a Miletus dominated by Ahhiyawa and the Hittite country. From later negotiations it appears that the envoy of the Hittite king to Ahhiyawa was a man of distinction who had ridden in the chariot with him, and with the King of Ahhiyawa's brother, when the latter was on a visit to the Hittite court.

The chief interest for the problem of the Ekwesh lies in the close connection between Ahhiyawa, the people of Miletus and of the Lukka Lands, and their mutual concern with corsairs, piracy and the sea. In another text a ship of Ahhiyawa seems set for a Syrian port. The 'Land of Ahhiyawa' has been placed in western coastal Anatolia near Miletus, in the Troad, in mainland Greece, in Rhodes, and in one of the larger islands, perhaps Crete. It is clear that the Ahhiyawans were a powerful sea-going people who at one time claimed equal status with the Hittite king himself, and who were frequently interfering in coastal Anatolia. Whether we place the controversial Madduwattas Indictment, with its references to the Mycenaean world, in the 13th century, where politically it would fit very well, or whether, as the linguists prefer, we date it some two centuries earlier, does not greatly affect this particular issue. There are linguistic objections also to the traditional direct identification of Hittite Ahhiyawa and Homer's Akhaiwoi (Achaeans) even without

68, 69 Among all the inscriptions and reliefs at Medinet Habu scarcely any enemy group is named in isolation; exceptions are the Peleset of 86 and Denyen of 87, who are virtually indistinguishable. It is therefore invaluable to have six named 'captive chieftains' with very different characteristics at Medinet Habu (*above*). Although this relief appears under the heading of a Syrian war, it is not historical but a symbolic representation of Pharaoh's victories over his main enemies. From left to right there are a Hittite, an Amorite, a Tjeker, a Shardana (the two latter shown also *below*), a partly obliterated name beginning 'Sh' that could be Shasu (Bedouin) or Shekelesh (the space is short for Shekelesh but the type is not that usually given to Shasu), last a Teresh. The Peleset further to the right is lost so neither Denyen nor Peleset are shown (but see 86, 87, 113).

bringing in the Egyptians' Ekwesh. One plausible explanation is that the Hittites may have understood the names Ahhiya(wa) rather differently at different stages in their history, just as Keftiu changed its meaning for the Egyptians, and later still Ionia and the Ionians. Ahhiyawa may have embraced all the Mycenaeans known to the Hittites, or only certain colonies in western Anatolia. This leaves a very wide door open to the Ekwesh, who could equally well have come to Egypt from western Anatolia, from one of the Aegean islands, or from mainland Greece.[4]

A Hittite text of Tudhaliyas IV (1250–1220) refers to Ta-ru-(u)i-ša (Taruisha), which may be the same as the Teresh, who also took part in the attack against Merneptah in 1220, and as the Tyrsenoi known to the Greek world. This is another name new to the Egyptian texts; but unlike the Ekwesh it seems that the Teresh were again on the attack in 1186. Ramesses III does not

70, 71 In Sicily in the early 12th century long-standing links with the Aegean (LH IIIB and Thapsos pottery) were broken and a new quite individual style of potting appeared in inland Pantalican settlements like Cassibile (*right*). The bowl on a high foot from Pantalica (*left*) is a superb example of the potter's craft that owes nothing to the Mycenaeans. These pots have a high red burnish reminiscent of Anatolian wares. For the inspiration of ill. 71 bottom cf. 106 and 114. High-footed bowl, ht 106 cm. Drawings, hts, top to bottom, 15 cm, 13.7 cm, 13 cm.

name them specifically among the raiders but a captive chief of the Teresh is shown among his prisoners. The Hittites located their Taruisha near the Troad, but they have also been placed in central western Anatolia from where, according to Herodotus, the Tyrrhenians migrated to central Italy. This would link the Teresh-Taruisha-Tyrsenoi with the Etruscans. On a relief at Medinet Habu of the time of Ramesses III, the prince of the Teresh has a quite different physiognomy from the other named captives. Teresh (Tursha) are mentioned with Peleset 'from the midst of the sea' in a rhetorical stela of Ramesses III (ch. 7).

The Hittite texts are not entirely silent concerning the Shekelesh. Recently discovered tablets from Ugarit include a letter from the Hittite king to a chief minister of Hammurabi, the last king of Ugarit, which refers to a certain Lunadusu who had been taken prisoner by the Šikala (Ši-ka-la-liù-a) 'who live in ships'. Lunadusu must have been rescued or ransomed, for the Hittite king wishes to question him about these Šikala before returning him to Ugarit.[5] The Shekelesh made their first appearance on the Egyptian scene as an enemy in 1220, and were attacking the Delta again in 1186. The same relief which had a portrait of the chief of the Teresh shows a prince either of the Shekelesh or the nomadic Shasu as bearded, with a thin prominent nose and a swept-back turban, or

68 possibly hair; unfortunately the name is damaged. The same
13 headgear was worn by allies of the Hittites at Kadesh, and by
74 part of the Egyptian guard in Ramesses III's first war against the Libyans, in year 5 (1189); and again among troops returning
14 from a (fictional) war in Syria (Amurru). But just as the Shardana are linked with Sardinia, and the Teresh with the Etruscans, so the Shekelesh have for a long time been identified with the inhabitants of south-eastern Sicily. Eighth-century Greek colonists found people known as 'Sikels' in the island, whom they thought had come from southern Italy after the Trojan War. Archaeologically there is no break after the appearance of the people of the Pantalica culture that followed Thapsos with its many Mycenaean connections (mostly LH IIIA with some IIIB). The small peaceful Thapsos villages were scattered round the coast and on offshore islands, but Pantalican sites lie inland, in rough country. Though fewer they are larger, with huge cemeteries of rock-cut tombs, so returning to a native tradition. This has the look of a political, not an economic change. Population has not decreased, but men are wary. They no longer live on terms of peaceful commerce with the Aegean. Mycenaean

pottery has vanished, but some Aegean bronzes are still copied. A high-quality red-burnished monochrome ware was produced on the wheel. It has some similarities with the native Thapsos pottery before it but none with Greece. If foreign styles are reflected at all, it is the fine monochrome pottery of Bronze Age Anatolia and certain so-called 'Philistine' pots (chapter 7). If Sikels and Shekelesh are in fact the same, they might have formed part of the larger confederation which, breaking up after its defeat by Merneptah, scattered over the East Mediterranean, a part being washed up on the coasts of Sicily, where it joined with a revived native culture from southern Italy and inland Sicily. Yet others may have joined Ramesses III's troops for his Libyan wars. This is of course highly speculative.

In the Great Karnak Inscription, as we have seen, the allies are referred to together as 'northerners coming from all lands'; and

70, 71

114

Table I

again the Shardana, Shekelesh and Ekwesh are 'of the Countries of the Sea'. Another inscription, the Athribis stela, seems to make it clear that *only* the Ekwesh are 'of the Countries of the Sea'. Much depends on how we, or rather how the Egyptians, understood 'the Countries of the Sea' (see chapter 7). The Hittites may also have been involved in some way that is not very clear, since they are blamed for ingratitude on the Karnak Inscription, and are named among the defeated on the Memphis Victory Stela, though this need not be taken too seriously. Unfortunately none of the raiders of 1220 – Shardana, Lukka, Ekwesh, Teresh and Shekelesh – are portrayed on the contemporary monuments. The Meshwesh, neighbours and allies of the Libyans, are known from texts of the Amarna period (early 14th century) as great herdsmen whose bulls were much valued in Egypt. In the Libyan war they were armed with very long tapering swords.

This whole group of attackers, apart from the Shardana and Lukka, have names with the same termination, and one authority, the late G. A. Wainwright, thought this might be an argument linking them all with western coastal Anatolia.[6] The Egyptian texts are not entirely consistent, but the Ekwesh, with 2201 prisoners against 742 Teresh and 222 Shekelesh, would have been the most important of this group.

The wider historical and archaeological problems involved in Merneptah's Libyan war must be left aside till later. Wherever they came from these allies of the African Libyans and Meshwesh are all 'northerners' in Egyptian eyes. It is an interesting question how they came to be so well informed about what was happening beyond the southern shore of the Mediterranean. An alliance between the tribes of Libya and the inhabitants of the northern islands and Anatolia is, on the face of it, surprising; but in fact there is a long history of toing and froing across the Libyan Sea to Crete and the Aegean, as well as of coastwise traffic. At various times the Aegean seems to have had direct relations with the North African coast independently of Egypt. A black troop of soldiers in Crete, an ostrich egg in one of the Mycenae shaft-graves, are pointers. They might have come through Egypt, but not necessarily so. That the Egyptians had some knowledge of Cretan and mainland topography is shown by the Theban Topographical List of Amenophis III of around 1400; and there are of course the Egyptian tomb-paintings, the earliest of which, early in the 15th century (reign of Hatshepsut), show incontrovertibly the visits of Aegean envoys. The so-called 'foreign coasts' of the Theran wall-painting which was destroyed at the end of the 16th century were thought by the excavator, the late Spyridon Marinatos, to be North African. The vegetation though not exotic is like the 'Nile Scenes' on niello-encrusted daggers from Mycenae and Pylos. However, a Cretan or even nearer locality is now thought more likely. All this belongs to an earlier epoch, but relations once established are easily renewed. Cyprus could also have been a clearing house for foreign intelligence. The long swords of the Meshwesh, defeated by Merneptah, are not likely to have come   110 to them by way of Egyptian craftsmanship, but might well have come from any of the northern islands, including Sicily and Sardinia. A north wind could carry shipping on the Aegean-Tyrrhenian routes straight to North Africa, as would have happened to St Paul if his ship had not struck Malta.

Peace and war in Egypt

Two Egyptian texts, one of the late 13th and the other of the middle 12th century, give as neat a picture of contrasting black and white, war and peace as the two cities on the Shield of Achilles. The first description comes from Merneptah's reign, on a stela which has the only mention on the Egyptian monuments of the name Israel – the so-called 'Israel Stela'. It   62 was written after the narrow victory of the Libyan war of *c.* 1220, at a time when Egypt could still indulge dreams of security and of the pleasures of peace which have not yet the hollow sound they will have in the time of Ramesses III.

> Men can walk the roads at any pace without fear. The fortresses stand open and the wells are accessible to all travellers [messengers]. The walls and the battlements sleep peacefully in the sunshine till their guards wake up. The police lie stretched out asleep. The desert frontier-guards are among the meadows where they like to be. The cattle roam freely where they please, and cross the streams in safety at flood time. There is no sudden cry at night 'Halt, see, here someone comes, someone with a stranger's voice.' There is coming and going and the people are singing and no great cry of mourning. Towns that were empty are settled again. The man who ploughs will eat the harvest. *Re* has returned to Egypt.[7]

This idyll is followed by a list of all the countries and tribes that are pacified or, more probably, that are not at the moment

72 The Papyrus Harris is the longest extant papyrus writing referring to Egypt's early history. Composed at, or just after, the death of Ramesses III, it gives a flattering account of his state and reign, ending with an historical review of his 'victories' real and supposed. The account given of the wars with the Sea Peoples differs in some respects from the Medinet Habu inscriptions, naming Shardana among the enemy.

actually at war with Egypt; these include Libya, Hatti, Canaan Ashkalon and Gezer, Yanoam (near Galilee), Israel, Hurru (northern Canaan) and the people of Egypt itself.

This picture of peace – secure roads, sleepy battlements and men quietly at work in the fields – may even then have been more dream than reality; but there is no doubt about the sharp truth of the second, the war picture. It comes from the Papyrus Harris, which is the largest extant papyrus, 40.5 m long with 117 columns of 12 to 13 lines. Only the last part is historical, and gives a retrospective summary of the events of the reign of Ramesses III, written soon after his death in *c.* 1162. It is a last will and testament compiled through the piety of his son and successor Ramesses IV. The summary of events starts with this dreary picture of the 'Interregnum years' around 1200 at the end of the 19th dynasty, before peace was restored by Seknakht, father of Ramesses III.

The land of Egypt was abandoned and every man was a law to himself. During many years there was no leader who could speak for others. Central government lapsed, small officials and headmen took over the whole land. Any man, great or small, might kill his neighbour. In the distress and vacuum that followed there came a Syrian, a foreigner who set himself up over the whole land, and men banded together to plunder one another. They treated the gods no better than men, and cut off the temple revenues.[8]

For the temple scribe the last item was no doubt the most painful of all.

Here was the usual sequence of exhausting war followed by economic disaster and general breakdown, leaving the society vulnerable to usurpation from outside or revolution from below. It does not matter whether the tyrant who set himself up after the period of chaos was a Syrian or a native Egyptian; it is the detail that matters, the picture so like Hesiod's 'Age of Iron'. Things became so bad around 1200, and the breakdown was so complete, that records were not kept nor years counted. There were shadowy Pharaohs before the Interregnum, then a partial   Table I
recovery with Seknakht the first Pharaoh of the 20th dynasty and his son Ramesses III, who followed him after one, or perhaps two, years.

Ramesses III's war against the northerners

Ramesses III probably reigned from *c.* 1194 to 1162. The contemporary inscriptions on the temple walls at Medinet Habu   73
are the prime source for the history of the times. The language has been called 'poetical' but is more justly described as 'bombastic'. It is a murky substitute for straightforward historical narrative, but that is something the ancient world never set out to give.

The inscriptions recount the events of Ramesses' Libyan war of year 5, about 1189. Egypt's western neighbours were still threatening, and had in fact gained a foothold in the Nile Delta. They were raiding as far as Memphis, and Ramesses was forced to act. He defeated them with great slaughter. The reliefs that   74
illustrate the campaign show contingents of Egyptian troops. The Shardana are probably there amongst the Egyptians with their horned helmets and cheek protection. Also amongst the 'Chiefs of the Guard' are men with the sort of tall headgear that

122   has been called a 'feathered crown' (see below). All these are clean-shaven, but there is also a bearded contingent with a headband and turban or hair swept back. This latter variety of headgear is usually connected with the northerners, though it

13   had been known to the Egyptians since Kadesh. The headbands of the kilted contingent, following the Shardana, are most like

68   the one worn by the Shekelesh or Shasu chieftain on a later monument at Medinet Habu, already referred to. None of the northerners were among the Libyan enemy of Ramesses in year 5, but the possibility must be considered that some of the old

enemies of Merneptah's Libyan war – Ekwesh, Teresh, Shekelesh – were now enrolled in the Egyptian army and fighting against their former allies.

Only three years later, in about 1186 or year 8 of Ramesses' reign, matters had altered profoundly, and the events took place that are commonly, though not very accurately, called 'the Great Land and Sea Raids'. At the beginning of the Introduction to this essay there was a brief quotation from the inscription at Medinet Habu describing the events of year 8, with the mustering of the enemy for the attack. A fuller quotation must now be given.

After some lines of panegyric and bluster the real situation is sketched:[9]

> ... as for the foreign countries, they made a conspiracy in their islands. All at once the lands [i.e. the people] were on the move, scattered in war. No country could stand before their arms. Hatti, Kode [Kizzuwatna], Carchemish, Arzawa and Alashiya. They were cut off. A camp was set up in one place in Amor [Amurru]. They desolated its people and its land was like that which has never come into being. They were advancing on Egypt while the flame [perhaps the Egyptian navy or a reference to scorched earth tactics] was prepared before them. Their league was Peleset, Tjeker, Shekelesh, Denyen and Weshesh, united lands [i.e. people]. They laid their hands upon the lands to the very circuit of the earth, their hearts confident and trusting: 'Our plans will succeed'.

Then Pharaoh describes his preparations:

> I organized my frontier in Djahi [probably in southern Palestine or between Egypt and Palestine]. [I] prepared before them: princes, commanders of garrisons, *maryannu*, I caused the river mouth [the Nile Delta] to be prepared like a strong wall with warships, transports and merchant-men, they were manned entirely from bow to stern with brave fighting men, and their weapons. The troops consisted of every picked man of Egypt, they were like lions roaring on the mountain tops [this was certainly a great emergency and *all* had to go to the defence of their native land]. The chariotry consisted of runners, of picked men, of every good and capable chariot-fighter ... as for those who reached my frontier their seed is not, their heart and their soul are finished forever.

The point is, however, that they *did* reach the Egyptian frontier.

73 The Great Temple of Ramesses III at Medinet Habu (viewed here from the south-east) is covered with inscriptions and reliefs, among which are those executed to glorify Pharaoh. Some are purely symbolic but many show unique scenes of war not met anywhere else – the boats of the invaders, the ox-carts and the strongly differentiated human types among the most important.

74 In year 5 of Ramesses III's reign (*c.* 1189) he waged a war against the Libyans who were once more trying to settle in the Delta. Amongst the Egyptian troops shown here we already see men with the high headdress ('feathered crown'?) worn by the enemy in the raids 3 years later (75), while others have the 'Shardana' horns and disc on a native Egyptian helmet – these troops carry swords and spears, the second contingent have bows and spears. See also 122.

119

After the land battle the inscription describes the attack by sea:

> As for those who came together on the sea, the full flame was in front of them at the river mouths, while a stockade of lances surrounded them on the shore [or 'canal']. They were dragged ashore, hemmed in and flung down on the beach [or 'they were grappled, capsized, laid out on the shore dead'], their ships made heaps from stern to prow and their goods. . . .

The inscription ends with a hymn of praise, a long boast of Ramesses. As a historical record it is meagre. The relief scenes on the walls at Medinet Habu, with their battle-pieces and lines of captives, provide a tantalizing supplement; tantalizing because it is so hard to know how far they can be taken literally, and to what extent the same ambiguities and idealizations exist as in the texts. Allowance has to be made here also for a sort of visual bombast. Nevertheless there is much that is new in the relief scenes, and the details were undoubtedly portrayed with as much truth as the artistic conventions of the day permitted.

The land battle

The land battle evidently took place before the sea battle, though where is uncertain. If the camp in Amor (Amurru) was in the nature of a base-camp set up to gather and restore the invading forces and prepare for the attack on Egypt, then this attack could have taken place somewhere north of the old Egyptian province of Canaan, perhaps immediately north of Tripoli. But it is unlikely that Egypt had at this time sufficient interest so far north, and Ramesses actually speaks of 'my frontier', so that it is more likely that the battle took place near the line of frontier fortresses that guarded the Delta on the eastern side. In the language of the inscriptions the approach of Pharaoh appears to the enemy 'like the heat of the sun over the two Nile shores'. The battle itself is shown as fought between the Egyptian troops and chariots and their Shardana auxiliaries, wearing the characteristic horned helmet, and, on the other side, the enemy, some of whom also fight in chariots, but in the Hittite manner of three men to a chariot, whereas the Egyptian chariot had only the driver and one combatant.

The battle is a confused melée with charioteers and footmen fighting hand to hand; but one is immediately struck by the ox-carts with their load of women and children. This is a people on

75 In the land attack of the northern enemy against Egypt in year 8 of Ramesses III's reign (c. 1186), most of the enemy wear the puzzling head-dress sometimes called a 'feathered crown' (see also 76, 77 and 86, 87); the kilt is identical to that of the attackers with horned helmets (cf. 112 left).

112

10

76, 77

the move in search of new homes. Either their camp has been surprised, or they have been caught and attacked on the march. The carts in themselves tell us something about the people. The beautiful horse-drawn chariot has always attracted more interest than the plodding carts and waggons of common use. The few war-chariots that have actually survived are extremely fragile objects. If a wheel meets an edge of rock or deep rut the chariot capsizes. Mycenaean tablets show chariot-bodies and wheels dismantled, and this would be the sensible way to transport them over rough country. But the ox-cart too is easily damaged. The carts at the land battle are not the normal heavy transport vehicles which were four-wheeled waggons pulled by two, or occasionally four, oxen in pairs. There are many bronze and clay models of such waggons in Anatolia and the Near East, while actual waggons survive in burials in the foothills of the Caucasus near Lake Sevan; and more are scratched diagrammatically on the rocks in the same region.[10] But what we have here is quite different, and possibly unique, a two-wheeled ox-transport drawn by a span of oxen yoked four abreast. It is an awkward arrangement, and the most likely explanation is that the extra pair were yoked on to the sides to cope with breakdowns, and also because they *had* to come. The wealth of an agricultural people usually lies in the number of head of cattle they own, which limits the amount of land that can be worked. These are not semi-nomadic bands, like those so long familiar to the Levant, but farmers, uprooted and bringing their families and their livestock with them. Their situation is quite different from that of the corsair and raider, whether on land or sea, who operates from a base. For the pirate in his ship family and belongings are an encumbrance that must be left behind.

78

The oxen are the humped zebu which were used in Anatolia and Mesopotamia, but not in Palestine or the Aegean, though they may have reached Cyprus. Recent experience with oxen in South Africa and in North America throws some light on their performance. The ox is slow-moving, and has an absolute maximum progress of 18 miles a day, with 10 more usual. Wheels smash easily, axles break, sudden storms flooding the gullies can halt them for hours, if not days. Ideally an ox requires 8 hours a day to graze and another 8 hours to rest, which only leaves 8 hours for work. In Natal during the Zulu War of 1879, when ox-transport was relied upon, the teams could not do more than 10 miles a day. The American settlers, who took the Oregon Trail in 1843, did not do much better although they still managed to

76–8   The main enemy attack on Egypt in *c.* 1186 was on dry
land, either east of the Delta or else perhaps further north on the
borders of Amurru. The enemy seem to have been taken by
surprise while on the move with their heavy ox-transports, women
and children; or possibly the camp was attacked. The battle is
confused with chariots on both sides as well as foot-soldiers. Some
ox-carts have solid sides, some wicker; in one (*opposite, above,* a
detail of 76) a woman with Anatolian features hangs on to a child.
This type of cart with solid wheels and wicker body can still be
seen in Anatolia (*opposite, below*), but with a more normal yoke of
two oxen; the extra pair in the drawing are probably only hitched
on in order to keep them with the others.

cover 2000 miles in 5 months.[11] The comparison with Natal is closer because the terrain is more like that of the Levant, but neither in Natal nor in America were the teams travelling through a fairly closely populated countryside with many walled cities defended by well-armed garrisons.

Without the protection of cavalry or strong contingents of foot soldiers ox-carts were dreadfully vulnerable. In this case there is no cavalry and the foot soldiers are hardly proving adequate protection. This is, however, the forward spear-point of the attack, which had left behind it a trail of desolation and ruin in Syria and Palestine (see chapter 7).

75

In the Egyptian reliefs one cart has three grown women in it with two children, and one child fallen or falling out of the cart. The mother holding a naked boy by the arm to yank him up has the type of profile that Egyptian artists gave to the Hittite race. Another cart holds one fighting man, and possibly a second, also one woman and a child, while a third, more damaged in the relief, appears to have two women and two children. It does not look as if there is any room for baggage but the weight would be about right for a normal ox-team load.

77
68

The sea battle

The sea battle, in which the invaders were routed again, probably took place within the Delta. For the invaders it was a disaster, with boats capsized and men drowning. The scene is vividly illustrated on the north wall of the Great Temple at Medinet Habu. The accompanying inscription partly recapitulates the account of the battle already quoted.

6

80–4

> Now the northern countries [i.e. people] which were in their islands were quivering in their bodies. They penetrated the channels of the river mouths [the Nile Delta]. They struggle for breath, their nostrils cease. His Majesty is gone out like a whirlwind against them fighting on the battlefield like a runner, the dread of him and the terror have entered their bodies, they are capsized and overwhelmed where they are. Their heart is taken away and their soul is flown away, their weapons are scattered upon the sea. His arrow pierces whom he wishes, and the fugitive is a drowned man. . . .

Five of the attacking ships are shown and one has already capsized. They are hard-pressed by four ships of the Egyptians

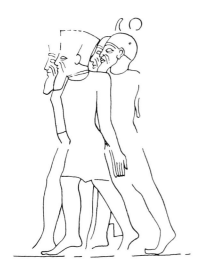

79 The Shardana both with and against Egypt are usually clean-shaven, although since the battle scenes are formalized this may not hold good in general; an important exception is the named captive chieftain (*right*, detail of 68), another is in a group of prisoners returned from a (probably fictitious) campaign in Syria (*left*). The same individual might be represented in both and the wearing of insignia (disc) could mean that this was an ally turned traitor. Note the earring.

which appear to be driving them on to the shore where they are met by Egyptian bowmen. Underneath the battle scene the prisoners are lead off in fetters.

Three of the attacking ships, including the one that has capsized, are manned by men who wear the same high headdresses as the defenders of the ox-carts in the land battle. 84
The men on the other two ships wear horned helmets which 82
have, perhaps mistakenly, been connected with the horned helmets of Pharaoh's Shardana bodyguard. In fact horns are all that they have in common with the bodyguard, otherwise the kilts and strap-corselets are identical with those of the other attackers. The Shardana are not named among the enemy in the account of year 8 quoted above, though they are in the Papyrus Harris (see below). The principal link between the men in the boats and the name 'Shardana' is the chieftain whose portrait, 79
identified by name, is shown among those of the other captive 68, 69
chieftains, but since these include a Hittite not too much can be built upon this association. The 'Shardana' chieftain wears the same helmet as the attackers in the boats, with the curving low sides, but between the horns there is the spike and disc, or sphere, which was the insignia of the Egyptian bodyguard. He is bearded, which none of the attackers are, any more than the Egyptian troops, but again too much should not be read into what may be no more than an artistic convention. He also wears large earrings. He could be a bodyguard turned traitor.

The boats of the raiders, with their heads of water-birds on bow- and stern-post, at first glance look quite new, and quite unlike the Egyptian boats. The latter are the traditional Nile 81, 83

80–2   A general view of the sea battle on the north
wall of the Great Temple at Medinet Habu (*left*) is
intended to show enemy ships driven towards the shore
where they are met by Egyptian bowmen lined up in
front of the gigantic, symbolic figure of Pharaoh. The
water is full of drowning men and one of the enemy's
bird-headed boats has turned turtle. Two attacking
boats are manned by men in horned helmets (not
necessarily Shardana) and three, including the capsized
boat, by men in high headdresses, the so-called
'feathered crowns'. There are four Egyptian boats and
all nine vessels symbolize a much larger force. The
Egyptian boats have rowers and bowmen and one
(*opposite, below*) already has a number of prisoners
hauled up out of the water (see 83). The Egyptian
vessels seem to be larger than the attackers', but the
rigging, superstructure and crow's-nest are identical. It
is still the old square rig of the Thera boat (II) that is
used, unable to tack and needing rowers. The attackers
(*below*) wield long swords, but some have curious
horned blades like Aegean swords of much earlier; it is
possible that they are intended to represent dirks such as
109. In the lower two registers prisoners are led away by
Egyptian officials.

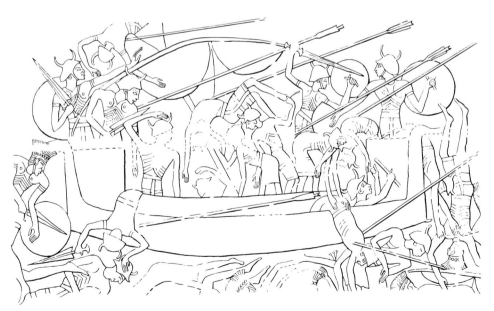

83, 84 An Egyptian boat (*right*) with lion-head ram is grappling the enemy boat immediately to the right of it (*below*) (details of 80, top left corner). The Egyptians are armed with bows and maces and the enemy with swords; each have their peculiar sort of shield. One man in the Egyptian boat is throwing grappling hooks that are tangled in the enemy's sail, perhaps to bring down the mast and capsize the boat since sails are furled and would be useless in such close fighting. The enemy look-out is dead, probably pierced by an arrow, and the water all round the boats (above and below) is full of drowning men. According to the inscription they were 'dragged, hemmed in, prostrate on the beach and made into heaps'.

boat, strengthened and adapted to a rig which is in fact identical with that of the enemy: loose-footed sails, and probably brails for shortening instead of a fixed yard, and with the same deck, upper works and look-out. The Egyptian vessels are manned by ten or eleven rowers on each side and by bowmen who are doing dreadful execution upon the raiders. The raiders' boats are not very different from the Syrian merchantmen of the 14th century and later. No rowers are visible, but with the simple square sails carried by both fleets these vessels could never have reached the Nile, or anywhere else, without oars. They were unable to tack and the sail could only supplement oar-power when the wind was blowing from behind (see chapter 1). The steersman in the illustration is in his proper place near the stern, though mortally wounded, and so is the look-out. The boats seem to be a little smaller than those of the Egyptians, and the rowers no doubt had to double as fighting-men. When it came to boarding and landing, they dropped their oars and fought with swords, spears and great round shields.

11

67

85 Besides the reliefs at Medinet Habu there are no other representations of actual full-size boats with bird's head on stern-post and bows, though animal heads were used in later centuries from the Mediterranean to the Baltic, and there are many small-scale models of such boats particularly in the 1st millennium in Danubian lands. One of the very few nearly contemporary representations with a bird or animal head is painted on a 12th-century Mycenaean pot (LH IIIC) from Skyros in the northern Sporades.

The double-ended hull is not new in the East Mediterranean but the bird-heads at prow and stern probably are. A very similar boat with a bird's head at the prow alone is painted on the side of a 12th-century Mycenaean pot from Skyros (LH IIIC). These boats could be ancestral to the Phoenician *hippos* of several centuries later, and to certain Assyrian boats with double animal heads. There are also rock scratchings of not dissimilar boats in the Caucasus that may be of the 12th century, or not much later. It is reasonable to conclude that, wherever the double-ended boats with bird's heads were built, it was somewhere in the Levant and near enough to the shipyards that built the Egyptian boats for the new and improved rig to have been already familiar to Egyptian shipwrights. Perhaps this was at Tyre or Byblos, or even Ugarit or Cyprus.[12] The King of Ugarit had a fleet of 150 ships at one time, and we know from the diplomatic correspondence that from time to time Egypt commissioned the building of boats in Cypriot shipyards (chapter 2). A section of the Papyrus Harris describes the building of a fleet of cargo boats, equipped with bowmen and armed troops, for the northern trade with Syria and 'the countries of the ends of the earth'.

The aftermath of battle is the display of prisoners and the reliefs show them in three lines being presented to the gods by Pharaoh. The upper line, according to the accompanying inscription, are 'leaders of every country', the middle line are 'the fallen ones of Denyen', and the bottom are 'the fallen ones of Peleset'. All wear the high 'crowns' and identical kilts with tassels.

Pharaoh boasts: 'My strong arm has overthrown [those] who came to exalt themselves: the Peleset, the Denyen and the Shekelesh.' On the preceding relief the Tjeker wear the same dress and head-crowns, so either we have to accept that Peleset, Denyen, Shekelesh and Tjeker were virtually indistinguishable, or that the representations are symbolic. These are the same names that, together with the Weshesh, appear as the confederacy of the land immigration, so it is not surprising that they are also indistinguishable in the relief of the land battle.

The despairing Tjeker exclaims: 'O mighty King . . . greater is thy sword than a mountain of metal. . . . Give to us breath.' On another relief, already referred to more than once and which is of a more symbolic nature, representative chieftains are shown in distinctive dress and headwear; unfortunately neither the Peleset nor the Denyen have survived.

86, 87 After the victory comes the counting of spoil and numbering of prisoners. At Medinet Habu Ramesses is portrayed presenting captive Sea Peoples to the gods Amon and Mut. The prisoners are in three lines and are indistinguishable from each other in appearance. The top line according to the inscriptions are 'leaders of every country'. Over the middle line (*right*) is written: 'Words spoken by the fallen ones of Denyen, "Breath thou good ruler, great of strength like Montu in the midst of Thebes;" ' and over the bottom line (*above*): 'Words spoken by the fallen ones of Peleset, "Give us the breath for our nostrils thou King, son of Amon." '

The boast of Ramesses

There is a repetition of the account of the same events under the inscription for year 5 (*c.* 1189) which is chiefly concerned with the first Libyan war of Ramesses III, in which northerners do not seem to have been concerned, but the later part must refer to year 8.[13]

... the northern countries quivered in their bodies, namely the Peleset, the Tjeker [?] ... they were cut off from their land and coming, their spirit broken. They were *teher* on land [*teher*: an uncertain word connected elsewhere with Hittite troops]. Another group was on the sea. Those who came on land were overthrown and slaughtered.... Amon-Re was after them destroying them. Those who entered the river mouths [the Nile Delta] were like birds ensnared in the net ... their leaders were carried off and slain. They were thrown down and pinioned. ...

The rest is pure panegyric.

The Papyrus Harris also contains a great boast of Ramesses:[14]

I extended all the boundaries of Egypt. I overthrew those who invaded them from their lands. I slew the Denyen [who are] in their isles, the Tjeker and the Peleset were made ashes. The Shardana and the Weshesh of the sea, they were made as those that exist not, taken captive at one time, brought as captives to Egypt, like the sand of the shore. I settled them in strongholds bound in my name. Numerous were their classes like hundred-thousands. I taxed them all, in clothing and grain from the store-houses and granaries each year.

There follows an account of a victory over the Shasu people from Edom, living in tents with their cattle: 'I gave them to the gods as slaves in their houses.' Ramesses had other wars in Asia and another Libyan war in the west, but the northern people are not heard of again. Some of the Shardana were still within the Egyptian fold. Among the 'good works' of Ramesses at home he claims:

I made the infantry and chariotry to dwell [at home] in my time; the Shardana and Kehek were in their towns, lying the length of their backs; they had no fear, for there was no enemy from Kush [nor] foe from Syria. Their bows and their weapons were laid up in their magazines, while they were satisfied and drunk with joy. Their wives were with them, their children at their side [for] I was with them as the defence and protection of their limbs.

The care with which character and expression are portrayed by the Egyptian artists encourages us to trust them. The type of the attackers in both the land and sea battles is thin, bony, harsh and imperious. This is very striking among the men in the boats

88, 89 Wounded and dying men of the attacking allies. The left-hand warrior has the curious high headdress of feathers or material and a neckguard. The figure with the horned helmet is drowning, having fallen from one of the attackers' boats (see 83 bottom right). The strongly marked features are in total contrast to the Syrians and Hittites as portrayed by the Egyptians. Note the banded body-armour worn by both (cf. 60).

and drowning in the sea battle. It is very different from the rather fleshy Hittite type, and from that of the Syrians and Amorites. That the headgear of the Peleset was a 'feathered crown' has passed into the literature, but not unchallenged. We have just seen that identical headgear was worn by the Tjeker and possibly the Denyen and Shekelesh as well.[15] The 'crowns' on the reliefs are not obviously made from feathers, whereas when feathers are worn by the Libyans they are unquestionably shown as such. Other suggestions for the crown have been leather, folded linen, a sort of rushes or a special way of dressing the hair. Representations on glazed tiles, ivories and pots show a great variety of hairstyles, from swept back and held by a band, to a form of stiffening so that the hair practically stands on end. It may not be out of place to recall that Celtic warriors used to stiffen their hair with lime. A statuette of Baal from Ugarit has a turban of some soft material; if the band that holds the folds together near the top were slipped down to the crown of the head we would get something very like the 'feathered crown' of the Egyptian reliefs. The Tjeker chieftain wears a 'chef's cap' or

68

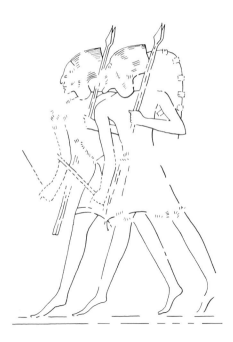

90–2 Hair stiffened and held by a headband, clearly *not* feathers, is worn by Egyptian troops from southern Palestine, fighting the Libyans (74) and accompanying Ramesses III on a symbolic lion hunt between the land and sea battles (*top right*, see also 13 last man). Prisoners (*top left*) depicted on glazed tiles found in the Palace of Ramesses III have, as well as similar hair, a long skirted robe under the usual kilt, and a medallion (cf. the 'Shekelesh' of 68). There is little likeness to the headgear of the northerners (86–8). Differing headgear, including obvious feathers, are painted on LH IIIC sherds showing rowers from the Seraglio, Cos (*bottom*). The turbaned Baal statuette of *middle right* can be compared with a fighting man from the Mycenae Warrior Vase (*middle left* and 119) and the figure on the Kition rhyton (19). Rowers, ht 8.5 cm.

93, 94 Ramesses, returning from an idealized, and probably fictitious northern campaign, drives before him representatives (*above*) of all the lands he claims to have conquered. Led by a Libyan there is an easily recognizable 'crown' (see 88) in the top row, several Syrians in long robes, a possible Tjeker (middle row back, cf. 68) and Peleset (bottom row back, see 113). There is no horned helmet but the turban with two humps (bottom row, man with medallion), was seen among Egyptian troops (14) and worn by two prisoners presented to a Canaanite (?) prince on an ivory inlay from Megiddo (*below*). (At Persepolis several hundred years later a similar turban is worn by Armenians.) Ivory, ht 5 cm.

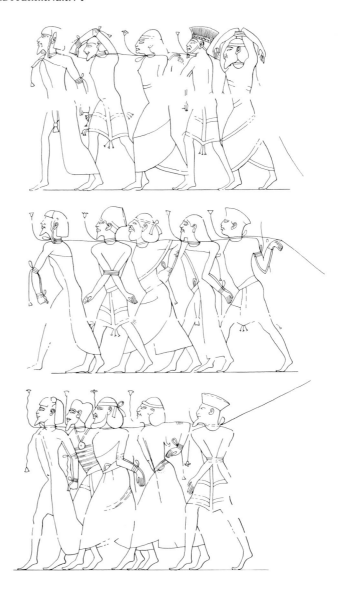

turban, certainly *not* feathers; on the other hand some LH IIIC
sherds found in Cos have crudely painted rowers with what   92
certainly look like feathers on their heads. In Herodotus' account
of the muster of the Persian army by Xerxes in the 5th century
BC, the Lycians are described as wearing 'a hat encircled with
plumes'. These Lycians could have been descended from our
Lukka, or from some one or other of the Anatolian branch of 'Sea
Peoples'. The question of the headdress must remain open, but
either feathers or folded material appear the more likely
candidates. The conventional representation at Persepolis in the
5th century BC of the linen headdress of the Persian Imperial
Guard is a fair comparison in a similar medium.

There is also a low turban with two humps sometimes secured
with a headband. It is worn by a prisoner returning from the
(probably apocryphal) campaign of Ramesses III against Amor,   93
and also by some of Pharaoh's own troops shown marching to the
second Libyan war and on parade with 'northerners', including   14
some with horned helmets. It may be the same as the headgear of
two naked prisoners on a Megiddo ivory as well as that of two of   94
the line of representative Hittite allies at Kadesh, including the   13
kilted leader with his 'Pontic' shield. There is no indication in
the texts who these men were. A flatter version sometimes is
worn by Shasu nomads, and at a much longer shot we might
recognize a similar turban on 'Armenian' tribute bearers at
Persepolis.

This is as far as the Egyptian reliefs and inscriptions take us.
In the next two chapters we will look forward to these events
from a northern vantage point and at the same time attempt to
catch some of them at an earlier stage in their history. What we
have gained in this chapter is at least the names, and an idea of
the looks, of some of the chief actors. What we want to know now
is where they came from, and why.

The crisis in the East Mediterranean
II: Anatolia, Ugarit and Cyprus

Hatti and Ugarit

In the last chapter we looked at the crisis from the wrong end because, studying the Egyptian records, we could suppose ourselves still in the domain of history. Individuals had names and titles, and were seen to act. But the trap that led to many of these actions was sprung far away in the north, by men without names, whose activities can only be surmised. Here and there we may see points of light, little patches of literacy, but for the most part we are groping and guessing.

The waning of Hittite power was probably a prime cause of much that followed in the Levant and the Aegean. In spite of the strength of its defences, the fortress, Büyükkale, fell when the rest of Hattusas fell; it had been so strong that one must suspect treachery. One Hittite text, probably of the last Suppiluliumas, catalogues the distresses of a sovereign as from direct experience: desertion by the army, the royal bodyguard and the people themselves, the king's men taken prisoner by an enemy, desertion by the nobles, the king sick, or embarked on a long campaign, or something unnamed even worse than this. The king accuses unknown persons of standing aloof when things went badly.

33
36

> You were not beside me. Did I not go alone to Nihirija and when the enemy tried to capture a part of Hurri Land [Hatti] I was left totally deserted in the town of Alatarma.

So long as the Hittite rulers had a sufficient grip on the political situation, external and internal, to hold the central Anatolian plateau, northern Syria too could look after itself; it did not have to face the cold realities of enemy attack except from the east. But at the beginning of the 12th century this was no longer so. Some of the misfortunes of the later Hittite kings were sketched in chapter 2. Now a sort of crisis point was reached. It was a great

95 Cypriot potters had evolved a light-hearted decorative style based on fairly distant Mycenaean models just before the vast changes that brought an end to the Late Cypriot II cities. A tall LH IIIB crater from Shemishin has lions flanking a tree. Ht 41.3 cm.

deal worse than the endemic defensive warfare against the Kashka in the north, or the aggressive campaigning of Assyria or Mitanni in the east. There were many unscrupulous and ambitious minor rulers ready to set up confederations to undermine the Hittite Empire. Troubled relations with the King of Ahhiyawa, and the menace of individual free-booters like that Piyamaradu who had plagued Hattusilis a couple of generations before, all show a country falling apart from the centre.[1] The Lukka Lands and Arzawa were the focus of the unrest. In the strong Egyptian phrase they 'quivered in their bodies'.

Two factors especially worked against the Hittites. First, theirs was never a maritime power: they depended on Ugarit and the untrustworthy Lukka for a naval force; secondly, their reliance on a feudal system gave much power to great vassals and subject rulers, while their feudal army was dangerously dependent on its chariotry, an over-specialized force.

The Great Inscription of year 8 of Ramesses III's reign (c. 1186) which was given in chapter 5, and which describes the overthrow of the northern countries, is open to more than one interpretation. First of the lands that could not stand before the northerners was Hatti, then came Kode and Carchemish, Arzawa and Alashiya, in that order. The fall of Hatti probably implies here the destruction of Hattusas, the far-off capital on the Anatolian plateau, though one suggestion has been that it applies rather to the Neo-Hittite kingdom of
III   northern Syria.[2] Excavations at Hattusas have uncovered signs of a terrible destruction after which the site was virtually abandoned for several centuries. After Hatti the next state named is Kode, Hittite Kizzuwatna, the coastal parts of Cilicia. An ancient highway runs almost due south via Hittite Kanesh,
96   through the Cilician Gates to Tarsus and Adana in Kizzuwatna, with a branch continuing east to Carchemish. So the lands mentioned on the Great Inscription follow a logical progress south and then east. But the last two names, Arzawa and Alashiya, are off the route from the mountains to the north
2   Syrian plain. Arzawa lies in western Anatolia inland from Miletus, Caria and the Lukka Lands, while Alashiya is the island of Cyprus, and therefore overseas.

If there had been only one invasion all the raiders and migrants from western Anatolia, some of them possibly from as far as the Troad, would have travelled a very roundabout way in the descent on Syria, and eventually Egypt. It seems more likely that there were at least two separate parties. One party made a

land trek and had no use for boats; the other operated in the coastal regions and was, at least partly, sea-borne.

It was the activities of the latter force that caused the Hittite king to make the appeal to the King of Ugarit for help which is to be inferred from the latter king's correspondence with Alashiya (see below). There is no certain way of deciding the order of events described in the cuneiform texts from Hattusas and Ugarit. They give a fascinating but discontinuous view, a jumble of flashbacks without a storyline. There is for instance a boast of Suppiluliumas II that he defeated certain ships of Alashiya in a sea battle.

> I mobilised, with speed, I Suppiluliumas the Great, I reached the sea. The ships of Alashiya came up against me and gave battle, three times out at sea . . . when I arrived on dry land the enemy came against me to do battle in multitudes . . . I fought them . . .

96 The Taurus Mountains are a formidable barrier between the Anatolian plateau and the south coast of Cilicia-Kizzuwatna. Through them Anatolian-Syrian trade and diplomacy had to make its way, and after the fall of Hattusas so did the fleeing Hittites and the pursuing enemy. The road through the great gorge called the Cilician Gates is one of the most ancient and the most frequented routes leading directly to Tarsus and Adana.

This defective text ends with the setting up of a rock sanctuary. This was not the final phase of the troubles. No King of Alashiya is mentioned, and it has been thought that the enemy ships were those of the Sea Raiders. If so they could have been using Cypriot harbours as temporary bases, as the Lukka had done for centuries. They need not have overrun the whole island.[3]

The next light comes from Ugarit. Two important points arise from the correspondence concerning the 'Šikala who live in ships' referred to in chapter 5. First, they are people as yet unknown to the Hittite king, about whom he wants information, so that they must be newcomers to the coast of Anatolia; and second, they are a real potential danger. We now have a short exchange of letters between Hammurabi, the last King of Ugarit, and the King of Alashiya or his chief officer. The date is not certain but the situation fits well with Ramesses III's northern war (c. 1186), since it immediately precedes the destruction of the city, probably by the confederates.[4]

The first letter from 'the High Steward' of Alashiya to Hammurabi of Ugarit, might refer to the sea battle of Suppiluliumas II, and so slightly predate the events of 1186.

> Greetings to yourself, and to your country. As to those matters concerning the enemy. It was indeed men of your country and your boats that did it, your people were indeed responsible for that offence, but don't complain to me. The twenty boats that the enemy left previously in the mountainous parts did not stay there, but they went off suddenly, and now we don't know where to look for them. I write to inform you, and to put you on your guard.

Either nominal subjects of the King of Ugarit had gone raiding, or the 'enemy' is not the same as the offending men of Ugarit, or there may have been a temporary alliance between the two.

The next two letters are written under the threat of a much greater danger and may be taken as answering each other. From the King of Alashiya to Hammurabi:

> Thus says the King to Hammurabi King of Ugarit. Greetings, may the gods keep you in good health. What you have written to me 'enemy shipping has been sighted at sea'. Well now, even if it is true that enemy ships have been sighted, be firm. Indeed then, what of your troops, your chariots, where are they stationed? Are they stationed close at hand or are they not? Who presses you behind the enemy? Fortify your towns,

bring the troops and the chariots into them, and wait for the enemy with feet firm.

The reply is a mixture of desperation and sarcasm:

> To the King of Alashiya. My father, thus says the King of Ugarit his son. I fall at my father's feet. Greetings to my father, to your house, your wives, your troops, to all that belongs to the King of Alashiya, many many greetings. My father, the enemy ships are already here, they have set fire to my towns and have done very great damage in the country. My father, did not you know that all my troops were stationed in the Hittite country, and that all my ships are still stationed in Lycia and have not yet returned? So that the country is abandoned to itself. . . . Consider this my father, there are seven enemy ships that have come and done very great damage. Now if there are more enemy ships let me know about them so that I can decide what to do [or 'know the worst'].

Violent events may have overtaken the writing of this letter, which was probably never sent, for it was found in the kiln in the palace at Ugarit. Seven ships seem rather few to have caused so much panic, but this may have been only one in a mounting series of attacks. It is unlikely that the King of Ugarit would have sent his entire fleet away to Lycia. It may have been dispersed by storm or other mishaps, or even have joined the enemy. In any case the letter from Alashiya will have given little comfort to the distressed people of Ugarit.

If the enemy were attacking in two bodies, and the Hittite king was engaged with them in Lycia or Caria, his appeal to the King of Ugarit (above) may have been caused by news of an independent attack on Hattusas, his own capital. This would have forced him to abandon Arzawa and the Lycian coast. Loyally Hammurabi (who was evidently still sufficiently under Hittite domination to feel he had to comply) did his best, and failed. The two separate enemy contingents may then have joined forces in northern Syria, going on to overrun and destroy Ugarit, and many other cities. One group of the attackers trekked on towards Egypt, destroying the Amorites on the way; but another large contingent probably remained north of the Orontes.

There is a lot of evidence, both archaeological and linguistic, for a southward shift of Anatolian people from the plateau to northern Syria, with groups from Caria, Lycia and perhaps

Arzawa carving out new small states on the fringes of the old Hittite Empire. This may account for the surprising absence of the Lukka from the sea attack on Egypt of 1186. Their lands had been at the centre of the disturbances for centuries, and they had been deeply engaged in the war against Merneptah (chapter 7).

Cyprus

Cyprus played a vital role in these confused and violent times. Between 1200 and 1050 population withered, old settlements were abandoned, traditional types of artifact disappeared; at the end there was only a handful of settlements 'enjoying a material civilization whose origins owed at least as much to the dying Bronze Age world of Crete, continental Greece and of Syria-Palestine as to [their] own Cypriot background'. It was probably during this 150 years that the Greek language took hold in the island.

Cyprus is a bridge between the Mycenaean world, Egypt and Palestine. Enkomi and Kition are our best guide to events. In chapter 2 the destruction of the Late Cypriot IIC (level VI, late-13th-century) fortification wall at Enkomi was referred to. It marked the end of an epoch. Pottery of LH IIIB style was still in use when it fell. About this time new settlers established themselves on promontories which they fortified, and on which they built in ashlar. At Maa-Palaeokastro they have been fully studied. The occupation was short but the evidence is unequivocal that ashlar buildings precede the new LH IIIC pottery. At Enkomi too it appears that the first ashlar buildings were put up at about this time and before the introduction of IIIC pottery by what was probably a new wave of settlers having closer ties with the mainland of Greece, the so-called Achaean settlement.[5] At Kition the 13th-century city was rebuilt after a little minor delapidation had taken place, and after a short interval without any signs of violent destruction. Pottery in the style of the earliest LH IIIC wares does not appear to have been found at either site, though it is found inland at Sinda and may have come more immediately from the Dodecanese.

The new town plans of Enkomi and Kition, as well as the building material, now the finest ashlar, were quite different from the old ones. When the new buildings went up the rich tombs of earlier generations were sealed over, although a few were plundered. Enkomi at this time was a curious mixture of the oriental and the Aegean, although the oriental was the

95

97 Ivory mirror handles
richly carved in a
Levanto-Mycenaean style
are found in Cypriot
tombs (Late Cypriot III).
On one from Enkomi
(tomb 24), a man with a
round shield and sword is
stabbing a griffin; he
wears the kilt and body
armour of the attacking
Sea People of 84 and 89.
The winged griffin might
possibly stand for a
Mycenaean enemy(?). Ht
20 cm.

stronger partner. The crowded town plan and the style of the temple buildings were still eastern. The temples at Kition have an open court and garden like those at Ugarit, with an inner 'holy of holies'. The cult itself seems to be oriental, as are the temple workshops for smelting and working bronze. Faience and ivory-work is probably Levantine though to some extent common also to the Aegean (the workshops at Mycenae have been referred to). Bronze tripods and bracket-lamps are peculiarly Cypriot, but some of the weapons, especially swords and greaves, are the same as those found at this time in the Aegean, including the distinctive type IIa flange-hilted sword (chapter 4).

97

98–101 After the
Treasury of Atreus at
Mycenae (26) there is
virtually no more ashlar
building in the Aegean for
many centuries. By
contrast at Ugarit the
13th-century palace is
almost entirely faced with
ashlar masonry and some
of it, including court V,
has blocks with drafted
edges (*opposite, below*). In
Cyprus, at about the same
date as the destruction of
the palace at Ugarit
(probably early 12th
century), a new phase in
ashlar begins. At Enkomi
and Kition this is at the
end of Late Cypriot II
(LH IIIB/C). The ashlar
at Enkomi was rubble-
filled but not at Kition,
where the blocks have
sockets for lead rivets and
probably stood 3 to 4
courses high. Much of the
work is very fine, and at
Kition the inner facing
blocks of temple 2 have
drafted edges (*right
above*). Perhaps the
earliest examples of this
technique are at a spring
sanctuary in Anatolia,
Eflatun Pinar (*opposite,
above*), which is probably
late Hittite. Incomparably
the finest drafted masonry
is from a Phoenician
temple at Kition (*right
below*). In the opinion of
the excavator the blocks
are reused from one of the
Bronze Age temples; some
of them measure 3.50 m
by 1.50 m and have graffiti
of ships.

V The horned god of Enkomi, cast solid in bronze, is a superb technical achievement, the largest and most important bronze to come from Cyprus or the Aegean in the 12th century or indeed until classical times. The gesture too is unique. Ht 54.2 cm.

But what gives these cities their Aegean cast is the pottery. Although native Cypriot pottery was still made, the LH IIIB/C and the later IIIC styles were now ubiquitous. This and the architecture show that we are in a new period, and probably to some extent among new people. At Kition the 13th-century mud-brick fortification wall was rebuilt, and has been traced for 1600 m; the streets still have the ruts of chariot wheels. When the old towns were levelled some of the rich 13th-century tombs were rifled. Temples as well as houses were rebuilt and in ashlar masonry. When the twin temples at Kition numbered 2 and 3 were remodelled, or rebuilt, temple 3 became temple 1, an impressive building 35 m by 22 m. It has an open court constructed of ashlar blocks 3.50 m by 1.50 m with drafted 98 (chisel-dressed) edges. Some of the blocks have Cypro-Minoan 99 signs, others have graffiti of ships. At the same time temples 4 and 5 were built, one for a god the other for a goddess. The sacred garden that had existed between temples 2 and 3 was laid out again with a pool, a table of offerings and horns of 20, 22 consecration. The votive anchors and ox-hide ingots found in the temple precincts have already been referred to (chapter 2). Temple 4 had a foundation deposit like most oriental temples, and in temple 5 there are ox-skull masks for use in the cult.

Enkomi experienced another great destruction perhaps a 132 generation later (Late Cypriot IIIA–B), followed by yet another connected with a strong Aegean influx in the 11th century (see V chapter 8). The bronze figure of a horned god, standing over half a metre high, is an astonishing object to come out of the troubled 12th century at Enkomi, but this is where it seems to belong, together with LH IIIC pottery. Some have seen the figure as an Aegean work, but it is unlikely that such a large and complicated casting could have been made at this time by Aegean bronze-founders, for nothing comparable has been found there. The gesture is unique, it stills and calms with the authority of the Apollo from the west pediment of the Temple of Zeus at Olympia, but no earlier figure is at all like it and the rather fleshy face is foreign to Mycenaeans and 'Sea Peoples' alike. The scale is odd with the massive legs and short body; it has been compared most aptly with the griffin-slayer of a Cypriot mirror 97 handle.[6]

At both Enkomi and Kition the oriental elements are not very informative, being what one would expect from the close proximity of the island to the Levant; but the ashlar masonry and the pottery might give a pointer to the identity of the inhabitants.

Ashlar and the end of Ugarit

Between the building of the ashlar palaces of Crete and early-12th-century Cyprus the gap is too great for any direct links to be sought between the two; and in Crete there was no trimming of the blocks to give a drafted border. On the Greek mainland the ashlar masonry and recessed entrance of the Treasury of Atreus may be as late as the early 13th century. At Pylos and Tiryns thresholds, and the lowest course of the palace walls, are good ashlar, but the usual building material is roughly dressed stone, rubble and occasionally mud-brick (chapter 3). There is nothing at all comparable to the temple walls at Kition, and there is no drafted masonry. Hittite buildings are usually of stone and are truly monumental, sometimes cyclopean, although the trimming is rough. There is superior work in the Great Temple at Hattusas, where there are orthostat courses with *raised* trimmed borders, and pilasters. In later work the blocks become larger: temple V is built of very large blocks indeed, trimmed *in situ*. Probably the finest Anatolian masonry, however, can be found at a spring sanctuary at Eflatun Pinar on Lake Beyşehir, just within the borders of Arzawa. The retaining wall of the sanctuary stands four courses high and is of fine workmanship, but the courses are not evenly bedded, and though there *is* drafting of the edges on one face, it does not approach the finish of the Kition temple buildings.

Bronze Age Canaanite cities such as Hazor (the last Canaanite city) and Megiddo (stratum VIIb, just pre-13th century), made use of basalt orthostats in the lowest course, but most walls were of mud-brick. In northern Syria at Alalakh (Tell Atchana) the practice was much the same, with only temples and palaces having orthostats; the blocks have lewis holes for handling. Back in the 18th century, however, the level-VII palace was ashlar built. At Tarsus the lower courses of the Hittite period walls were cyclopean below and mud-brick above. Nowhere, apart from Eflatun Pinar, is there any sign of drafted masonry, nor is there any in Egypt, where the beautiful stone-work is used on different lines; and even in Egypt, in later times, ashlar work was reserved for temples and palaces: secular buildings were of mud-brick.

The key to the problem lies in one place alone: Ugarit. Here the palace, built after a major disaster in the first half of the 14th century, was still standing throughout the 13th century. It covered approximately 10,000 m² compared with the 5,000 of

VI The Taurus Mountains that separate the Hittites of Central Anatolia from the rich and productive land of Hittite Kizzuwatna (Cilicia) and the Levant, though formidable, were no barrier to commerce.

26, 27

III

100

Büyükkale at Hattusas and 4,000 for the palace at Alalakh; while at Mycenae the whole area within the walls was no more than 30,000 m². The palace is constructed of fine ashlar throughout, with six and more courses of large blocks still standing today and originally twelve stairways to upper floors. It was remodelled several times and doubled in extent during its lifetime. Some of the latest building was around court V where the archives were stored and the kiln that held the last dispatches before the catastrophe was found. Also in the same area was a sword of a new type, with on it the cartouche of Merneptah.[7] The external

101 walls of the palace, today still six to ten courses high, had drafted edges. The open area of court V held a pool, or tank of water, and was probably planted as a garden. The links with Cyprus: drafted ashlar masonry, temple and garden, and the correspondence in the archives, are close and direct. Fine as the

98 Ugaritic ashlar is, it is no finer than that of Enkomi and Kition, and the trimming of the drafted borders is inferior to the temples at Kition. We have to wait for Omri's palace at Samaria, c. 872, for comparable work; and there it has been called a supreme example of the mason's craft. The masons at Samaria were Phoenicians, and the style of building is 'Phoenician'. The foundations have drafted blocks very much like those at Ugarit. Some eighty years earlier Solomon's temple at Jerusalem, nothing of which survives, was probably built in the same technique, and reputedly, by Phoenicians. But none of this work matches the excellence of the drafted sandstone blocks at Kition which can be compared with Herodian buildings in Jerusalem, themselves probably a refinement on Solomon's building.[8]

Enkomi did not long survive the 12th century, but Kition lived through various disasters and vicissitudes to be rebuilt in

99 the 9th century as a Phoenician city. Twelfth-century blocks were re-used in the temples which, perhaps significantly, contained a great deal of Samarian pottery. So by the time that Phoenician masons were building in Jerusalem and Samaria, Cyprus was very largely a Phoenician island. The inhabitants of Bronze Age Ugarit, if not Phoenician by name, were forerunners and collaterals of the Phoenicians. Ugarit disappeared at about the time that the city of Kition and its temples were rebuilt. It therefore seems a plausible proposition that in 13th-century Ugarit and 12th-century Cyprus we have the forerunners of the school of Phoenician masons who were later to produce their masterpieces in Samaria and Jerusalem.

For the purposes of this history it is important to know when the exodus from Ugarit to Cyprus actually took place. The oriental characteristics of Enkomi and Kition in the 12th century have been referred to. Some of these characteristics were of long standing, others were probably due to new incursions; but what was the role of the Aegean and the ubiquitous Mycenaean pottery in these changes?

The disaster that overwhelmed Ugarit was total, buildings were abandoned with pots still in the kilns. It is pottery therefore that can give a few useful cross-datings. According to J.-C. Courtois, just before Ugarit was destroyed the 'lion craters' (mixing bowls) were fashionable. These rather ornate pots were made locally, but in the Mycenaean LH IIIB style. They have links with Miletus where similar pictorial craters were found in the latest level. Though locally made they imitate the Mycenaean (LH IIIB) pottery of the Argolid. This pictorial style was followed in Cyprus by a poorly executed sequel, some-times referred to as 'rude style', which Courtois has recognized at Ugarit, and which is a far cry from the LH IIIC style of the Argolid, a local phenomenon of mainland Greece. Other variants are found in Cyprus, coastal Anatolia (Tarsus) and even Palestine; they are generally made locally and become less and less Aegean. The destruction of Ugarit, according to Courtois' findings, took place after the appearance of at least one pure 'rude style' pot in a level immediately above a lion crater. In Cyprus 'rude style' appears in the new buildings after the destruction of 13th-century Enkomi. If the 'pictorial style' of Ugarit and its 'rude style' sequel inspired the 'rude style' pottery of Cyprus the story told by pottery agrees with that of architec-ture; and there is no need for a hiatus between the departure from Ugarit and arrival in Cyprus.[9] When the refugees left behind in the ruins of Ugarit the older, finer, LH IIIB-style pots, some of which were still in use, and started pot-making in their new homes, what they turned out were local imitations of LH IIIB and 'rude style' pots; only later did the LH IIIC at Enkomi and Kition appear and come to form ninety per cent of all pottery excavated.

Unfortunately we do not know who these people were, for to call them 'Achaeans', as some suggest, begs the question and is inaccurate. There may well have been Carians and Lukka among them, and Mycenaeans from Miletus and other coastal sites, for all shared the Mycenaean tradition in potting that evolved into the various local styles inspired by the early LH IIIC pottery of Greece. At Tarsus, where Hittites and

103
104

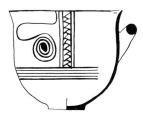

102 A deep bowl with antithetic spirals and a lipless cup from post-Hittite Tarsus (LH IIIC), where Mycenaean pottery shows continuous links with the Greek mainland and particularly with Cyprus where a similar style was very popular.

103–6 Mycenaean·
pottery from Ugarit just
before its destruction, and
from Cyprus at the
beginning of the Late
Cypriot III phase of
rebuilding. Tall craters
(LH IIIB or IIIB/C, *right
above* and *below*) were
popular in Ugarit in the
last phase. A family
likeness has been seen
between this pottery and
the Mycenaean wares of
the Dodecanese and Caria
(Miletus), with each
developing its own
preferences in decorative
subjects. The crater from
the Petit Palais at Ugarit
(*right*, with ornamentation
developed) has dolphins,
wild goats and a man
holding two horses; his
sword may be compared
with one found in Egypt
(110 right). A deep bowl
from Sinda in Cyprus
(*opposite, above*) is mar-
ginally later and comes
from the Late Cypriot III
rebuilding, while the jug
with sieve spout from an
unknown Cypriot site
(*opposite, below*) has
characteristic decoration
(see also 114). Hts: 103,
45 cm; 104, no scale; 105,
26.2 cm; 106, 11.5 cm.

Mycenaeans had probably met, the Hittite temple was destroyed
by people using LH IIIC pottery; but unlike Ugarit Tarsus was
reoccupied. There may also have been adventurers from Rhodes
and Cos among the new arrivals. Archaeologically the last phase
at Ugarit was one of very open trade. Where formerly the
Argolid had been the chief source of Mycenaean pottery it now
came from Attica, Euboea, Caria (Miletus) and possibly Crete.
All the northern islands and coasts were 'on the move and scattered in war'; or so it seemed to the Egyptians. If we go back
now to the Egyptian texts, is it possible to put names to any
of the authors of the archaeological changes that we have been
looking at?

102

N

TAURUS MTS

KIZZUWATNA

CILICIA

Seyhan

Ceyhan

Euphrates

Karatepe

Adana

Sinjirli

Tarsus

Mersin

Carchemish

HATTAY
DANUNA?

AMANUS MTS

Alalakh
(Tell Atchana)

Aleppo

MUKISH

Ugarit
(Ras Shamra)

Sinda

Salamis
Enkomi

CYPRUS

Kition

Hala Sultan Tekké

Tell Sukas

Orontes

AMURRU

Kadesh (Tell Nebi Mend)

Byblos

MEDITERRANEAN

PHOENICIAN COAST

SEA

Sidon

Tyre

Damascus

Tell Dan (Laish)

Hazor

Acre

TJEKER?

Tell Abu Hawam

Mt Tabor

CANAAN

Dor

Megiddo

Taanach

Beth Shan (Bashan)

Tell es Saidiyeh
Deir Alla

Samaria

Jordan

PELESET DANUNA?

Tell Qasile

Gezer

Ai

Jerusalem

Amman

Ashdod

Ashkalon

Lachish

Gaza

Tell Eitun

DEAD SEA

Tell Fara
(Beth Pelet)

El Kantara

Via Maris

0   150 Kms

0   100 Mls

0   200 Kms

0   120 Mls

El Kantara

Memphis

Nile

Medinet Habu
(Thebes)

Karnak

Luxor

156

The crisis in the East Mediterranean III: northerners in the Levant

'Northerners coming from all lands'

The northern allies of the Libyans defeated by Merneptah
c. 1220 were Shardana, Lukka, Ekwesh, Teresh and Shekelesh
(chapter 5). The Ekwesh were probably the largest contingent,
but they do not appear again. They are designated as 'of the
Countries of the Sea' on two separate inscriptions. The
Shardana and the Shekelesh are only so described on the Great
Karnak Inscription. Wherever the Ekwesh came from they were
peculiarly men of the sea, and since the Lukka do not have this
designation in spite of their long history as a sea-going people, it
looks as though the Ekwesh really were from the islands, or an
island. If they are the Ahhiyawans, and if the Ahhiyawans are in
some sort Achaeans, they may have come from anywhere in the
Aegean. We found the Lukka in south-west coastal Anatolia,
probably Caria, and the Teresh north of them, perhaps in the
neighbourhood of the land that became Lydia. On the Shekelesh
little was certain, apart from a possible identity with the Sikels of
southern Italy and Sicily (chapter 5).

None of the raiders are very likely to have taken their
household pots to North Africa. Whether they took the
potmakers, wives or otherwise, we do not know, but it seems
unlikely; so it is not much use looking for their identities among
the potsherds in Egypt and Libya. As fighting men we should
know them by their swords and other accoutrements, and first in
importance is the type IIa, flange-hilted sword, northern-made
or Aegean-copied. It had spread, as we saw (chapter 4), all over
the Aegean, to Cyprus and even to Egypt. In the Aegean it came
into use alongside LH IIIB pottery and so could be contemporary with Merneptah as well as Ramesses III. We also
have the sword of a quite different type, found at Ugarit, with a
cartouche of Merneptah on its blade, which is more like Italian
swords of Monza type, than any other. If the Shekelesh really

107 A map of the
Levant showing the
principal sites mentioned
in the text and the Via
Maris running from the
Phoenician coast to the
Delta. The siting of
Peleset, Danuna (Denyen)
and Tjeker refers to their
probable situation in the
later 12th-century settlement. In the *early* 12th
century Danuna may have
been in the Hattay. The
inset shows the position of
the Egyptian monuments
with reliefs at Thebes,
Karnak and Luxor.

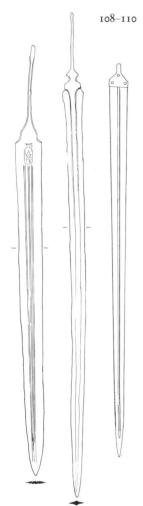

108–110 came from southern Italy or Sicily this need not be so surprising; it also suggests a possible source for the long swords of the Meshwesh, none of which have survived. There is another small group of distinctive bronzes, which could belong to this time, but which on grounds of its distribution, should rather, I think, be placed in the hands of Ramesses III's attackers. This is the short sword or dirk of 'H' type in the Aegean series. The sword has a tapered blade, flanged tang and quillons. One was found at Siana, Rhodes and another probably near Pergamon in western Anatolia. With the Siana sword there was a one-edged knife with a flanged tang that looks like a product of the same workshop. One was found at Ialysos in Rhodes (Old Tomb 27), another almost identical one at Colophon on the Carian coast and yet another at Troy. The dirk could have developed out of the Aegean series of short swords (type G). A closely related type of dirk was found at Ugarit, in the same court V which has already been referred to several times (chapter 6), and there was one in the latest levels at Alalakh, both in northern Syria. A third came from a tomb at Tell es Saidiyeh in Palestine, east of the River Jordan.[1] Yet another 'western' type of sword has been found in Egypt at El Kantara and may appear on a Mycenaean pot from Ugarit (ill. 103).

In the land and sea battles of Ramesses III we find once more engaged: the Shardana (probably but not certainly among the attackers, as well as being Egyptian auxiliaries), the Shekelesh, and probably the Teresh. Then there are four new names: Tjeker, Denyen, Peleset and Weshesh. Although the Denyen did not take part in Merneptah's war they were already known in the East Mediterranean (chapter 2); about them and the Peleset there will be more to say shortly. But of the shadowy Weshesh virtually nothing is known, unless they had any connection with the 'Wilusa' (Wilusiya) of Hittite writings, that may have lain in south-western Anatolia, or with 'Ilios' (Troy) in the north-west. The Tjeker have also been connected with the Teucri of the Troad, and with the Greek Teucer, the legendary founder of Salamis in Cyprus, after the Trojan War.

The main historical inscriptions at Medinet Habu mention islands, though they give greater emphasis to the approach of the land contingents from the north. An inscription of Deir el Medineh states that Ramesses III 'has trampled down the foreign countries, the isles who sailed over [or 'against'] his [boundaries?] . . . [gap] the Peleset and Tursha [Teresh] [coming?] from the midst of the sea'. There is no doubt that in

the eyes of the Egyptians these people came from 'overseas'.[2]
What is less certain is exactly what they understood by this.
From the Egyptian point of view the northern seas were full of
islands. Cyprus they knew well, and beyond Cyprus probably
Crete. They might have known something directly of Rhodes
and Cos, but more probably by hearsay only. Egyptian jewellery
has been found in Mycenaean graves on both islands, but it could
have come through Cyprus. Beyond this, to anyone sailing north

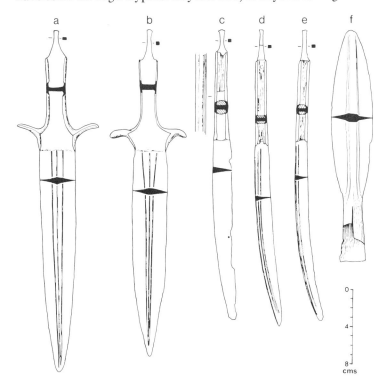

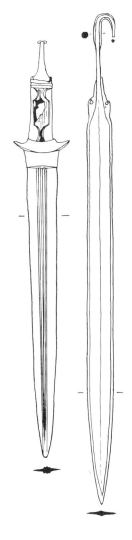

108–110   Around the end of the 13th century
there were many experiments in weaponry; new
types of sword and dirk were evolved to counter
new tactics (e.g. 55). A long slender sword was still
needed: some now have a rod-like tang for hafting,
such as the one (*opposite, left*) in a room of the
Palace at Ugarit which must have been manufac-
tured between *c*. 1224 and 1214 as it carries a
cartouche of Merneptah. Compare this with the
Monza type of sword found chiefly in northern
Italy and France (*opposite, centre*, from the Yonne
at Sens). Another slender sword of a related pattern

with three rivets (*opposite, right*) comes from
a Thapsos-culture grave at Plemmirio in Sicily, and
is probably 14th to 13th century. A sword from El
Kantara, Egypt, with a broader blade, has a similar
tang turned over (*above, far right*, cf. 103). A short
dirk (type H), of which there are two variants
(*above, a, b* from Aegean, and *second from right*
from Ugarit) and which is linked by its hafting to a
type of knife (*c–e*), has an interesting coastal
distribution. 109 *a* Pergamon; *b, c, f* Siana, Rhodes;
d Ialysos, OT 27, Rhodes; *e* Colophon. Lengths:
108, 74–5 cm; 110, *left*, 46 cm; *right*, 56 cm.

In the Aegean, among the Dodecanese and the headlands, gulfs and promontories of the Anatolian coast, the eye is confused and it is hard to distinguish island from mainland. The view from Ayvalik in Turkey looking west towards Lesbos is typical.

into an unfamiliar Aegean, the capes and promontories of the Anatolian coast viewed at deck-level would be indistinguishable from islands, so that too much should not be read into Egyptian topographical epithets such as 'of the sea' and 'in the midst of the sea'. The Egyptians include the Denyen among islanders from the north, and this they almost certainly were not.

The disappearance of the Lukka and the Ekwesh is surprising, though there is always the possibility of contingents fighting under names not their own. In the Hittite writings a Lukka land is referred to, and 'the Lukka' may have been too heavily engaged in their own country, if we follow the lead given by the Ugaritic correspondence (see above). The presence of some Shardana among the attackers is implied in the Papyrus Harris, and is not surprising, but it still gives us no indication of their homeland. In chapter 5 their characteristic dress and accoutrements – horned helmet, short kilt, round shield and spear or sword – were all found at home in northern Syria, and especially at Ugarit. A small bronze figure, the so-called 'ingot-god' found at Enkomi in a 12th-century sanctuary, conforms to the usual picture of the Shardana warrior. He wears his kilt a

66, 65

12

112

VIII

little long, but he has the familiar horned helmet, and is armed with a round shield and a spear. He probably wears greaves which were standard at this time in the Aegean, and sometimes worn in Cyprus. He stands on a copper ingot which probably makes him a god, and perhaps a patron of metal-workers and the copper trade.[3] This figure has nothing really in common with the 'horned god' of Enkomi except the horns. In the one case they are attached to a pointed helmet and the gesture threatens; in the other they emerge from a fleecy cap, and the gesture, equally commanding, commands peace.

The eclectic appearance of the figure (Aegean greaves, Cypriot ingot, probably northern Syrian helmet) make it appear likely that a strong contingent of Shardana (under whatever name) were among the settlers who arrived in Cyprus after the destruction of Ugarit. Not the main refugee contingent, but a (possibly disruptive) element within it. It seems likely that after making Cyprus their home for a time they moved on to Sardinia, taking with them their name and some characteristically Cypriot bronzes like the miniature tripod-stands; and taking, if we may judge by the 'Sardinian bronzes' of later years, their peculiar dress and weapons as well (ills. 129, 130).

112   Warriors of the 13th to 12th century belong to a common type, from the Greek mainland through the Levant to Egypt. All are armed with a spear and round shield and wear a short kilt. More particular characteristics are the helmet insignia of the Egyptian bodyguard from the land battle at Medinet Habu (*left*), the greaves of the Greek from a Pylos wall-painting (*centre*) and the ingot on which the 'god' from Enkomi is standing (*right*). See also 75, 129 and VIII.

The Denyen

When the Egyptians recognized Denyen among their adversaries, these were people they already knew something about. A 'land of Danuna' is referred to in the Amarna correspondence, in the early 14th century, where it is named immediately before Ugarit, Kadesh and Amurru. The list runs from north to south, so we may infer that wherever the 'land of Danuna' was it was north of Ugarit and the Orontes, but not too far distant. In the northern Syrian campaigns of Suppiluliumas I (1373–1335) Halpa (Aleppo) and Carchemish are referred to in the east, and Alalakh and Ugarit in the west, also Kizzuwatna (Cilicia) to the north. By a process of elimination this only leaves the Hatay for the 'land of Danuna'; unless it is much farther north than the Amarna correspondence seems to place it.[4]

In the 8th century BC a 'Land of the Danuna' (Dnnym) had its capital at Adana, from where its ruler held some sort of suzerainty over Karatepe on the Ceyhan river, overlooking the coastal plain. Both were closely allied to the people of Cilicia and the Neo-Hittites of Carchemish and Sinjirli with whom they shared the Luwian family of languages and the 'Hittite' hieroglyphic script. According to 8th-century Luwian texts a ruler of Karatepe, Asitawandas, described himself as 'of the House of Mpš' (Phoenician) (or 'Mukshash' (Hittite)). Mukshash was named in a particularly defective portion of the Madduwattas Indictment, but the Phoenician form may be the same as Mopsus who in Greek legend was ruler of Colophon. Colophon had Mycenaean links and a Mycenaean tholos tomb that held the knife referred to above. Mopsus is supposed to have joined a party of Greeks returning from Troy, and led his people south through Pamphylia, founding cities at Aspendus, Phaselis and in Cilicia; and then, according to the Lycian Xanthus, he trekked south to Ashkalon in Palestine where he died.[5] A part of the legend may be based on history supported, as it is, by the Luwian texts from Karatepe. Unfortunately there is no separate Egyptian representation of the Denyen, who cannot be distinguished on the reliefs from other groups. The death of Mopsus at Ashkalon could be a memory of events following the defeat on the Egyptian frontier, or in the Delta when numbers of attackers recoiled into Palestine. Whether the earlier home of the Denyen had been in south-western Anatolia, or in the Hattay, or in both, the shift to Karatepe and Adana was not a great one, but parallels that of Hittite groups from the plateau to Carchemish and Sinjirli. This is the movement described in the text of Ramesses III of year 8 concerning the overthrow of the northern countries (chapter 5). If it was the Denyen, or more probably some other northern contingent that joined with a part of the Denyen, who overran the Lukka Lands, and so were the immediate cause of the Hittite king's appeal to the King of Ugarit (chapter 6), then this would help to explain the absence of the Lukka from among the attackers of 1186. The Denyen, who

109e

4
VI

87
86

107

were making their first appearance *in* Egypt amongst the attackers of that year, could have taken their place. As for the legendary Mopsus and his companions from the Troad, there is the suggested connection of the Weshesh with Wilusa, and the Teresh with Taruisha (Ta-ru-(u)i-ša), both possibly sited in the Troad, to give it a semblance of support. There is no linguistic objection to the introduction of people from Lycia into northern Syria; for the Luwian family of languages was spoken in both regions, though in northern Syria overlaid with a veneer of Hittite names. Unlike Greece there was no loss of literacy here.

Before leaving the Denyen we must look at an intriguing twist to their story that is almost a continuation of the Mopsus legend but based on completely separate premises. This is a bold suggestion that links the Denyen-Danuna of Egyptian texts with the Biblical Tribe of Dan.[6] When Deborah, Barak and a combined force of Israelites defeated the Canaanite commander Jabin and his chariotry at Mount Tabor sometime in the 13th or 12th century, as told in the Book of Judges, the muster of the Israelite forces comprised Ephraim, Benjamin and Issachar. But in the clan of Reuben there was searching of heart, 'Why did you tarry among the sheepfolds to hear the piping of the flocks?' Gilead stayed away in the east, 'and Dan, why did he abide with the ships?' (Judges 5, 17). The puzzle has been how Dan should have come to have ships at all, for none of the other Israelite tribes were seamen. So the obvious meaning – that the Danites were a maritime people and were busy with their ships, just as the shepherds of Reuben were busy with the flocks – has been dismissed. In both instances Deborah's call to war was refused because of more profitable business. If Dan was not originally one of the tribes of Israel who crossed the Jordan from the east, then the text 'Dan shall judge his people as one of the tribes of Israel' (Genesis 49, 16) means strictly what it says. Formerly Dan was not one of the tribes, but henceforth he is admitted into the Covenant, *like* one of the Tribes of Israel. There are other odd things about the Danites. They appear to have changed their religion (Judges 18), to have had no objection to carved wood and cast metal images or to foreign priests. A group of southern towns in the neighbourhood of Jaffa is connected with Dan, and at Jaffa is Tell Qasile, an important 11th- and probably also 12th-century coastal town with a temple and much pottery of the sort that is connected with the Sea Peoples ('Philistine' pottery, see below). Quite a large piece of the land is in question which later the Jews knew as Philistine (Joshua 21, 24). According to the theory this would have been before the northward migration which settled the Danites in the old Canaanite city of Laish, where the native population 'dwelt in security after the manner of the Sidonians, quiet and unsuspecting'. Their sense of security and the distance from their Sidonian allies was their undoing, for the Danites took the city and rebuilt it. This city of Dan is moreover the farthest north that the so-called 'Philistine' pottery has been found.

The Biblical narrative is a tale of action, a success story, but the atmosphere is probably true enough to how things were in that troubled 12th century when the identities of desert nomads, northern migrants and sea-raiders, could be confused. One detail of the northward trek of the Danites in search of a home recalls the reliefs at Medinet Habu. Six hundred armed warriors made a camp and then set forward 'putting the little ones and the cattle and goods in front of them' (Judges 18, 21). Sidon was defeated by Ashkalon about 1100 (Tiglath Pileser I of Assyria) so these events should have taken place in the 12th century.[7] Perhaps behind these speculative reconstructions we may see shadowy outlines of 12th-century history, and of a little-known people, which came, like the Philistines, to be absorbed by the Israelites.

76

Peleset, Philistines and 'Philistine' pottery

I think it is better to treat as three separate entities the Peleset of the Egyptian texts, the Philistines of Biblical narrative, and the so-called 'Philistine' pottery. All three have been brought together as a unity giving rise to much speculation with wide-ranging conclusions based upon it.

The Peleset

A linguistic connection between Egyptian *plst* (Peleset) and Philistine must be conceded, but the connection is a good deal more complicated than the simple identity sometimes assumed. Egyptian texts naming the Peleset have been quoted already (chapter 5); but none gives any indication as to where they came from. They appear first in year 8 of Ramesses III, and are never named apart from some one or other attacker. They are not specified as 'of the sea' except in one passage, an historical stela of Ramesses III from Deir el Medineh, already quoted.

He [Ramesses III] has trampled down the foreign countries, the isles who sailed over [against?] his [boundaries?] . . . [gap]

the Peleset and Tursha [Teresh] [coming?] from the midst of the sea.

Even here they are not isolated, but linked with the Teresh, who were probably from the Anatolian coastland. They share a trans-Mediterranean origin with the other enemy their constant associates. The Egyptians looked on them all as 'Peoples of the Sea', but this does not get us very far (see above). The only individual Peleset, named as such, on the Egyptian monuments is the bearded prince at Medinet Habu who is a prisoner of Ramesses III. One authority on this period, the late Père R. de Vaux, has stated unequivocally of the 'Sea Peoples' 'rien ne nous dit qu'ils aient eu derrière eux une tradition de gens de mer'.[8] Nothing more is heard of the Peleset apart from the Papyrus Harris which states that Ramesses III used Peleset along with Shardana, Weshesh, Denyen and Shekelesh as garrison forces and as mercenaries. Peleset are unknown to the Hittites, at any rate by this name.

113   There is only one Peleset named in isolation, and beyond confusion with other Sea Peoples, on the Egyptian monuments – the captive 'prince' from the northern colonnade at Medinet Habu. What manner of hairstyle is hidden by his cap is wholly problematic, but he does *not* wear a 'feathered crown' for certain.

The Philistines

Of all the Land and Sea Raiders of Merneptah's and Ramesses III's wars the Bible knows only the Philistines. This is probably because, by the time the Israelites felt themselves strong enough to attack the plains and the coastal cities, in the 10th century, it was the Philistines who were their chief antagonists. They possessed the land to which they have given their name: Palestine. The five cities of the Philistines – Gaza, Ashkalon, Ashdod, Ekron and Gath – are all in the coastal plain or the foothills of the Shephelah. Gath and Ekron are not certainly identified, but ancient Ashdod has been dug and gives a most valuable stratigraphy (see below).

A gap of 400 years separates Ramesses III from the earliest Biblical reference to the Philistines, which may be based on genuine Philistine tradition. 'Did I not bring up Israel from the land of Egypt, and the Philistines from Caphtor and the Syrians from Kir?' (Amos 9, 7). This coupling of Philistines and Israelites has been taken to imply that the Philistines were no more native to Caphtor than the Israelites to Egypt, but that they had arrived immediately *from* Caphtor like Israel *from* Egypt. The same tradition is thought to lie behind the reference in Jeremiah, written about 600 BC, to the Philistines as 'a remnant of the coastland of Caphtor' (Jeremiah 47, 4). A similar reference in Ezekiel is merely repetition. But according to Genesis (10,

13–14) the Philistines came from Casluhim whose 'father' was Egypt, which is little help, though it might be a memory of the setting up of garrisons in Palestine by the Egyptians, or of the retreat from the Delta. The authors of Jeremiah and the Genesis passage may not have known where Caphtor was, and so have given 'coastland' instead of island, since Caphtor should be linked with the Keftiu of Egyptian texts and the Kaptara of Syrian writings. The Egyptians in the mid-2nd millennium, knew that the Keftiu came from Crete but later the name, like Kaptara, seems to have broadened its meaning to that of Aegean lands in general, or even parts of the Anatolian coast. In the Old Testament the Philistines are sometimes linked with the Cherethites and Pelethites; or the Pelethites may be Philistines. There was a 'Negev of the Cherethites' (or 'Kerethites') that may have lain in the hinterland of Gaza (I Sam. 30, 14).[9]

There is not a great deal to be won from Biblical descriptions of the Philistines that will help with 12th-century problems. They were uncircumcised, but in Biblical times their religion was Canaanite. The very little that can be surmised about their language seems to point to Anatolia. Later Philistine rulers have Semitic names, but Luwian affinities have been suspected. The Philistine oligarchy, the five lords of the five cities, were known as *Seren*, which may be related to Neo-Hittite *sarawanas-tarawanas*, and, less plausibly, to Greek *tyrannos*, so too the Philistine Akish may be a Hurrian name from Cilicia, rather than Greek Anchises.[10] In material culture the Philistines were indistinguishable from their neighbours of the 1st millennium. They fought in chariots, and so did their neighbours, only the greaves of Goliath may have come from the Aegean or Cyprus, the rest of his armour could also be Canaanite. The Philistines may have formed no more than a ruling class soon absorbed by the native population, but if so there *is* something genuinely northern in their make-up.

'Philistine' pottery

The style of pottery that has come to be known as 'Philistine' is a hybrid. On one side it owes much to Mycenaean potters, especially to those who originated the LH IIIC of the Argolid 'decorative style'. The shapes of many of the vases, as well as the designs painted on them – antithetic spirals, birds and various panelled patterns – are inspired by Mycenaean originals. On the other hand some shapes are native Levantine, as are the clay

114
115
106

and the matt paint, since Mycenaean paint is lustrous. There is a
particular preference for a bird looking backwards, which is very   114
rare in the Aegean, though not altogether absent. Other points of
difference are the use of two colours, usually red as well as black
(bichrome pottery) and the employment of a whitish ground,
either a wash or self-slip that disappears in the kiln, used perhaps
to compensate for the lack of brilliance compared with
Mycenaean wares. In some pots, particularly the later ones, it
has a greenish tinge. Both characteristics come from a long-
standing native tradition of bichrome pottery which goes back to
the 16th century, and which occasionally had birds and trees, as
well as wheels, and other similar motifs.[11] Clay analysis has   115 left, centre
shown that 'Philistine' pottery was made in the coastal parts of
Palestine. It was traded inland from Ashdod, and probably other
cities, to Tell Eitun near Tell Beit Mirsim, and farther east. A
little has been found at Beth Shan and Deir Alla in the Jordan
valley, and at Megiddo, Hazor, and even Tell Dan (Laish) in the
north.[12]

It is because so much of this pottery comes from southern
Palestinian sites known to the Jews later as 'Philistine' that the
pots have been called 'Philistine'; but the situation established in
the 10th century cannot be translated back into the 12th. We
have reason to think that as well as the Peleset there were Tjeker,
Denyen, Shekelesh, and possibly other tribes, active in Palestine.
When looking at the dress and headgear of the different attackers
we found it very difficult to distinguish one from another,
particularly those wearing 'feathered crowns' (chapter 5). Some
of these people were retained by the Egyptians to garrison
strongholds in Palestine and the Jordan valley. I think that on
all grounds it would be less misleading to call this 'Philistine'
pottery 'Sea Peoples'' pottery or 'foreign' pottery, without
commitment to any particular group.

The Mycenaean IIIC1b pottery with which 'Philistine'
pottery was linked by Furumark, as well as being found in the
Aegean, the Dodecanese, a few Anatolian coastal sites and
Cyprus, also reached the Levant. A little has come from   106
Canaanite cities such as Beth Shan, Sarafand and probably Tell
Ibn Hani. But in the majority of sites the destruction levels still
only have LH IIIB pottery. It is also imitated at Ashdod. This   103, 104
site is so important for the chronology of the Levant that it will
be looked at again below.

It is no good looking for a clue to the 'origins of the Philistines'
in the pottery. What we find is evidence for an intermingling of

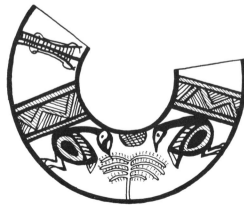

peoples from the north among whom an Anatolian element was very strong. One writer has said that 'Philistine' pottery is 'nothing more than a regional variation of Mycenaean IIICı',[13] but this underestimates the native side of the hybrid, the bichrome pottery of Syria-Palestine which, contrary to views once held, did survive long enough to play its part in the formation of this new style. At its best 'Sea Peoples'' pottery is inferior to good LH IIIC 'Close Style', and to some IIIC in Cyprus, which may have been a direct source. This whole phenomenon is of mixed Aegean, Anatolian and native Canaanite elements, and the product of a settled people who had, at least for a time, found a homeland. Further than this I do not think it is safe to go.

If we return now to the 12th-century Peleset – the land force on the walls at Medinet Habu – we see that they had ox-carts and spare ploughing oxen, which are the impedimenta of a slow-moving agricultural people in search of new land to cultivate. These specifications fit northern Syria, Anatolia, even possibly the foothills of the Caucasus, better than the Aegean islands and far-off Greek mainland. Europe across the Hellespont, and the distant Danube are, I think, out of the question, though pressures in northern lands may have been a source and symptom of the general unrest that was transmitted through many intermediaries, each adding its quota to the sum of aggression. Nothing in Biblical narrative connects the Philistines with the sea; but the invasions did have a maritime side, though it was probably not quite so important as the Egyptian texts imply. It was far stronger in *c.* 1220 than in 1186. Unlike the cities of the sea-going Phoenicians such as Byblos, Sidon and Tyre, the Palestinian coastal sites – Ashdod, Gaza, Sharuhen,

114, 115 So-called 'Philistine' or 'Sea Peoples' pottery is a hybrid between the native tradition stemming from bichrome pots of the mid-2nd millennium (*opposite, below left* from Beth Shan, *centre* from Megiddo) and the late Mycenaean style (LH IIIC). The characteristic pots from Tell Eitun (*opposite, above left* and *this page*) and Beth Shemesh (*opposite, above right*) have the bird, often looking backwards, that was very popular in Palestine. Like the native wares and unlike the Mycenaean, this 'Sea Peoples' pottery also has two colours (cf. 106, 105 (shape) and, more distantly, 70). *Above*, max. ht 32.3 cm; *below*, max. ht 30 cm.

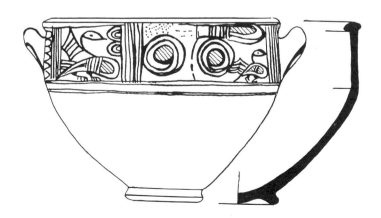

Tell el Ajjul, Tell Mor – were all a few miles inland with swampy country and dunes between them and the Mediterranean. There is no natural bay or anchorage south of Jaffa. The harbour of Ashdod was in a small river estuary a short distance off. But all these towns lie on the ancient Via Maris from Egypt, a great commercial route linking that country with the rest of the civilized world.

The Tjeker

The Tjeker may or may not have had some connection with the Teucri of the Troad, and with Greek Teucer, the traditional founder of Salamis in Cyprus, but they certainly have a better right than the Peleset to a sea-going reputation, and quite as good
84 a right to the so-called 'feathered crown'. At some time after the attack on Egypt in 1186 they settled in the country around Dor, south of Mount Carmel. They were there in about 1100 BC, as we learn from the almost-contemporary Egyptian Tale of Wen Amon; nor had they lost their buccaneering ways. Wen Amon's mission was, following ancient practice, to procure timber for ship-building from the Phoenician Prince of Byblos; but he found that Egyptian prestige was pitifully declined, and the unfortunate envoy had little more than bluster to see him through. On the way to Byblos he fell foul of the Tjeker from Dor; more corsair than merchant, they evidently had the freedom of the seas, and were able to pursue him to Byblos. This is a real sea-story with its nights on ship-board moored in the harbour, its sea-captains and troublesome harbour-masters, its loadings and unloadings and, most evocative of all, the audience with Zakar-Baal, Prince of Byblos 'sitting in his upper room with his back turned to the window so that the waves of the great Syrian Sea broke against the back of his head'. This arrangement naturally revealed the face of the unhappy Egyptian. The conversation that followed shows that Zakar-Baal was in undisturbed possession of the throne of his grandfather, which takes the family back at least to the mid-12th century, and the aftermath of the Land and Sea Raids (Pritchard 1969, 25–9).

Chronological cross-points:
Ashdod, Beth Shan, Deir Alla

In this final section the archaeology of the Levant must be looked at very briefly in the light of the Egyptian historical texts. Any correspondences have an importance that stretches far beyond the Levant, for virtually all the dates used in the Aegean are reckoned back from these points. Among Levantine cities I select three sites as particularly useful: Ashdod, a 'Philistine city' in southern Palestine, and Beth Shan and Deir Alla in the Jordan valley.

Bronze Age Ashdod was the capital of a Canaanite city-state lying on the Via Maris from Egypt. It was a large city of twenty acres and, lacking a harbour (see above), it owed its importance more than anything else to this highway, although it was also in touch with Cyprus through an anchorage on the little river Lachish. The last Canaanite city (Late Bronze II, level XIV) at Ashdod was destroyed by fire. The rebuilt city, Ashdod XIII, had two phases, the earlier, XIIIb, containing imitations of IIIC pottery made locally. According to the excavator it imitates fairly closely Late Cypriot pottery of Aegean inspiration (Sinda II (and ?III)). The following level XIIIa still had copies of the IIIC style, but also quite a lot of the new 'Philistine' or 'Sea Peoples'' pottery. The level XII town was partly remodelled and fortified, and contained a shrine with a figure of a small seated goddess that has both Cypriot and Aegean relatives. The 'Sea Peoples'' pottery makes up fifty per cent of the whole. After level XII the character of the site changed again, and although there was architectural continuity the aspect is far more indigenous Levantine.[14]

The question is, which of these levels is contemporary with the wars of Ramesses III? The excavator, Moshe Dothan, interprets the destruction of the Canaanite city, level XIV, as

Table III

116   A clay figure, part woman part chair, from Ashdod level XII (*left*) is claimed to show strong Mycenaean influence. A rather similar figure, unpainted (*centre*) comes from tomb 28 at Katyd-hata, Cyprus (Late Cypriot III, probably 13th century). Compare with these a well-known type of Mycenaean seated figure from chamber tomb 91 at Mycenae (*right*); there are only a few of these figures and the chair was found separately. Hts: *left*, 17 cm; *centre*, 9.5 cm; *right*, 15 cm.

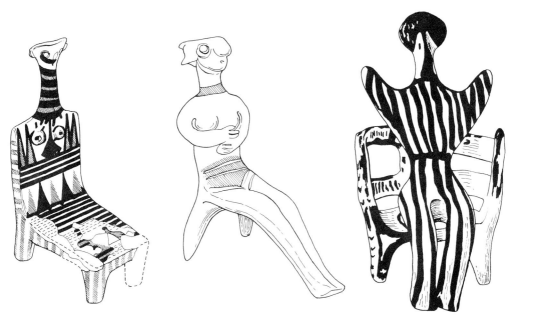

falling within Merneptah's lifetime, while the 'Philistine' pottery of level XIIIa would belong to the aftermath of Ramesses III's victory of 1186, with a resettlement of the defeated Sea Peoples in Palestine. It could be however that the level XIV destruction marks the passage of the northern invaders to the Egyptian border in 1186, especially if it coincides with destructions at Ugarit, Tell Sukas and in Cyprus, as claimed. There is a choice here, and it is the crux of the problem.

At Beth Shan the Egyptian connection was particularly close, in spite of the city's position in the Jordan valley. An Egyptian garrison had been housed here since the days of Seti I and may have remained in some such capacity till the end of the 12th century.[15] The Canaanite (Late Bronze II) level VII city received Mycenaean (LH IIIA2 and IIIB) as well as Cypriot pottery (the usual Base-ring and White-slip styles (BRII and WSII)), perhaps by way of Megiddo to the north. There was a violent destruction but the following city, level VI, was rebuilt immediately with the same layout, a sign of continuity, and with new houses for the Egyptian commanders and an inscription of the Great Steward of Ramesses III. Local imitations of IIIB were found, and some IIIC-inspired pots possibly imported from Cyprus, but there is practically no 'Philistine' pottery at Beth Shan, although there is a little, and very late, in tombs. Now that the anthropoid coffins have been relegated to their proper place as Egyptianizing funeral furniture, it is likely that the coffins of this sort found at Beth Shan were those of an Egyptian garrison. This garrison may well have included various 'northerners' after 1186, though whether the latest and 'grotesque group' of coffins are really wearing the 'feathered' headdress of the attackers on the Egyptian monuments is very questionable.[16] Historically the Philistines were not held to be at Beth Shan till the days of Solomon in the 10th century, by which time distinctions between the different northern peoples had dissolved (see above). There is no evidence for 12th-century Peleset in particular at Beth Shan, but the Tell es Saidiyeh tomb (see above) points to the presence of northerners east of Jordan in some capacity or other.

Deir Alla may have been a sanctuary not a city; it was destroyed by a violent earthquake a little after 1200, since a faience vase with a cartouche of Tausert, the widow of Seti II, last Pharaoh of the 19th dynasty, was found on a floor burnt in the earthquake that destroyed it.[17] Some LH IIIB pottery was found in the same pre-earthquake level. After this there were two

118
117

117, 118 At one time clay coffins with anthropomorphic lids were taken as evidence of Sea Peoples, specifically 'Philistines'; but they stem from an Egyptian tradition (*left*, from Tell el Yahudiyeh, Egypt) and those found in Palestine, like the one (*right*) from the northern cemetery at Beth Shan, were probably the coffin lids of Egyptian garrison troops, many of whom were undoubtedly recruited from the ranks of the northern raiders. The head ornament has been compared with the enemy of e.g. 88.

unsuccessful attempts to rebuild the site, which remained unoccupied for a space. When it *was* rebuilt 'Philistine' pottery found its way here. The disastrous interregnum described in chapter 5 followed Seti II and Tausert, and may coincide with the temporary abandonment of Deir Alla after the earthquake.

If these sites are set side by side a good case emerges for connecting the destruction of Ashdod XIV with Ramesses III rather than Merneptah, although the nature of the material is still too imprecise. There is a dangerous temptation to link destruction levels together in the interests of tidiness and economy, but history is seldom tidy or notably economical, however it may be with philosophy. This is one of the reasons why history should not be written by philosophers or sociologists. In practice the various Sea and Land Raiders, and migrants from the north, had many competitors: Israelites and others from east of Jordan, not least. A change in the styles of pottery made and used may be the archaeologist's only recourse; it is often made to bear more historical weight than is justified.

VII In a symbolic scene
on the south-eastern
corner of the Great
Temple at Medinet Habu
Ramesses III is smiting
'the chiefs of all countries'
before the god Amon. The
kneeling chiefs show their
different nationalities by
the profile of their faces
and physiognomies.

Table II
Table IV

It is even more hazardous to attempt to bring Cyprus into line with the Egyptian record of events. We may, if we please, correlate the end of Ashdod XIV with the destruction between Enkomi VI and Enkomi V, Late Cypriot IIC and IIIA, or in the following generation between Enkomi V and IV, Late Cypriot IIIA and IIIB and the corresponding Sinda II and III. Ingenious juggling will make either work quite well. Destruction in Cyprus, and at Ashdod and other Palestinian sites, *may* be the result of the same events, or they may not; they *may* be connected with the wars of a Ramesses or a Merneptah, or they may not. It must be faced that we are guessing. The earthquake and fire that destroyed 13th-century Deir Alla should be a warning against reading an act of war into every tumbled wall. The anarchy and disruption of the years of Interregnum between the 19th and 20th dynasties, with which northern people apparently had nothing whatsoever to do, are another warning. The Israelites are not likely to have been attacking large cities in the coastal plain or in the Jordan valley so early as the first half of the 12th century, let alone the 13th; but their presence was another symptom of unrest and insecurity.

Chamber tombs at Tell Fara in the south of Palestine are thought to be more Aegean than native, but their introduction may antedate the main attack in the 12th century, while in Cyprus Aegean-style tombs probably did not appear till the 11th century.[18]

Footnote on iron

The Philistines have been credited with the spread of iron technology on the strength of one rather ambiguous Biblical reference, which does not in fact specifically name iron, though it is implied by the context.[19] During the 12th century iron was certainly coming into use throughout the Levant. It occurs in tombs at Tell Fara, and in at least one case it is associated with 'Sea Peoples" pottery. At Tell Qasile on the coast near Jaffa, in stratum XII, probably of the 12th century, there is an iron knife with an ivory ring handle and bronze rivets. There is also iron at Ai and Tell Reddon, and in rock-cut native tombs at Tell Eitun, the latter not likely to be later than the 12th century.[20] Most of these sites have 'Sea Peoples" pottery as well. In Cyprus there is iron in early-12th-century tombs (Evreti 8) with Late Cypriot IIIA pottery, and rather more after the destruction that brought to an end the first ashlar city at Enkomi (level V) in the following

Late Cypriot IIIB and IIIC levels. In Greece and Crete small iron objects occur at the same time, especially knives with bronze rivets, found at Knossos (Gypsades), and Perati in Attica. But everywhere in the 12th century bronze still dominates the metal industry.[21]

This widespread dispersal of a rather tentative technological innovation takes it out of the hands of any one people. Now that the old theory of a 2nd-millennium Hittite iron monopoly has been refuted we can judge better the history of its introduction and spread as, first of all, a curiosity and luxury article and, later, as possibly reflecting a real scarcity of tin and even copper for bronze-making. There was certainly a shortage in the Aegean and the fact that sub-Mycenaean (11th-century) settlements had no access to the enormously rich supplies of tin north of the Danube (chapter 4) is a strong argument for the isolation of the area and its freedom from Balkan domination in the Dark Age.[22]

The early technology of iron did not produce a commodity superior to bronze until a form of carburization was tried, leading to the production of a steel-like metal. It was the cheapness and comparative abundance of iron ores that was the root of their popularity. The Sea Peoples do not seem to have had any special interest in iron production, though they may have had an indirect influence on its spread through the dislocation of trade-routes, and the machinery of supply and demand. The diaspora that followed the raids took rarities, including iron, to islands and countries overseas that might have had to wait much longer for them. In Palestine the northern peoples (not only the Philistines), were undoubtedly active users and spreaders of iron, but so were the Canaanites and probably the Neo-Hittite states and the Israelites as well; while iron may have reached the Balkans and Macedonia from northern Anatolia by way of the Kashka lands.

VIII The god standing on an ingot of bronze from 12th-century Enkomi. He is cast solid, with repairs on the legs, an attachment at the back to fasten him to a wall and with a peg below the ingot. See also 112, 129 and cf. 91. Ht 35 cm.

Crisis in the Aegean

Breakdowns and destructions

In chapters 5, 6 and 7 we traced the swirl of disaster back from Egypt to Anatolia and Cyprus, to the more shadowy islands and lands beyond; while in chapters 3 and 4 we saw prosperity beginning to ebb in those more northerly lands. Now we must look at the crisis as it struck them too, and the onset of the dark centuries, when

> Father will have no common bond with son
> Neither will guest with host, nor friend with friend
> The brother-love of past days will be gone. . . .
> Men will destroy the towns of other men.
> The just, the good, the man who keeps his word
> Will be despised, but men will praise the bad
> And insolent. Might will be right and shame
> Will cease to be. Men will do injury
> To better men by speaking crooked words
> And adding lying oathes, and everywhere
> Harsh-voiced and sullen-faced and loving harm,
> Envy will walk along with wretched men.[1]

This was the chill reality behind the heroic legends of Mycenae, Thebes and Troy in the days of the brigands and pirates who sailed the Aegean. Though Hesiod probably wrote towards the end of the 8th century BC and appears to describe the present, this 'Age of Iron' reads like sharp memory of a not very distant past rather than present evils. The 'Age of Heroes' is an intruder among Hesiod's other 'ages', but memory went back to the men 'strange and full of power who loved the groans and violence of war'. No longer well-to-do land-owners and bureaucrats, 'their hearts were flinty hard, they were terrible men'. Of such was the last generation of Mycenae and Tiryns after the overturning of the old citadels when life was different.

119 A Mycenaean version of the 12th-century fighting man, perhaps a mercenary from overseas since the helmet is Levantine not Greek. He is one of a troop on the Warrior Vase from Mycenae (developed LH IIIC 'Close Style' preceding 'Granary', perhaps second quarter of the 12th century). See 124, 125 and 91.

How did things come to this condition and why did they take so long to recover? Hesiod's description is so like the disastrous Interregnum in Egypt (chapter 5), yet Egypt made some sort of recovery which Greece did not; why did it not? There have been two comprehensive studies of the Greek Dark Age in the last few years, and it is no part of this essay to reconstruct the history of those centuries.[2] It is the point of crisis, its immediate cause, and the part of the 'Sea Peoples' in both, that is our subject. The problem of the Dark Age is the absence of events, the problem of the years preceding it is a plethora of events. Almost all the great Mycenaean sites suffered ruin and disaster at some time, though many partially recovered. A table based on cross-references to pottery styles is the best way of obtaining a general picture.

Table III

Leaving aside an earlier destruction at Thebes during LH IIIA (the 14th century), which was probably due to interstate warfare, we get a wave of trouble with destruction at Mycenae (outside the walls), at Tiryns, Zygouries, Berbati and possibly Pylos too, with a second destruction at Thebes at some uncertain date. This was while LH IIIB pottery was still current in the second half of the 13th century, and it coincides with an intense interest in the Levant, and much IIIB pottery reaching Cyprus, Ugarit and other sites (chapters 5–7). This was followed by another wave of destructions in the Argolid at the end of the 13th or beginning of the 12th century; this too may have been when Pylos fell. Some sites suffered further trouble in the course of the 12th century: Iolkos, Korakou, Mycenae, Tiryns and, rather late, Lefkandi on Euboea, and perhaps Teikhos Dymaion near Patras. But the whole of the southern and central Greek mainland was not overwhelmed at the same moment, as might have happened if there had been a massive attack by invaders from beyond the frontier. The evidence of the pottery fits better warfare between Mycenaean states prolonged over a considerable stretch of time, along with internal breakdown. The painstaking construction of a wall (if indeed it is a wall) across the Corinth Isthmus speaks of a danger that was anticipated. Pylos may have escaped the earlier threat. As we have seen the palace was unfortified to the end; but the tablets seem to show exceptional concentrations of materials, and listing of resources, as though under threat of some new danger. They do not show the breakdown itself. When the catastrophe did come it was all the more shocking, and it clearly took the inhabitants by surprise. It may have come from the sea. Messenia has a very long coastline which was, after some sort, defended. Certain tablets

120   A linear B tablet from Pylos that lists a naval force sent to Pleuron, perhaps the Pleuron in Aetolia (near Thermon on map (44)); lines 2 to 6 name the place of origin of the rowers. This action may have been a preliminary to the fall of Pylos, possibly near the end of the 13th or at the beginning of the 12th century.

121   Twelfth-century Aegean shipping was of many kinds. The top boat, from a clay box at Pylos, has sail and ram; graffiti from Cyprus (second down) may depict the same type of boat; the bottom one, painted on a pot from Asine, has an animal prow but is very sketchy. Only the decked round boat with important persons on board (third down), from a Cypriot pot, is at all like the bird-headed boats of 82 and 84; it is probably the earliest although all are 12th century (LH IIIB/C).

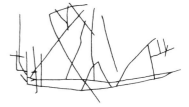

refer to 'rowers'; about 30 men from 5 different towns are listed to go to Pleuron, which may be the Pleuron in Aetolia. Another defective tablet gives more than 570 'rowers' which, if 30 rowers manned a single ship, would give a fleet of over 20 ships. The ships used by the attackers in the Delta, unless very inaccurately recorded, were much smaller. The number of oarsmen can only be guessed at, but the total complement would seem to have been considerably under 30.

84

There may have been a sea battle in which the fleet was destroyed, but if so we have to ask who was in a position to raise a fleet large enough, well enough organized and, most important, having sufficient incentive, to carry out the massive devastation on land, as well as the action on the sea? The Lukka had been capable of action on a considerable scale when they destroyed Cypriot cities, but these may have been quite small. There would have been little incentive for Ugarit or Cyprus itself to mount such an expedition. No northern power would have been likely to do it. Only men already bred to the sea and with some knowledge of these treacherous coasts could have made the attempt. A confederation of Mycenaean princes might have done it, a sort of Trojan War in reverse, or the whole fleet might have been lured away to join one of the great attacks on Egypt, either that of 1220 or 1186; but in that case how are we to account for the devastation of the palace, the whole state, and its subsidence into insignificance?[3]

It is more likely, I think, that an attack on land coincided with a temporary absence of the fleet, a situation not unlike that at Ugarit. The ruin of Pylos might have been a long time hatching, with internal collapse bringing it to a head. If the fleet was not destroyed, or at any rate not entirely so, it could have been used by the defeated aristocracy and military to sail away to safety among friendly, and still secure, neighbours; or if these hardly existed any more, to possess themselves of the land and cities of weaker states. There was no rich city and harbour a few miles across the sea to tempt the men of Pylos, as Cyprus tempted those of Ugarit, but there was Athens undestroyed and, a much longer shot, Cyprus itself, Egypt and the Levant.

Depopulation

Depopulation is a sign of troubled times, especially in old centres of over-population like Messenia. But depopulation in Greece was not uniform, it cut a central swathe from Boeotia, Phocis, Corinth and the Argolid, through to Laconia; whereas Attica did not lose, and eastern Attica may even have gained, new inhabitants, as did Achaea and the Ionian islands. The great island of Euboea prospered. Lefkandi has a smoother history in the 12th century than most mainland sites, with no destruction at the end of LH IIIB, but an access of population, and rebuilding on a superior plan during the century (LH IIIC), and two destructions, probably towards its end. The pottery hints at overseas connections with Kea, Chios, the Dodecanese, Tarsus(?) and possibly Cyprus, as well as Attica.[4] Indeed in the 12th century there was something of an east-west axis from Attica through Euboea and the Aegean islands to Tarsus. In the Ionian islands of the far north-west there was an influx perhaps at about the same time that disaster struck Messenia, which would seem to argue against the north-west as the home of the destroyers. Kephallenia and the islands look west to Italy as well as south-east to Attica, and possibly the Levant.

Where population was maintained, as in Attica and Euboea, it was not unchanged. The later Athenians claimed that their city had been a refuge in times of trouble. A stubborn tradition brought the ruling house of Pylos, the Neleids, to the east coast of Attica, where Perati too was in touch with Cyprus and the Aegean islands. There is also archaeological evidence for refugees from Pylos reaching Eleusis, Athens and Salamis though they did not reach the latter till the sub-Mycenaean 11th century.[5] The men who lived on these coasts were seafarers, either raiders or something less reputable. Their activities included visits to Cyprus.

Depopulation should not be thought of as absolute, but rather as meaning a return to that subsistence farming that leaves nothing in life or death for the archaeologist. The small-holding of the 12th century BC would be indistinguishable from that of the 12th century AD. Depopulation means the disappearance of the ruling and bureaucratic classes, and probably of the craftsmen too. Some of these people undoubtedly found their way to Cyprus, where a large Mycenaean influx took place in the later 12th century, but still more in the 11th, from which time probably much of the island adopted the Greek language.

The economic crisis

In chapter 3 we looked at the economic danger-points that emerged in the course of the 13th century in the Mycenaean states: an over-specialized economy, too great a dependence on a central administration, the necessity for safe and efficient transport and communications, over-population and exhaustion of the land. What the economy fatally lacked was that balance based on exploitation of local resources that can sustain itself for long periods and survive short-term climatic change and even catastrophe. The end came when the marginal land was exhausted and the farmers had no surpluses to trade to the palace-centres. Some men would drift away, while others would revert to subsistence farming, dropping out of the bureaucratic system. The palaces no longer had resources for export, nor were they able to control or defend the outlying parts of their territory. It has been said that 'the boom conditions of the 15th and 14th centuries almost inevitably produced the slump after the end of the 13th'.[6] Without entirely agreeing with this *wholly* economic solution, nor with the concept of an *irreversible* process of dissolution, this was undoubtedly one cause of collapse. But there were others. Events overseas in Egypt, Anatolia and the Levant, had their repercussions. For that was where the richest markets had been. Apart from a very few Hittite documents, wherever there *are* references to the Aegean in the correspondence of the powers, and to Keftiu or Kaptara (Crete), it is always in connection with *commodities.*

With one doubtful exception there are no marriage-treaties such as formed the staple of Near Eastern political correspondence: the absence of Aegean names from the Ugaritic archives is notorious. Most of the evidence is indirect: Semitic words for commodities in the linear B texts, and the wide dispersal of Mycenaean pottery in Cyprus and the Levant. There was a rich man's club and it looks as though the Aegean rulers were not full members. It depended on a system that worked, and had worked for a long time; but the question we have to ask is: what happens when the system breaks down? If

24, 28 the comparative peace and real prosperity in which the Mycenaean rulers of the 14th and early 13th century lived was only partly of their own creation, and depended much upon their relationship to Egypt, Cyprus, Ugarit and, less directly, the Anatolian powers, then when trade was no longer welcome and the stuff of exchange was not there to handle, these lords of Mycenae and the islands were at a loss. Not themselves equipped to be self-supporting, like small farmers and cultivators, they could not go back to the land, but would have said, like the rich man's steward, 'I cannot dig, to beg I am ashamed.' All that was left to them was to rob their neighbours, to live the life of the corsairs for as long, but *only* as long, as the amassed wealth lasted among the strongest. They had lived, most of them, by benefit of a borrowed bureaucratic system; and when it disappeared, along with the surpluses which had given them the leisure to practise their martial arts and breed their beautiful horses, the only asset

123 that they were left with was their swords and their boats. It is a situation that accounts for the many shifts of population that have been found at this time. Some of them may well have taken

85, 53 those boats and swords to Cyprus and even to Libya and Egypt. Some of the swords were descended from those 'northern

54 bronzes' that were described in chapter 4.

Dorians and Heraclids

Argument concerning the 'Dorian Question' has been based on the history and distribution of dialects, since Dorians have totally eluded the archaeologist's net. (The cist-grave is now following the old diagnostic criteria of cremation and the use of iron on to the scrap-heap.) The pattern of dialects has been taken to support a Dorian homeland somewhere within Greece, but outside the centres of Mycenaean population, and probably in the north-western highlands. From here the speakers of Dorian dialects would have shifted gradually south into the Peloponnese, and eventually overseas to Crete and the Dodecanese, when the land was already partly depopulated, towards the end of the 11th century, the movement having started perhaps a century earlier. As well as the general move southwards there would have been certain lateral shiftings.

A new look at the problem sets out to explain it rather differently.[7] This supposes that alongside the standard Mycenaean language of the palaces and administration there was a secondary dialect spoken by the lower classes, and that on the collapse of the Mycenaean aristocracy 'standard Mycenaean' was replaced in the Peloponnese by 'sub-standard Mycenaean', but not of course in Arcadia. Elsewhere there would have been a good deal of mixing. One could therefore argue that the standard dialect that survived in the Cyclades was the high talk of displaced nobles, or rather brigands; and the sub-standard dialect of Thessaly was the language that had become native to a great part of Greece. This solution allows us to scrap the complicated pattern of minor migrations that criss-cross the Greek mainland in a confusing and unconvincing fashion, but it is still highly speculative.

The 'Dorian Question' is still more complicated by its, probably artificial, connection with the Heraclids (the descendants of Heracles), and their 'returns'. Out of this whole story we were best to salvage no more than the fact of a civil war among Mycenaean states at the time of the LH IIIB/C watershed out of which the Athenians emerged intact, while Mycenae, like many others, was grievously diminished, though not extinguished.[8]

The re-emergence of Middle Helladic features, such as cist-grave burials and dress-pins, may be part of that return to an older, more basic sort of subsistence farming, and lower living standards, which we suspected on economic grounds. Neither Dorians nor Heraclids have much to do with Sea Peoples, which is the excuse for treating both rather cavalierly. The legends that surround them are the attempt by later men to understand their confused memories of the Time of Troubles. The descendants of the last stable Mycenaean rulers have more right to the name of a

Sea People: those who took to the sea as refugees fleeing from breakdown and chaos at home, or those who as corsairs set out to salvage something from the ruin. If there was a diaspora it was limited to one class, the lords and their immediate followers. Craftsmen were often mobile and a law to themselves. They may have found new markets and new masters overseas, and not only in the south: some may have found their way to Italy and the central Mediterranean, which would account for certain bronze knives and swords from Italy and Greece, including Crete, that are very much alike, and are for the most part late-developed types of the end of the 12th and of the 11th century.[9]

Aegean corsairs

The opening scene of the *Iliad* displays to view the big-scale Aegean pirate – his arrogance, his choler, his *philotimo* and his power to dominate over other men. This was the heroic ideal of the 'sacker of cities'. If we take him for the moment as an historical fact, what does it really mean? It does not mean that he was after greater political power, or greater commercial power. The whole purpose of the hero's activity is spoil. 'Silver, gold, bronze, horses, cattle and sheep, women, above all treasure and women'.[10] Success did not mean the establishment of a state, however small, it meant a larger band of followers, and larger enterprises. The seven ships that attacked Ugarit in the last days may have been such a band. But these men were not a cause of the general breakdown, they were one of its results, and a not unimportant element among all those that inhibited recovery. Achilles and Agamemnon are not so much memories of the Mycenaean princes who had lived in palaces, in comfort and security, as of their near descendants: disinherited men whose comings home were either tragic or endlessly delayed.

The new corsairs did pretty well at first; but with the increasing impoverishment and isolation of later centuries, with the closing down of long-distance trade-routes, northern overland as well as southern maritime, the proud leader of a warband became a small-time bandit, happy if he could pick up a few Cypriot or Egyptian trinkets to give to his wife or bury with her. Archaeologically the evidence for piracy is difficult to catch, but the Cypriot, Egyptian and other trinkets that turn up in Dark Age sites and in graves may be just such evidence.[11]

Privateering and brigandage was a way of life, accepted if not condoned, by society from the earliest times. Aristotle recognized

40, 67
89

it as an alternative to commerce. The first modern history of the Mediterranean begins with an act of piracy.

There were many gradations between the big operators, the Homeric 'Sackers of Cities', an honourable title, and the 'three or four men in a small barque with a sack of flour, a skin of oil and a pot of honey', who between ventures, and when the weather was contrary, could support themselves almost anywhere. Braudel has made a point not always sufficiently remembered that there is a 'positive correlation between piracy and the economic health of the Mediterranean. They rise and fall together and not in opposition. Honest sea-captains and privateers were often the same men in different capacities.' They did not themselves cause the collapse of commerce and of the great powers, but were a result of that collapse. 'When piracy disappears altogether there is probably nothing worth taking'.

In a period of great turmoil and the breakdown of society wars, raids and insurrections are not likely to be confined tidily to one or two black years. They stretch over decades. This is what makes it dangerous to attempt to correlate disturbances in Greece with events in Egypt and the Levant. If we could not, with any degree of confidence, correlate destructions in Cyprus and Palestine with the wars of Merneptah and Ramesses III, it would be folly to try to do this in Greece. Bands of refugees and buccaneers from the Aegean could have been sailing all round the East Mediterranean, but it has to be admitted, reluctantly, that what we cannot do is put a finger on one or other of the enemy contingents that were given names and a memorial by the Egyptians, and say that *these* were men from Greece. What we *can* do is list the names not specifically Anatolian or northern Syrian: the Ekwesh of Merneptah's reign (chapter 5), probably the Shekelesh of Merneptah and Ramesses III, the Tjeker who have a possible link with Salamis and the Troad, and the Peleset (chapters 5–7). But the Peleset seem unlikely candidates since they formed a considerable part of the land trek through Syria in 1186. Both Anatolia and Cyprus may have acted as filters through which Aegean groups passed, and where they lost their names, if not their identities.

It is unfortunate that we have no contemporary portraits of the Ekwesh, and of Merneptah's other northern enemies, unlike those of Ramesses III; but in the Aegean some idea of what the fighting men of the first half of the 12th century looked like can be got from paintings on pots, especially the disciplined troop 124, 125, 119 that march round the Warrior Vase from Mycenae. Although the

122 If the relief at Medinet Habu is reliable there were already troops on the Egyptian side in the first Libyan war (year 5, *c*. 1189) dressed like the 'feather-crowned' attackers of year 8 (*c*. 1186), for this man is returning from that Libyan campaign.

portrayal is naïve and sketchy, certain essentials of dress and accoutrements stand out, and are curiously familiar. The helmet is the Asiatic 'Shardana' helmet worn in the sea battle of Medinet Habu and by the captive Shardana chieftain, but also by the ingot-god of Cyprus. We have traced the history of this helmet (chapter 5) which till now was not Aegean. The kilt is also familiar from Ugarit and the Egyptian monuments. The only oddity is the shape of the shield which, unlike the round shields of the attackers of Egypt and of the Pylos wall-paintings, and again of the ingot-god, has a concave lower edge. The Warrior Vase is later than the wars of Ramesses III, coming from around the middle of the 12th century (LH IIIC Pictorial Style). Contemporary sherds from Lefkandi in Euboea also have warriors with round shields, and a similar fringed kilt and tasselled sword and wearing greaves. Greaves distinguish these men from the attackers of Egypt, but connect them with Cyprus and with Sardinia. Greaves were an Aegean fashion, and it was probably Aegean fighting men who took them to Cyprus during the troubles. In a grave at Enkomi greaves and a flange-hilted sword (type IIa), belonged to one dead warrior (Enkomi tomb 18, LH IIIB/C). He could have been an adventurer from the Aegean or some other country. The traffic may not have been all one way, and mercenaries and adventurers could have come from northern Syria, Cyprus and Anatolia to Greece, as well as Mycenaeans from Greece to those parts. The armament industry is apt to be international, and a good weapon, or a good bit of protective body-armour, will travel quickly once its advantages are understood.

123–5 The naive draughtsmanship conceals the
fact that it is probably a grim enough troop of
spearmen who we see on the celebrated Warrior
Vase from Mycenae (*above* and *right*), men of
bronze and iron 'harsh-voiced and sullen-faced and
loving harm'. The warriors wear greaves and
fringed kilts with a corselet, and carry curious half-
moon shields. On one side the helmets are horned
and plumed (91 and cf. perhaps 19), on the other
side (*right*) a spiky or furry cap or wild hair is
worn; but see 92 left which is not hair and *opposite,
centre* from Mycenae, which may be – the
two men on this sherd (and on another from
Mycenae, *opposite, far left*) are standing in a
chariot. Another chariot (sherd from Lefkandi
opposite, below right) is unique though stylistically
related to the Warrior Vase. The other chariot
(*opposite, bottom left*) with multiple-spoked wheels
on a 'rude style' sherd from Ambelio, near Mor-
phou, Cyprus is a much more business-like affair
than the usual elegant contraption with a con-
ventionalized(?) four-spoked wheel (cf. 38 and 39).

Troy

Troy was a city like Miletus, like Tarsus, like Ugarit, that was attacked, ruined and forgotten, though only Ugarit was lost more or less without trace, and had no continuance. G. A. Wainwright, who wrote much that was eminently sensible about the 'Sea Peoples', said of the Trojan War,

> the Greeks were only interested in that part of the commotions in Asia Minor in which their ancestors had taken part, and that was in the Trojan War. That proves to have been only an episode in what we know to have been a long drawn-out period of wars, disasters, migrations . . . we have therefore to understand 'Troy' as western Asia Minor at the time of the Trojan War.[12]

In the memory of Iron Age Greeks the Trojan War is a paradigm of many sieges, many quarrels, many flights and many returns. In reality the location would have been far more dispersed. One instance has been cited: Tlepolemos, leader of the Rhodians, was killed on the plain of Troy by the Lycian commander Sarpedon. Now these two may have been old enemies, for at home they faced each other across the small strip of water that divides Rhodes from the Anatolian mainland.[13] Their enmity is logical but their tragedy could have been accomplished much nearer home. In the reducing atmosphere of history the splendours of Ilion, and the great Trojan adventure, shrivel like the 'truth' of Tombstone and the O.K. Corral beside a hundred 'Westerns'.

The 'Catalogue of Ships' is a part of the *Iliad* that may almost be treated as an historical document. Composed independently of the rest of the poem, it preserves, in the essentials, a memory of Mycenaean Greece.[14] In the *Iliad* the strength of the different fleets is used arbitrarily as a muster-list for the whole campaign, and the attempt of the poet to bring it up to date has led to many discrepancies and to anachronisms. Men are present who should be dead, and so on. The Catalogue was not meant to fit the poem; it describes events of a still recent past, whereas 'the rest of the *Iliad* is the result of a later and much freer handling of the traditional Tale of Troy'.[15] It reads like a much tattered fragment from some archive of the old bureaucracies before the administrative system had broken up. Internal evidence suggests that its composition follows the fall of Thebes, which is not mentioned in fact, but precedes the first round of major catastrophes at the end of LH IIIB, though it has also a number of later additions and adjustments. I think that it takes on a haunting interest if we see in it a record of Mycenaean greatness during the last decades before the scattering. As an evocation of past glory it became fixed and sacrosanct.

After the Greek Catalogue comes the list of the Trojan Allies. Much briefer, it probably does no more than name the most familiar enemies and trading partners of the Mycenaeans, for the names are clustered in the Troad, and around Sardis and Miletus, all of which had Mycenaean pottery or colonists. Beyond the Troad itself Carians and Lycians are named, and in Europe Thracians, Kikones and Paeonians. Discrepancies between the list and the rest of the *Iliad* are probably due to the same causes as in the Greek Catalogue, while the author's ignorance of some Anatolian names suggests a date before the Ionian migration of around 1000.

Handmade pots

If the arguments of this chapter have any validity, where do those northern invaders of Greece about whom we used to hear so much fit in? There was not much to attract northerners either in Dark Age Greece or in devastated Anatolia. It had been very different even at the turn of the 13th and 12th centuries when the 'northern bronzes' first appeared, and we thought of mercenaries and adventurers from the Balkans, and perhaps from as far as the Danube (chapter 4). The Dorians have shown themselves even more elusive, but there remains one further odd phenomenon, the handmade pottery.

Coarse handmade pottery has been found on many Mycenaean sites.[16] Perhaps the first thing to notice is its likeness to a sort of kitchen-ware that has turned up all over Europe from the Neolithic onwards. It has been given a name, *Kummerkeramik*, 'miserable pot'. It is much the same from eastern France to Romania, and it is usually *not* the most characteristic local pottery of its time. It is likely to have been made in the home by the cook herself, and only the almost indestructible nature of the material has given it a prominence it never merited.

The Mycenaean housewife was usually able to buy superior wheel-made cooking pots from professional potters, but there is a little evidence for the use of handmade pottery during earlier periods. When it appears in much greater quantities, alongside Mycenaean IIIC pots, at Korakou, Asine and to some extent at 126

126 Handmade pots from Korakou of a type found increasingly on a number of late Mycenaean sites (LH IIIC) but not unknown earlier. They derive from new or previously submerged elements, or are simply a throwback to a common sort of domestic pottery, *Kummerkeramik* (see also Noua pots, 49). Hts: *left*, 15 cm; *right*, 36 cm.

Mycenae too, the presence of 'northern invaders' has been suspected. It does not supersede the late-Mycenaean pottery; and at Asine, where there was no destruction, it was evidently made by people actually living on the site; but they appear to have been 'only incidental to the life of the settlement where the Mycenaean way of life and culture continued to be wholly dominant'. One explanation put forward is that the coarse pottery was made by a small body of rather backward new settlers who were accepted into the Mycenaean town, without influencing it to any great extent. This could be so, but the same result could come from a breakdown, perhaps only temporary, in the fabric of life, and the rise of a new strata of the population with little interest in a superior sort of pot-making. At the same time the professional potters would no longer have been able to distribute their wares, so that, to replace her losses, the latter-day Mycenaean housewife would have been thrown back on her own resources, which did not rise above this inelegant kitchen-ware. This would also account for the continued use of wheel-made pots alongside the poorer stuff, as at Korakou. There are strong arguments also for an Adriatic source for some of the handmade pottery found at Tiryns and even in western Crete.[17]

The situation with Troy is rather different. Troy had been in close touch with the Mycenaean world for several centuries. Level VIIa contained only one imported LH IIIB sherd but many local imitations, as well as a little quite uncharacteristic LH IIIA, while some may copy very early LH IIIC. This would fit well with the traditional date of the destruction of this level around 1185.[18] Whether or not this corresponds to the destruction of Homer's Troy is another matter. In the immediately following level VII Bi there is no longer any imported Mycenaean pottery but there is some locally made IIIC. There is again no agreement over the date and contents of the following VIIBii level, which, according to Carl Blegen, the excavator of the site in the 1930s, had some LH IIIC as well as a new pottery called 'knobbed ware', while others maintain that the two are not contemporary. Not all the handmade pottery is in fact new, but the 'knobbed ware' itself, and some of the incised pottery, is. Both styles, but especially the latter, have been found extensively in Bulgaria, and in Romania at Babadag in Dobrogea, Pšenicevo, Gabarevo and other sites in the Maritsa plain near Plovdiv.[19]

127, 128

The distribution of this pottery justifies our calling it 'Thracian'. There is no longer any need to go far north of the Danube to find its home. The fluted and knobbed pots came out of the south-eastward movement of Hungarian 'Gava' urnfields, along the lower Danube and into north-western Bulgaria. The other group, the incised and impressed pottery, has a double inheritance with, on the one side, the rough pots of the Noua culture and their Coslogeni extension in north-eastern Bulgaria (chapter 4), and on the other the finer incised wares of the later Middle Bronze tradition on the Danube: Cîrna, Gîrla Mare and Monteoru. This led to a pottery characteristic of the Late Bronze Age, which is found from the Dobrogea to the Rhodope and the Troad. It is not easy to date its appearance but it probably did not reach the Troad till some three generations or more after the 'northern bronzes' had appeared in the Aegean and almost as long after the Land and Sea Raids on Egypt. It has nothing whatsoever to do with them. Whatever the last act at Troy was it was witnessed by Thracian tribesmen from north of the Rhodope. These tribes played some still undetermined part in the rise of the Phrygians, and they controlled the ore deposits of the Rhodope.

49,

47

The handmade and fluted pottery of Macedonia may have a slightly different background from that found at Troy. There is more of the fluted ware than the incised wares though both exist at Kilindir, for instance, and Saratsé, where characteristic quirks and running spirals are incised, as well as painted, on good-quality pots (Kilindir and Tsaoutsitza). For their ancestry we should probably go up the Vardar and over the passes to the Morava, where a similar local pottery has been found near Niš, at Mediana. Behind this are the same Hungarian urnfields of Gava type, also a plainer local pottery (Slatina).

127 Handmade pottery from Troy and the Balkans: *a* is the new type of intrusive pottery of Troy VII Bii, with incised patterns, ribbing, bosses and handles; *b*, for comparison, pottery from the defended settlement of Babadag in the Dobrogea (all except the handled cup with impressed decorations are from the earliest occupation level). Similar pottery is found elsewhere in Romania and in Bulgaria. Not to scale.

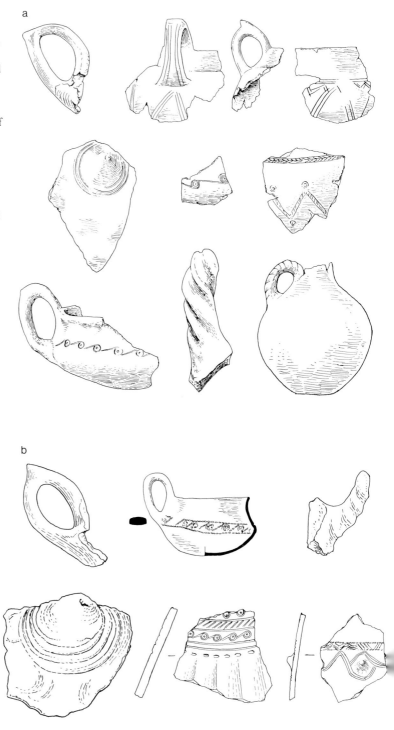

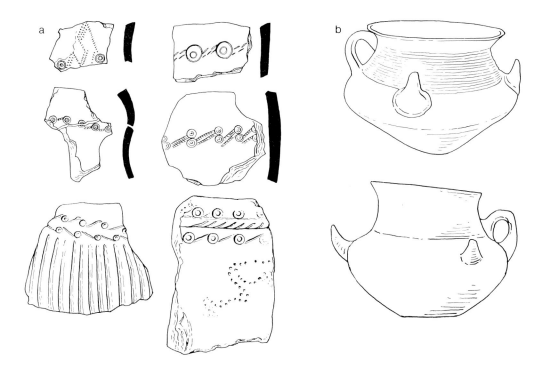

None of this had much to do with 'Sea Peoples', but it is evidence of pressures, steady and unrelenting, rather than immediate and overwhelming; and it was these pressures that for so long a time inhibited recovery. As well as the north there were irritants in the west, and an often-neglected source of danger in the highlands of Anatolia from where the Kashka had harassed the Hittites. The Kashka, who may have played a decisive role in the overthrow of the Hittite Empire, possessed a land rich in iron ores, and may possibly have inspired the precocious but primitive iron industry of Greek Macedonia, which enjoyed a period of relative prosperity during the whole of the Dark Age. But Iron Age Macedonia, the decorated Bouboustí pottery, the problems of Vardaroftsa and the people buried at Verghina, belong to another story.[20]

128 Handmade pottery from Bulgaria and Troy: *a*, sherds with impressed decoration from a defended site at Pšeničevo in the Maritsa valley, Bulgaria (note the linked circles similar to Babadag and Troy (127)); *b, above*, an urn with cremation from Gabarevo in the Maritsa valley and *below*, a pot from Troy VII Bii – this type of pot has a Danubian ancestry. Not to scale.

9
Conclusions

There are no clear-cut solutions to the problems discussed in these chapters, no rolling up of the map by a Genghis Khan or Attila, only a number of very complicated actions and interactions. In Greece a seemingly inevitable economic breakdown was precipitated by contraction of commerce at home and overseas, disruption of communications through natural and political disaster, and over-population in the mountain regions causing internal pressures which were reinforced by hostile action from frontier tribes who were themselves suffering infiltration and attrition from tribes in regions still farther north (chapters 1, 3, 4 and 8). An essentially artificial way of life, which had been cultivated in the great political centres, was unable to take the strain. Collapse was gradual, lasting through several generations, and ending up with marked, though not I think complete, depopulation of old centres such as Messenia and the Argolid. 'In the Mediterranean the soil dies unless it is protected by crops'. This characteristic statement of Braudel's is true, and from it a chain reaction starts which leads straight into the so-called 'Dark Age'.

In Anatolia central government collapsed, partly through attack from beyond the frontiers (the Kashka and the Assyrians), but probably rather more through the revolt of border provinces, establishing their own independence, through the great vassals throwing off their allegiance to a harassed central authority, and quite possibly through too great a dependence on a professional army of chariot-troops. What precipitated the final crisis is not known, but the feudal basis of society had been showing signs of strain for some time (chapters 2, 6 and 7). There was also the dangerous lack of sea-power and dependence on the help of ambivalent maritime powers – the Lukka and Ugarit – combined perhaps, but this is guesswork, with family feuding and weakness at the centre.

In Egypt there was exhaustion too: economic and political breakdown went hand in hand, reinforcing each other. Here

129, 130 A bearded bronze figure of a god (*left*) comes from 12th-century Enkomi. He is armed like the fighting-men of the time with rounded shield and spear and wears a kilt, possibly greaves and 'Shardana', or perhaps Ugaritic(?) horned helmet. He stands on an 'ox-hide' ingot, so although a warrior he is also probably god of metal-workers whose workshops were attached to the temples at Kition (see VIII, 112 and cf. 91).

Some four centuries later another warrior (*right*, from Sulcis) is one of many found in Sardinia with round shields, horned helmets and spear, sword or bow; this one has greaves and body-armour as well. Here may be another link with the Shardana. 'Ingot-god', ht 35 cm.

there was an even more fatal dependence on foreign troops, on a military aristocracy like the *maryannu*, and on past raiders turned mercenary and ally like the Shardana, who in the end may have opened a door to their compatriots. In the Levant the situation was explosive. Withdrawal of the great powers had given head-room to a number of smaller independent or semi-independent states, each ambitious for itself. Here too there was the same reliance on the loyalty of great vassals and on a class of charioteers who were often foreigners. The general weakening of authority and loss of the old great-power equilibrium opened the way for semi-nomadic bands of shepherds and raiders – *hapiru*, Shasu, Israelites and others – who were a constant source of instability between the desert and the sown, drifting hither and thither, able to assert themselves at will, but by reason of their way of life hardly discernible to archaeology.

Of the 'Peoples of the Sea', and their part in the history of the times, the pattern is splintered and infinitely complicated. What we have found is in part, but only in part, a continuation of the endemic piracy and small-state warfare that had existed for centuries in the East Mediterranean – a symptom more than a cause of the Dark Age that was coming. We have found evidence of a diaspora which has a special interest because of its part in forming the modern map of the Mediterranean, with Sicilians, Sardinians, Etruscans, Philistines, Greek Cypriots and Thracians planting their names where they still are, or were to be found for some long time. Other names have vanished, Danuna, Tjeker, Weshesh.

The hall-mark of the times is movement. About this at least the Egyptians got it right; this too was what the later Greeks remembered most of these troubled centuries. Thucydides recalls rampant piracy by Greeks and barbarians alike and men carrying arms as a survival of the old freebooting life, the 'weakness of olden times . . . that before the Trojan War Hellas, it appears, engaged in no enterprises together'. Few of the war-like bands active in the East Mediterranean appear to have made a single move, raid or flight from a first homeland to a 'final' settlement; but rather, like the Peleset who came to Palestine 'from Casluhim' (Egypt) or the Shardana who probably reached Sardinia by way of Cyprus, they were homeless wanderers for perhaps a generation, perhaps longer, perhaps a shorter time. The land-invaders, especially the allies who passed through the length of the Levant around 1186 with their cattle and their families, seem to have been engaged in a much more deliberate search for farms and homes not too distant from where they started. The same may be true of the Thracians and Epirots north of the Pindus, but we know terribly little about what was happening there.

If we take in turn, very briefly, the contingents known to the Egyptians, our very limited results are somewhat as follows. The Shardana had been known first as raiders who then became mercenaries and garrison troops in Egypt only to return again to raiding. They were good fighters, especially with sword and shield. Footloose and potentially dangerous, there is some reason to think they came originally from northern Syria, and that after the attack on Ramesses III's Egypt they stayed for a time in Cyprus, perhaps arriving there with the refugees from Ugarit. From Cyprus they, or a part of them, found their way to 129 Sardinia to which island they gave the name which it had 130 acquired in the 9th century BC, as we know from an inscription found at Nora, which seems to describe an expedition from Tyre to protect Phoenician mining interests in Sardinia. The Phoenician presence in Cyprus at this time, and the earlier and collateral Phoenician relationship with Ugarit, fits well this picture. How soon after 1186 the descent on Sardinia took place we do not know. There may have been several expeditions, either quite small or more numerous. Sardinia was already known to the East Mediterranean as a source of copper, and was engaged in the trade in 'ox-hide' ingots. There is always the possibility of 58 even earlier settlements and trafficking, as was argued for Corsica by Dr Grosjean. In any case the likeness in dress and arms between the sea-raiders of Medinet Habu in the Nile battle, and 82 the gods and warriors portrayed by 8th-century and later Sardinian bronzes, is too close to be ignored. Helmets, corselets, 130 round shields, swords, bows, the only difference is that the Sardinians wear 'Aegean'-style greaves, but these could have been adopted in Cyprus (chapter 6).

For the Shekelesh we have an historical connection through Greek writers with the Sikels of Sicily, and before that perhaps with southern Italy. At the same time there is the archaeological break between the coastal Thapsos sites in south-eastern Sicily, with their Late Helladic pottery, and the Pantalica sites of the interior, between which and the Aegean there appears to be very 70, 71 little connection at all, unlike southern Italy where there was still a tenuous link with LH IIIC and sub-Mycenaean Greece (chapter 4). From this it seems very unlikely that the new element in the Pantalica population, probably that of the Sikels,

131 Detail from the ivory box (18) from Enkomi. There is no more reason to call this man a Tjeker than 132 a 'Philistine', although both are among the Sea Peoples (see the sea battle 81, 82 (top left) and 83). The axe is unusual for a huntsman and is a type also found in Sicily, so we might call him a Shekelesh(?).

came from Mycenaean Greece. If it came from farther than the Ionian Sea it is more likely to be a result of upheavals in Anatolia and the Levant. We have noticed a curiously Anatolian finish to some of the finer Pantalica pottery. In any case Pantalica begins at a time when the sea-lanes had become unsafe through piracy and raiding, for it repeats the shift in Crete from coastal to defensible inland sites. This was the state of the Mediterranean after the Land and Sea Raids against Ramesses III and also, but to a lesser extent, already after Meneptah's Libyan war. From about the time of that war, around 1220, there is some evidence for activity across the Libyan Sea, activity in which Sicily and southern Italy, possibly even Sardinia, could have been involved, along with Cyprus and the Aegean.

The Teresh or Tursha are even more elusive. They are a shadowy presence in western Anatolia connected either with Lydia or the Troad and, according to some opinions, with the antecedants of the Etruscans. They are referred to once (in 1186) along with the Peleset as 'from the midst of the sea', which could mean some temporary island refuge, and need not deny them an earlier Anatolian homeland. That the Lukka came from western Anatolia is most likely, with the Carian coast and Lycia preferable to anywhere further north or inland, though both have also been suggested (chapter 2). The dubious reputation of the Lukka in the 2nd millennium was inherited by the Carians in the 1st millennium.

Among the most interesting of the contingents named by the Egyptians are the Ekwesh who, like the Lukka, do not appear after Merneptah's reign; indeed the Ekwesh *only* appear then, and they are singled out as especially connected with the sea (Athribis stela). Much depends on whether we accept their identification with the Ahhiyawa of the Hittite texts, or with at least a part of them, and with the Achaeans. If so they are securely placed either on, or not far from, the western coast of Anatolia, very likely in one or other of the islands, though it can be argued that at certain times the Hittites were referring to the mainland of Greece and most probably the kings of Mycenae by this name. Their designation as 'of the Countries of the Sea' would suit islanders; but too much should not be made of these Egyptian labels (chapters 5 and 6). If Mycenaeans are lurking under this name, what are we to make of its strange disappearance from all the records after 1220? The disappearance of the Lukka at the same time is even odder, but the possibility must not be forgotten of shifts of name and title, or the merging of one name into another, so there is a special interest about the *new* names of 1186.

The new raiders of Ramesses III's time – the Denyen or Danuna, the Tjeker, Peleset and Weshesh – attacked by land as well as sea, with the main land invasion following one or possibly two routes from Anatolia through Syria-Palestine to the Nile Delta. Their aspect is that of farmers uprooted and looking for land, like the Libyans in their wars with Egypt. The Denyen may have come from no farther than the Hatay, and their later history, whether or not we credit them with a prolonged existence in Palestine as 'Danites', does place them firmly and historically in the extreme north of Syria where I suspect the Shardana once lived. The Tjeker probably came from as far as the Troad, perhaps by way of Cyprus, and they too were settled on the Palestinian coast north of the Danites at the end of the 12th century. For the Weshesh information is almost wholly lacking apart from a hinted connection with 'Ilios' (Troy). Both may have had connections with the Teresh-Tursha.

The most controversial group of all is that of the Peleset who have given their name to Palestine, and who have sometimes been brought in ships from the Aegean and mainland Greece, or from the Caucasus, but who appear in fact to be more landsmen than any of the others. Their cities in southern Palestine were not harbours, and there is very little to connect them with the sea at all. What meagre linguistic evidence there is points to Anatolia rather than Greece or Crete (chapter 7).

So where after all are those Aegean refugees and pirates, those earlier vikings with their northern panoply spreading fire and ruin through the East Mediterranean? How is it that the picture is so confused, and that so much of the evidence seems to point to Anatolia rather than Greece or the Balkans? G. A. Wainwright thought that the invaders did in fact come from Anatolia, and others have followed him, but I think the reason may be not quite so straightforward.

If most of the activity was rather small-scale, then what we see in Egypt is the end of a chain reaction. Something set these bands moving from Anatolia, from Cyprus and northern Syria, and that something was the harassing of other bands setting off perhaps from Aegean ports, from Messenia and the Argolid, Euboea and Crete, for Miletus and Tarsus, the Dodecanese and Cyprus. Others may have come from much farther away, from the Troad and from southern Italy and Sicily. It would be a mistake to give too much weight to the handful of names that

67

132

happen to have reached the Egyptian monuments. They mark a high watermark, and behind that farthest wave we must think of a great confusion of nationalities and actions, criss-crossings, interlockings and repulsions, among which the exodus from Pylos and the fall of Troy were incidents. Destructions at Mycenae and Miletus, continuity on Cos, change and revival at Kition: there is no single great voice, but the 'sound of running history' is a babble of little streams. Somewhere at the edges are the mountain folk: the Epirots and Albanians, Thracians and Danubians, who never quite focus. But underneath the flux there is something older and stronger, an enduring source of stability: the small farmer, Hesiod's forefathers, and humbler folk, in Greece, in Anatolia and in the Levant. The land was still turned and crops were raised, but with contracted horizons, each man growing and working for himself, not troubled overmuch with what lay behind the mountains, except for the fear of pirates and robbers, descendants probably of his masters from a few generations back, who still could irrupt into his life, upsetting its old rhythm, to leave him destitute in the ruin of his home. But in a few years he, or his brother, or his son, is back again ploughing the same poor piece of land, as unambitious and as little changing in the 9th century as in the 19th, in BC or AD, till once more the great exotic growths appear, the bazaar cities, the great sanctuaries, the centres of refined civilization and sophisticated commerce. A new set of names begin to make their din: Athenians, Phrygians, Lydians, Phoenicians, Israelites, Aramaeans, Romans. The process is still going on today in spite of a new crescendo of change: 'the masters come and go, the rest remain'.

132 There is more evidence for Cyprus as a focus of the Sea Raiders in this black steatite seal from an ashlar building at Enkomi (under a Late Cypriot IIIA floor). This is presumably how the warrior liked to see himself, with large round shield, spear or sword, and 'crown'. See 122 for the same man, without a beard, as seen by the Egyptians at Medinet Habu. Ht 1.5 cm.

Chronological tables

EGYPT			HITTITES		SEA PEOPLES AND RAIDERS	ANATOLIAN PEOPLES OR PLACES
DATES			DATES			
LOW	MEDIUM					
					Land of Danuna (Denyen), Shardana, Lukka Meshwesh (Libya)	Ahhiya (Ahhiyawa) Lukka Lands
14th century or earlier						
			1306	Muwatallis		
1279	1290	Ramesses II				
1275	1286	Battle of Kadesh	1286	Battle of Kadesh	Shardana in Egyptian army	Hittite allies include Lukka, Dardany
			1282	Urhi-Teshub		
			1275	Hattusilis III		
	1269		Treaty of Peace			
	1256		Marriage treaty			
			1250	Tudhaliyas IV Wars with Assyria and Arzawa; Hittites overrun Cyprus?		Taruisha (Teresh?) Wilusa (Ilios?)
1213	1224	Merneptah				
1208	1220	Libyan war	1220	Arnuwandas IV	Libyan allies include Shardana, Lukka, Meshwesh, Teresh, Ekwesh, Shekelesh	
1203	1214	D. of Merneptah Amenmesses Pharaoh				
1199	1210	Seti II				
1193	1204	Siptah and Tausert Interregnum		Dynastic troubles?		
1185	1196	20th Dynasty: Seknakht				
1183	1194	Ramesses III				
			1190	Suppululiumas II?		
1179	1189	1st Libyan war				
1176	1186	Year 8: land and sea battles vs. northern allies		Sea battle off Cyprus? Fall of Hattusas?	Northern allies: Shardana, Shekelesh, Denyen (Danuna), Teresh, Peleset, Tjeker, Weshesh	Dynastic and border wars
1173	1183	2nd Libyan war				
1152	1162	D. of Ramesses III				

After 1100 erstwhile raiders settled in: Palestine (Peleset, Tjeker, ?Danuna-Denyen); northern Syria (Danuna-Denyen); Sicily (Shekelesh); Sardinia (Shardana); and ?Etruria (?Teresh).

Table I is the only table with any historical foundation in written documents. Dr Kitchen's low dates as well as the medium dates used in the rest of the book are shown for comparison (see Introduction n. 2). Names of raiders and northern allies are given on their first (*italic*) and subsequent appearances in the relevant Egyptian and Hitti e texts. For the dates and details of Egyptian reigns I have drawn on very helpful correspondence with Dr Kitchen.

EGYPT	BETH SHAN	DEIR ALLA	ASHDOD
Tausert c. 1200 (or 1193–85)	*Level VII*: Canaanite city with Egyptian garrison; LH IIIB and Cypriot pottery imported	'Sanctuary site'? LH IIIB pottery, cartouche of Tausert	*Level XIV*: Canaanite city (Late Bronze II)
Ramesses III 1194 (or 1183)	Violent destruction *Level VI*: immediate rebuilding on similar plan; additions to Egyptian garrison buildings Inscription of official of Ramesses III with cartouche of latter Some imported LH IIIC-derived pots;	Earthquake Two attempts to rebuild followed by fires Reoccupation with 'Philistine' pottery	Destruction by fire *Level XIIIb*: new building phase; local copies of LH IIIC (not earliest) pottery *Level XIIIa*: locally made 'Philistine'
D. of Ramesses III 1162 (or 1152)	further destruction and re-building immediately after		pottery; cult site

EGYPT AND THE LEVANT	GREEK PERIODS	GREEK DESTRUCTIONS AND REBUILDINGS	TARSUS, MILETUS AND LEFKANDI
Ramesses II Beth Shan VII Ashdod XIV	LH IIIB	Great period of building at Tiryns, Mycenae, Pylos	Tarsus a Hittite town
Merneptah		Mycenae defences, Lion Gate and cyclopean walls First destructions in Argolid: Zygouries, Berbati, Mycenae (houses outside walls destroyed)	Fortification and LH IIIB pots at Miletus
LH IIIB pots still to Levant Ramesses III Beth Shan VI	LH IIIC (early)	Building at Mycenae and Tiryns Pylos destroyed? General wave of destruction – Mycenae citadel burnt, also Thebes? Gla? Meneleion? Pylos? Some rebuilding, Pylos abandoned?	Miletus links with Ugarit Tarsus destroyed LH IIIC at Tarsus Lefkandi phase 1a
Ashdod XIII? LH IIIC at Beth Shan	LH IIIC (mid.) 'Close Style' developing	Mycenae granary 'Close Style' Warrior Vase	Destruction and rebuilding at Lefkandi 1b Lefkandi 2a: pictorial style pottery
	LH IIIC (late)	Destructions at Tiryns? Iolkos, Korakou 'Regionalism'	Tarsus LH IIIC (late) Lefkandi 2b
Death of Ramesses III		Mycenae granary destroyed Teikhos Dymaion destroyed?	Lefkandi 3

CYPRUS	ASHDOD ALTERNATIVE
LC IIC	*Level XIV* destroyed *Level XIIIb*
LC IIIA	*Level XIIIa*
LC IIIB	*Level XII*

Table II (*left*) attempts to lock the archaeological material from three key sites in the Levant into the historical framework (table I). The alternative low dates shown are those of Dr Kitchen, but see Introduction n. 2. Evidence for the table comes from the excavation reports (ch. 7 n. 15), with much additional help and advice from the Hon. Mrs Hankey.

Table III (*below*) is a very tentative correlation of events in Egypt, the Levant, central Anatolia (Hittites) and – more speculatively – Cyprus, the Anatolian coasts, Greece and the Aegean islands. Among the many sources Dr E. French's articles have been especially consulted, with additional help in correspondence; see also Introduction n. 5 and Dickenson, ch. 1 n. 4; also, though too recent for all but the most cursory consultation, J. Rutter in *Symposium on the Dark Ages in Greece*, New York 1977, 1–20.

CYPRUS	UGARIT	HITTITES
Late Cypriot IIC (Karageorghis IIB)	Ashlar palace and outer walls; LH IIIB pots	Tudhaliyas IV
Enkomi fortification wall built?	Merneptah cartouche	Arnuwandas IV
		Dynastic troubles
'Rude style' pots Enkomi destroyed Late Cypriot IIIA Ashlar buildings; Kition temples rebuilt	Pictorial craters link with Miletus Ugarit abandoned	Suppiluliumas II? Hattusas destroyed
Enkomi destroyed Late Cypriot IIIB		

GREECE	EPIRUS, THE NORTH-WEST, AND IONIAN ISLANDS	ITALY, SICILY	ALBANIA	MACEDONIA	TROY
LH IIIA2 14th to early 13th century	Tris Langadas IIIA2 in Ithaca	Luni, Ischia, Scoglio del Tonno (Taranto), Thapsos (Sicily)	Malic 4c Settlement?	Vardaroftsa (Axiochori), first Mycenaean imports	
LH IIIB early 13th to early 12th century	Mazaraki cists Kalbaki, Kastritsa Kephallenia chamber tombs	Luni, Ischia, Scoglio del Tonno, Thapsos		LH IIIB in coastal sites	VII A
		Peschiera, Surbo	Tumuli Vodhinë 17 Vodhinë 16?		
LH IIIC from early 12th century	Population increases Kastritsa	Pianello I Pantalica I (Sicily), Scoglio del Tonno, Torre Castelluccia (Protovillanovan)	Malic 4d? Vodhinë and Vajzë		LH IIIB and IIIC imitated VII Bi LH IIIC 'Granary Style' imitated
				Vardaroftsa Burnt level	VII Bii

EGYPT	CYPRUS UGARIT	GREECE	ITALY SICILY	TROY
13th century Ramesses II	LC IIC	LH IIIB	Thapsos	
Merneptah		First destructions in Argolid e.g. Mycenae houses outside walls		VII A
Short reigns *12th century* Ramesses III		Main destructions e.g. Mycenae citadel LH IIIC	Peschiera	
	Ugarit abandoned LC IIIA		Pantalica I	VII Bi
	LC IIIB			
		Mycenae granary destroyed		VII Bii

BULGARIA	ROMANIA	HUNGARY	MIDDLE DANUBE	REINECKE, MULLER-KARPE, MOZSOLICS SYSTEM FOR CENTRAL EUROPE
Middle Bronze Age: Gîrla Mare etc.	MBA: Otomani, Monteoru, Wietenberg etc.	MBA: Large cemeteries of tumuli	MBA: Tumuli	
	MBA traditions continue Noua moves into Moldavia, Monteoru destroyed	Hoards with some new bronze types Predecessor of type IIa sword; Forrø type hoards		Bronze C
Late Bronze Age: Noua-Coslogeni	LBA: first horizon of hoards, IIa swords	LBA: earliest IIa swords Bükk-Aranyon Peschiera bronzes Opalyi hoards	LBA: Riegsee Peschiera bronzes Baierdorf-Velatice Čaka corselet median-winged axes	Bronze D (Hungary: IVb1)
Gava advance	Second horizon hoards (Cincu-Suseni): beaten bronze	Val-Gava urnfields		
Pšeničevo	Babadag I			Hallstatt A1 (Hungary: IVb2)

BALKANS AND SOUTH-CENTRAL EUROPE	CENTRAL EUROPE
Middle Bronze Age traditions	Bronze C
Noua advance Type IIa swords Čaka burial Hoards	Bronze D (Hungary: IVb1)
Urnfield spread	
Pšeničevo Babadag I	Hallstatt A1 (Hungary: IVb2)

Table IV (*above*) extends the span from Italy to the Danube and Troy, and plunges still deeper into the mists of uncertainty. Correlations with Greece and the East Mediterranean lands are not much more than guesswork. The table is partly based on Rusu and Mozsolics (Romania and Hungary, ch. 4 n. 3), also on Bjetti-Sestieri (ch. 4 n. 12) and Wardle (ch. 4 n. 10).

Table V (*left*) attempts to give an approximate idea of relationships over the entire area covered by the book. It is not an amalgamation of the other tables because levels of probability are so variable; it merely sets out certain signposts and their very loose interconnections.

207

Notes

Abbreviations

AJA	American Journal of Archaeology
Annuario	Annuario della Scuola Archeologica di Atene (Rome)
Arch. Anz.	Archaeologischer Anzeiger
Arch. Delt.	Archaiologikon Deltion
Arch. Mold.	Archeologia Moldovei (Iaşi)
BCH	Bulletin de Correspondence Hellénique
BPI	Bullettino di Paletnologia Italiana
BRGK	Bericht der Römisch-Germanische Kommission
BSA	Annual of the British School at Athens

Eph. Arch.	Archaiologiki Ephemeris
IEJ	Israel Exploration Journal
JCS	Journal of Cuneiform Studies
JNES	Journal of Near Eastern Studies (Chicago)
MDOG	Mitteilungen der deutschen Orient-Gesellschaft
PPS	Proceedings of the Prehistoric Society
Slov. Arch.	Slovenska Archeologia (Bratislava)
Wresz.	Wreszinski, W. *Atlas zur Altaegyptischen Kulturgeschichte*, Leipzig 1935

Introduction *(pp. 9–13)*

1 From Edgerton and Wilson 1936, pl. 46, p. 53; and Wilson, J. 'Egyptian Historical Texts' in Pritchard 1969.

2 The whole of Egyptian New Kingdom chronology is still very much in the melting-pot. The crucial date is that of the accession of Ramesses II. The old 'high' date of 1304 still has many advocates, but a much lower date was put forward by Dr K. Kitchen. I am most grateful to Dr Kitchen for showing me in correspondence the various arguments for the dating schemes. The choice is between a 'middle date' for Ramesses II of 1290–1224, which would make Ramesses III 1194–1162, and a 'lowest date' with Ramesses II 1279–1213 and Ramesses III 1183–1152. Dr Kitchen writes of a slight preference for the lowest date and next to it the middle one 'subject to further investigations not yet completed'. For the sake of consistency I have adhered throughout to the middle date as proposed in Kitchen, K. A. 'Date, Nature, Content of Egyptian Sources on the "Sea Peoples"', in Crossland (forthcoming); see also Kitchen, K. A. *The Third Intermediate Period in Egypt (1100–650)*, Warminster 1972. Should the lower chronology be used, corresponding adjustments must be made to all events dated by reference to Egypt, and on the tables. The argument is very complex and even after fixing for one or other date there may be ten to thirty years' 'surplus' to be distributed piecemeal among Merneptah's successors (Kitchen *loc cit.*). It follows that I date Kadesh, year 5 of Ramesses II, 1286/5 and the peace treaty of year 21, 1269. The accession of Merneptah is 1224, and of Ramesses III *c.*1194. On Egyptian dates see also Hankey, V. and Warren, P. 'The Absolute Chronology of the Aegean Late Bronze Age', *Institute of Classical Studies, Mycenaean Seminar*, London 1973, giving alternative systems and their implications for the Aegean.

3 See ch. 2 n. 3, ch. 3 n. 4.

4 Dikaios 1969, vol. II, 441–536, table p. 496; Sjöqvist, E. *Problems of the Late Cypriot Bronze Age*, Stockholm 1940, 197 etc. Catling, H. 'The Achaean settlement of Cyprus', in *Acts of the International Symposium 'The Mycenaeans in the Eastern Mediterranean, Nicosia 1972*, Nicosia 1973, 34–9. Karageorghis 1976, table p. 173; Dr Karageorghis suppresses any LC IIC altogether and brings LC IIB down to 1230, Furumark's date for the end of LH IIIB.

5 The subdivisions and affiliations of late Mycenaean pottery – LH IIIB and IIIC – are at present being reassessed by among others, F. Schachermeyr, E. French, J. Rutter, C. Mee and S. Sherratt. While matters remain in a state of flux I have deemed it wisest to keep to a very broad terminology, only occasionally using Furumark's subdivisions LH IIIC1a and IIIC1b etc. where they occur within a context directly based on his argument. In future far greater precision should be possible in assessing the history of Mycenae itself and other late Mycenaean sites; this will be particularly crucial for Cyprus and the change from LC IIC to LC IIIA, and from IIIA to

IIIB (ch. 6 n. 9) and also for the end of Pylos for which see Chadwick, J. 'The Mycenaean Documents', in McDonald and Rapp 1972, 100–16; also Dickenson, O. *Antiquity*, xlviii, 191 (1974), 228–30. On problems of LH IIIB pottery most recently see French, E. 'Mycenaean Problems 1400–1200', *Institute of Classical Studies, Mycenaean Seminar*, London 1976.

6 See V. Hankey, ch. 7 n. 15.

7 On the limitations of radiocarbon dating see Snodgrass, A. 'Mycenae, Northern Europe and Radiocarbon dates', *Archaeologia Atlantica*, 1 (1975), 33ff., and Hood, M. S. F. 'Comparison of radiocarbon dates for the Aegean Late Bronze Age and the Egyptian New Kingdom', *Tenth International Congress of Pre- and Protohistorical Sciences, Nice 1976* (forthcoming). I am very grateful to Mr Hood for letting me see his text in advance of publication.

Chapter 1 *(pp. 17–27)*

1 Braudel 1972, 225.
2 G. K. Chesterton, Ballad of the White Horse.
3 Myres, J. L. *Mediterranean Culture*, Frazer Lecture 1943, p. 9 and passim.
4 Dickenson, O. 'Drought and the decline of Mycenae', *Antiquity*, xlviii, 191 (1974), 228 answering Bryson, R., Lamb, H. and Donley, D. *Antiquity*, xlviii, 189 (1974), 46; Wright, H. Jr. 'Climatic Change in Mycenaean Greece', *Antiquity*, xlii, 166 (1968), 123; Snodgrass, A. *Institute of Classical Studies, Mycenaean Seminar*, London 1975.
5 Braudel 1972.
6 Lethbridge, T. *Boats and Boatmen*, London 1952, 153.

Chapter 2 *(pp. 29–53)*

1 For Egyptian chronology see Introduction n. 2. For the battle of Kadesh see Breasted 1906, vol. III, 123–74; Gardiner, A. *The Kadesh Inscriptions of Ramesses II*, Oxford 1960, ch. 2 and Appendix.
2 Goetze, A. 'Warfare in Asia Minor', *Iraq*, 25 (1963), 124–30.
3 Otten 1963.
4 Güterbock, H. G. 'The Hittite Conquest of Cyprus Reconsidered', *JNES*, 26 (1967), 73–81; Otten 1963.
5 The fullest version of the Kadesh inscription is at Luxor but there are others at Abydos and Karnak; Gardiner (n. 1 above), and Breasted 1906, vol. II, para. 305 *et seq.*
6 For the location of the Lukka Lands I find the arguments put forward in Garstang and Gurney 1959, ch. VI, still to be more convincing than any other; but see Macqueen, J. G. *Anatolian Studies*, 18 (1968), 169–85, favouring north-western Anatolia, and Bryce, T. R. 'The Lukka Problem and a possible solution', *JNES*, 33 (1974), 395–404, advocating Caria *and* Lycaonia.
7 Nougayrol, J. 'Guerre et Paix à Ugarit', *Iraq*, 25 (1963), 110–23; Gray 1965, *passim*.
8 Astour, M. C. 'Ugarit and the Aegean' in

Hoffmann, H. (ed.), *Orient and Occident: Essays presented to Cyrus Gordon*, Neunkirchen 1973.
9 For Enkomi and Kition see Dikaios 1969 and Karageorghis 1976 respectively; see also Schaeffer 1952.
10 See n. 4 above.
11 Kitchen, K. A. 'Interrelations of Egypt and Syria', in Liverani, M. (ed.) *La Siria nel Tardo Bronzo*, Orientis Antiiqui Collectio IX, Rome 1969.
12 Muhly, J. D. *The Land of Alashiya . . . (Praktikon tou protou diethnous Kyprologikou Synedriou)*, vol. I, Nicosia 1972, 210–19.
13 Catling, H. op. cit. (Introduction n. 4); Cadogan, G. 'Patterns in the Distribution of Mycenaean Pottery in the East Mediterranean', *ibid.*, Nicosia 1973. Catling, H. 'A Study in the composition of Mycenaean pictorial pottery from Cyprus', *BSA*, 60 (1965), 212–24, with references. See also Hankey, V. (ch. 3 n. 11).
14 Stela Petrie Tanis II, pl. 2 no. 73, also Aswan Stela, in Kitchen, K. A. *Ramessid Inscriptions*, vol. II, Oxford 1958–74, 290, 1–4.

Chapter 3 *(pp. 55–79)*

1 See Introduction n. 5.
2 Killen, J. T. 'The Wool Industry of Crete in the Late Bronze Age', *BSA*, 59 (1964), 1–15. The 'D' series dealing with sheep, wool and the textile industry is the largest group of tablets. It refers to the numbers and make up of flocks, probably as target figures rather than actual numbers received. Sheep were allowed out by the overlord for herding by tenants as in the Middle Ages. There are indications of seasonal movements.
3 I am using 'ashlar' in the current architectural sense as 'clean-hewn' stone that is cut and squared on all surfaces with close-fitting joints; some writers have used the term for the much rougher shaping of the large stone courses at Mycenae and other Mycenaean sites.
4 The date of the Madduwattas Indictment and connected texts are discussed by Houwink ten Cate, Ph. H. J. in Crossland 1973, 141–53, with full bibliography; see espec. Otten. Die hethitischen historischen Quellen und die altorientalische Chronologie, *Abhandlung der Akad. Wiss, Geistes-Soz. Klasse*, Mainz 1968. Although the majority of philologists incline to date this text in the 15th instead of the 13th century, there are political and historical difficulties, especially with regard to Alashiya-Cyprus; I have therefore deemed it wiser to leave this material on one side until the problem is satisfactorily resolved. See also ch. 2 nn. 3 and 4.
5 Iakovides, Sp. *The Actual State of Research at the Citadel of Mycenae*, lecture given at the Institute of Archaeology, London 1976 (forthcoming); *idem*, 'The Centuries of Achaean Sovereignty' in Christopoulos 1974.
6 Littauer, M. A. 'The Military Use of the Chariot in the Aegean in the LBA', *AJA*, 76 (1972), 145–57;

Catling, H. 'A Mycenaean Puzzle from Lefkandi in Euboea', *AJA*, 72 (1968), 41–9.

7 Wheeler, T., Maddin, R. and Muhly, J. D. 'Ingots and the Bronze Age Copper Trade in the Mediterranean', *Expedition* (1975), 31–40. Cooke, S., Henrickson, E. and Rapp, G. 'Metallurgical and Geochemical Studies', in McDonald and Rapp 1972, 225–33. Muhly, J. 'The Ox-hide Ingots and the Development of Copper Metallurgy in the Late Bronze Age', in Bettancourt, P. (ed.) *Temple University Aegean Symposium, Philadelphia, February 1976*, 1976, 10–14. Muhly argues for a gradual increase in the use of sulphide ores during the Late Bronze Age in the Near East and the depletion of the superficial oxides; the Hittites were smelting sulphides in the early 2nd millennium. Cyprus did have an oxide zone, but Muhly suggests that there was something of a crisis at the end of the 13th century.

8 Bass, G. 'Cape Gelidonya: A Bronze Age Shipwreck', *Transactions of the American Philological Society*, n.s. 57/8 (1967); Maddin, R. and Muhly, J. D. *Journal of Metals*, 26/5 (1974).

9 Muhly, J. D. in a paper presented to the Fourth International Colloquium on Aegean Prehistory, Sheffield 1977.

10 Catling, H. *BSA*, 55 (1960), 108; *Archeometry*, 4 (1961), 31, and 6, (1963). See ch. 2 n. 13.

11 Hankey, V. 'Mycenaean Trade with the South-Eastern Mediterranean', *Mélanges de l'Université Saint-Joseph, Beyrut*, 46, 2 (1970), 11–30 and *idem* in Crossland (forthcoming); see also ch. 2 n. 8.

12 McDonald and Rapp 1972, Perspectives, 240–61 and other chapters *passim*, espec. Chadwick, J.

13 Hutchinson, J. S. 'An Analogical Approach to the History of LH III', *Institute of Classical Studies, Mycenaean Seminar*, London 1975; see also Bettancourt, P. 'The End of the Greek Bronze Age', *Antiquity*, l, 197 (1976), 40–7 with full bibliography.

14 Iakovides, S. 'Centuries of Achaean Sovereignty', in Christopoulos 1974, 268–302, Decline 293; see nn. 5 and 12 above.

Chapter 4 *(pp. 81–103)*

1 Piggott 1965, 126.

2 Florescu, A. 'Contribution à la Connaissance de la civilisation de Noua', *Arch. Mold.* 2–3 (1964), 143–216; Romanian with English summary.

3 Rusu, M. 'Die Verbreitung der Bronzehorte in Transylvanian vom Ende der Bronzezeit bis die mittlere Hallstattzeit', *Dacia*, n.s. 7 (1963), 177–210; Mozsolics, A. *Bronzefunde des Karpatenbeckens*, Budapest 1967.

4 Snodgrass, A. 'The First European Body-Armour', in Boardman, J., Brown, M. A. and Powell, T. (eds.) *The European Community in Later Prehistory*, London 1971, 33–50 with bibliography; for Čaka itself see Točik, A. and Paulík, J. *Slov. Arch.*, 8 (1960), 59–124.

5 The ancestry of the IIa sword: Cowen, J. D. 'The Origins of the Flange-hilted Sword of Bronze in Continental Europe', *PPS*, 32 (1966), 262–312; *idem Actes du VIII ème Congrès des Sciences préhistoriques et*

protohistoriques, Belgrade 1973, III, 26–8. Viable alternatives are described in Holste, F. 'Die Bronzezeitlichen Vollgriffschwerter Bayerns' *Münchner Beiträge zur Vor- und Frühgeschichte*, I, 1953; and Reim, H. 'Die Spätbronzezeitlichen Griffplatten-, Dorn-, und Griffangelschwerter in Ostfrankreich', *Prähistorische Bronzefunde*, iv, 3, Munich 1974.

6 Type II (IIa) swords in the Aegean, Catling, H. 'Late Minoan Vases and Bronzes in Oxford', *BSA*, 63 (1968), 89–131, and *idem PPS*, 22 (1956), 102–25; *Antiquity*, xxxv (1961), 115–22.

7 Northern bronzes in general, Snodgrass, A. M. 'Metal-work as evidence for immigration in the Late Bronze Age', in Crossland and Birchall 1974, 209–14; Desborough, V. R. d'A. 'The Greek Mainland *c.* 1150–1000', *PPS*, 31 (1965), 213–28; Bouzek, J. *Alasia* I, Paris 1971, 433–48.

8 Catling, H. *BSA*, 63 (1968), 103.

9 Morricone, L. *Annuario* n.s., 27–8 (1965–6), 136. Catling n. 6, Desborough and Snodgrass n. 7 above.

10 Snodgrass, A. M. The Problem of the Epirot Chronology, in Crossland (forthcoming); Wardle, K. *Institute of Classical Studies, Mycenaean Seminar*, London 1975, 420–5. The northern frontier of Mycenaean Greece: Papadopoulos, Th. 'The Bronze Age in Epirus', *Dodona* 5, Iannina 1976, 271–338.

11 Sakellarakis, J. *Germania*, 53 (1975), 153; this pottery is reported to be most like Attic pots from Vourvatsi.

12 Bietti-Sestieri, A. M. 'The metal industry of continental Italy, 13th–11th century, and its Aegean connections', *PPS*, 39 (1973), 383–424.

13 Van Buren, A. 'Newsletter from Rome', *AJA*, 68 (1964), 373.

14 Taylour, Lord William, *Mycenaean Pottery in Italy and Adjacent Areas*, Cambridge 1958, 128, 183ff.

15 Bianco Peroni, V. *Die Schwerter in Italien: Le spade nell'Italia Continentale*, Munich 1970, pl. 70, ABC; Hencken 1968, vol. II, fig. 466; see also for pins, Desborough, V. R. d'A. op. cit. (n. 7 above); Bianco Peroni should be read with J. D. Cowen's review in *PPS*, 37, 1 (1971), 244–6; also n. 12 above.

16 Surbo see Macnamara, E. *PPS*, 36 (1970), 241–60; for the latest discussion of the winged axemould from Mycenae, Bietti-Sestieri, op. cit. (n. 12 above), 399. However Dr E. French states that the context of the axe mould is as good as one can get: the building was destroyed in the mid-13th century and the axe mould deposited then.

17 Guido 1963, 110 ff. Balmuth, M. 'The "Sea Peoples" Cyprus and Sardinia: geographical and chronological problems', in Crossland (forthcoming); for ingots see also ch. 3 n. 7. Ridgway D. *BSA Archaeological Reports* 1979–80 p. 58; Lo Sciavo, F. and Vagnetti, L. 'Micenei in Sardegna', *Atti Academia Nazionale dei Lincei* 35 (1980), 371–92; Macnamara, E., Ridgway, D. and F. R. 'The Bronze Hoard from S. Maria in Paulis, Sardinia', *British Museum Occasional Papers* no. 45, London 1984. Another wreck with oxhide ingots has been found at Kas west of Gelidonya with better possibilities for recovering the structure of the boat: Bass, G., Frey, D. and Pulak,

C. *Nautical Archaeology*, 13, 4 (Nov. 1984), 271–79.
18 Grosjean, R. 'Récents acquis archéologiques et iconographiques . . . en Corse', in Crossland (forthcoming); among the late Dr Grosjean's publications on Corsica see *La Corse avant l'Histoire*, Paris 1966, and *Antiquity*, xl (1966), 190 with references, *ibid*. 318 (review).

Chapter 5 *(pp. 105–137)*

1 Breasted 1906, vol. III paras 251–351; for discussion of Egyptian dates see Introduction n. 2.
2 Borchhardt 1972; Schachermeyr, F. *Ugaritica* VI, Paris 1969, 451–9; discussed in Sandars, N. K. 'Contrasted roles of sea and land transport', in Crossland (forthcoming).
3 See ch. 2 n. 6.
4 Houwink ten Cate, Ph. H. J. 1973, see ch. 3 n. 4; on the locations of Ahhiyawa see also Huxley 1960, *passim*; Gurney 1969, 46 ff.; Page, D. L. *History and the Homeric Iliad*, Berkeley 1959, 13 ff.; Wainwright, G. A. 'Some Sea-Peoples', *Journal of Egyptian Archaeology*, 47 (1961), 71–90.
5 Gurney 1969, 56; Wainwright 1959; Kitchen, K. A. op. cit. (ch. 2 n. 14), 90–1. In correspondence Dr Kitchen has emphasized that the inscription referring to the Peleset and Tursha (Teresh) as 'from the midst of the sea' employs the normal semitic word for sea, *yam*. (See also ch. 7). Lehmann, G. A. 'Die Šikalāiū, ein neues Zeugnis zu den "Seevölker" Heerfahrten im späten 13 JG.v.Chr.', *Ugarit Forschungen* 11, Neukirchen-Vluyn 1979, 481–94; also *Ugarit Forschungen* 10, 1978, 53.
6 Breasted 1906 and Wainwright 1961.
7 The Hymn of Victory of Merneptah also known as the 'Israel Stela', probably dating from Merneptah's fifth year, was found at Thebes and a fragmentary duplicate at Karnak, Pritchard 1969, 376–8.
8 Breasted 1906, vol. IV, para. 398.
9 Breasted 1906, vol. IV paras. 59–82; Edgerton and Wilson 1936.
10 Piggott, S. 'The Earliest Wheeled Vehicles and the Caucasian Evidence', *PPS*, 34 (1968), 266–318; Karachian, G. O. and Safian, P. G. *The Rock-Carvings of Syunik*, Yerevan 1970 (Armenian with Russian summary); and Littauer, M. A. and Crouwel, J. H. 'Early Metal Models of Wagons from the Levant', *Levant*, 5 (1973), 102–26.
11 Morris, D. R. *The Washing of the Spears*, London 1966; for the account of oxen used in the Zulu War, see also Sandars, N. K. op. cit. (n. 2 above) for further refs.; also correspondence with Mrs Littauer who thinks the extra pair of oxen were not in fact working, but being transported in this way; also Dunbar, S. *A History of Travel in America*, New York 1937, 209 ff., and letter from Mrs Arthur B. Tourtellot.
12 Nelson, H. H. 'The Naval Battle pictured at Medinet Habu', *JNES*, II (1943), 40–55; Casson, S. *Ships and Seamanship in the Ancient World*, Princeton 1971, 22, 36, 38 etc.; Barnett, R. 'Early Shipping in the Near East', *Antiquity*, xxxii (1958), 220–300; for the Caucasus, Formosov, A. A. *Essay in Primitive Art*,

Moscow 1969 (in Russian), fig. 3; see also Lethbridge, T. op. cit. (ch. 1 n. 6).
13 Breasted 1906, vol. IV, para. 44; see also Edgerton and Wilson 1936, 30–1.
14 Papyrus Harris, Breasted 1906, vol. IV, paras. 397–412.
15 Schachermeyr, F. op. cit. (n. 2 above), also Galling, F. *ibid*., 247–65 with full bibliography.

Chapter 6 *(pp. 139–155)*

1 Otten 1963. Singer, I. 'Western Anatolia in the 13th century B.C. according to the Hittite sources', *Anatolian Studies*, 33 (1983), 205–17.
2 Edgerton and Wilson 1936, pl. 46; also verbal communication from Prof. R. Crossland on possible alternative interpretations.
3 Otten 1963; Güterbock, H. G. op. cit. (ch. 2 n. 4); the text is KbO III 38.
4 Nougayrol, J., Laroche, E., Virolliaud, C. and Schaeffer, C. F. A. *Ugaritica*, vol. V, Paris 1968, 83–6, 105, 701–3 etc.
5 Catling, H. op. cit. (Introduction n. 4); for Enkomi see Dikaios 1969, for Kition, Karageorghis 1976. Karageorghis, V., Demas, M., King, B. Excavations at Maa-Palaeokastro, 1979–82 *Reports of the Dept. of Antiquities, Cyprus* 1982, Nicosia 1982.
6 Dikaios 1969, vol. II, 527 ff., level IIIB 12th century; the comparison with a small bronze figure from Kampos, Laconia (Marinatos, S. *Arch Delt.*, 18 (1963), I, 95 and pl. 35), is not very convincing – the gesture is quite unlike, as well as the scale.
7 Schaeffer, C. F. A. et al. *Ugaritica*, vol. III, Paris 1956, 19, fig. 122, for the Merneptah sword; for ashlar building at Ugarit, Schaeffer, C. F. A. *Ugaritica*, vol. IV, Paris 1962, *passim*, figs. 29, 66, 67, 68, pp. 105 and 150, nn. 18 and 19 for ashlar references.
8 Kenyon, K. *Royal Cities of the Old Testament*, London 1971, 5–9, 76 and 39–40, pls. 44–5 and 18–19.
9 Courtois, J.-C. 'Sur Divers Groupes de Vases Myceniens en Mediterranée Orientale', in *The Mycenaeans in the Eastern Mediterranean*, op. cit. (Introduction n. 4), 137–65. Courtois uses Furumark's date of 1230 for the change from LH IIIB to IIIC which of course affects all his other datings. His emphasis on what he calls 'Carian craters' and their relations to the 'rude style' of Cyprus is not very generally endorsed, though a link between Miletus and Ugarit is allowed. I had valuable advice from Mrs Hankey and Dr E. French on this vexing problem, see Introduction n. 5 and Karageorghis, V. *Nouveaux Documents pour l'Étude du Bronze Récent à Chypre*, Paris 1966, 258.

Chapter 7 *(pp. 157–177)*

1 Sandars, N. K. 'Later Aegean Bronze Swords', *AJA*, 67 (1963), 140 ff. At Tell es Saidiyeh the dirk was in tomb 2.
2 Kitchen, K. A. op. cit. (ch. 2 n. 14).
3 Schaeffer 1971, 506–16; Catling, H. 'A Cypriot bronze statuette in the Bomford Collection', in Schaeffer 1971, 15–31.

4 Goetze, A. 'Cilicians', *JCS*, 16 (1962), 48.

5 Barnett, R. D., 'The Sea-Peoples', in *Cambridge Ancient History*, vol. II, 1975, ch. 28, 363 Mopsus and the *Dnnym*. There is also a remark of Stephanus of Byzantium that Gaza was once known as Minoa, see Strange, J. 'Biblical Material on the Origin of the Philistines', in Crossland (forthcoming).

6 Yadin, Y. 'And Dan why did he remain in ships?', in Best, J. and Yadin, Y. *Henri Frankfort Foundation*, I, Amsterdam 1973, part 2.

7 If the conventional reading of the Biblical passages is kept, one might have to envisage the Danites as already in the north at a rather earlier date. I am grateful to Prof. A. Malamat for allowing me the benefit of his views and doubts on this problem.

8 de Vaux, R. 'La Phenicie et les Peuples de la Mer', *Mélanges de l'Université Saint-Joseph, Beyrut*, 45/29 (1969), 481–98; *idem*, 'Les Philistins, Autres Peuples de la Mer en Palestine', *Histoire ancienne d'Israël*, part 3, Paris 1971, 468–80.

9 Strange, J. in Crossland (forthcoming). Dr Strange refers to the possibility that these names could be titles of classes of soldier, 'butchers' and 'élite troops'.

10 There is a very large literature on the Philistines, see Kitchen, K. A. 'The Philistines', in Wiseman 1973, 53–78, with bibliography, and n. 13 below.

11 Amiran, R. *Ancient Pottery of the Holy Land*, Engl. lang. edn, Jerusalem 1969, see espec. ch. X, the Late Bronze Age; an earlier adoption of certain 'Philistine' shapes is pointed out (p. 267) with the corollary that only the decoration is new. Epstein, C. *Palestinian Bichrome Ware*, Leiden 1966. The suggestion made in Hoffman, H. (ed.) op. cit. (ch. 2 n. 8), that Palestinian bichrome ware originated in Cyprus does not materially affect the situation in the 12th century.

12 Tell Eitun has interesting native-type rock-cut tombs with much 'Philistine' pottery, Edelstein, G. and Glass, J. 'The Origin of Philistine Pottery based on petrographic analysis', *Jubilee volume for Shmuel Yeivin*, Tel Aviv 1973, 125–31 (Hebrew, English summary). The native pottery at Tell Eitun is without sand while the 'Philistine' pots – bird-decorated deep bowls, strainer-spouted flasks, pilgrim flasks, small bowls with antithetic spirals – do contain sand from the Palestinian coast, as for example at Ashdod. I have had much help with this site from Dr Edelstein. See also n. 20 below.

13 Muhly, J. D. 'The Philistines and their Pottery', in Crossland (forthcoming). 'Philistine' pottery has been discussed with its importance for dating Aegean history since Furumark 1941, 118; see espec. Desborough 1964, 209–14; also Dothan, J. 'Relations between Cyprus and the Philistine Coast', in *The Mycenaeans in the Eastern Mediterranean*, op. cit. (Introduction n. 4).

14 Dothan, M. *'Atiqot*, English Series, Jerusalem 1971, 9–10; Ashdod II–III, *idem, IEJ*, 19/4 (1969), *passim*, and 'The Beginning of the Sea-Peoples and of the Philistines', in Crossland (forthcoming). Much comparative material for the dating of all these sites is found in Dothan, T. 1982.

15 For Ashdod and Beth Shan I have been greatly helped by Mrs Hankey who is at present working on the Mycenaean pottery from the latter site. I owe to her and to Dr E. French knowledge of revised views on the Beth Shan level VI (locus 1586) stirrup jar as 'mature LH IIIC' probably dating some 30–50 years after the beginning of IIIC in the Argolid, but still pre-granary (see table II). It comes from one of the Egyptian garrison houses and is probably from near the end of level VI which has one subdivision. See James, F. W. *The Iron Age at Beth Shan*, Philadelphia 1966, 240, fig. 49, 4; also Hankey, V. 'Mycenaean Pottery in the Middle East', *BSA*, 62 (1967), 127; de Vaux, R. 1971, op. cit. (n. 8 above), 443–85.

16 Oren, E. *The Northern Cemetery at Beth Shan*, Leiden 1973, chs. 5 and 6. Dr Oren seems to prefer Denyen-Danuna to Peleset at Beth Shan. Anthropoid coffins were at one time identified with the Sea Peoples, but are now known to antedate the raids, though late debased coffins lasted into the 11th century. They evidently stem from Egypt and were introduced to Palestine by Egyptian garrisons. Dothan, T. 'Egyptian and Philistine Burial Customs', in Crossland (forthcoming); *idem*, 'Anthropoid Clay Coffins from a Late Bronze Age Cemetery near Deir el-Balah', *IEJ*, 23 (1973), 129–46.

17 Hankey, V. op. cit. (n. 15 above), 131, and correspondence with the writer.

18 Tell Fara: Waldbaum, J. D. 'Philistine Tombs at Tell Fara and their Aegean prototypes', *AJA*, 70 (1966), 331–40.

19 Strange, J. see n. 9 above.

20 Edelstein, G. and Glass, J. (n. 12 above); for Tell Qasile, Mazar, A. *IEJ*, 23 (1973), 65–71; see also Hankey, V. n. 15 above for references to the older excavations. An iron knife from Tell Qasile has an ivory ring-handle rather like a well-known bronze knife found in a tomb at Ialysos, Rhodes; I am grateful to Dr A. Mazar for this information. Stratum XII at Tell Qasile is referred to the 12th century but could perhaps be a little later; it has produced 'Philistine' pottery, much of it very devolved. I am indebted to Dr J. Calloway for information on iron, probably 12th century, at Ai and Tell Reddon.

21 Waldbaum, J. C. 'Hittites, Philistines and the Introduction of Iron in the Eastern Mediterranean', in Crossland (forthcoming); Maxwell-Hyslop, K. R. 'Assyrian Sources of Iron', *Iraq*, 36 (1974), 139–54. At Hala Sultan Tekké an iron hook was apparently found in a LC IIC context: Åstrom P. et al. 'Hala Sultan Tekké I', *Studies in Mediterranean Archaeology*, 45/1, Göteborg 1976, 117, 123–5; Catling, H. 'Kouklia: Evreti Tomb 8', *BCH*, 92 (1968), 1, 162–9.

22 For iron in the Aegean see Snodgrass 1971, ch. 5; *idem*, 'Barbarian Europe and the Early Iron Age', *PPS*, 31 (1965), 229–40; Desborough 1972, 340.

Chapter 8 *(pp. 179–195)*

1 Hesiod, *The Works and Days* (transl. Wender, D.), Harmondsworth 1973, 182–95.

2 Desborough 1964 and Snodgrass, A. op. cit. (ch. 7 n. 22: 1971).

3 Chadwick, J. 'The Defence of Pylos against Sea-Borne Attack', in Crossland (forthcoming); *idem*, McDonald and Rapp 1972, the o-ka tablets p. 102; *idem* 1976, 191.

4 Popham, M. R. and Sackett, L. H. (eds.) *Excavations at Lefkandi, 1964–66*, London 1968.

5 Souvinou-Inwood, C. 'Movements of Population in Attica at the end of the Mycenaean period', in Crossland and Birchall 1973, 215–24.

6 Hutchinson, J. S. op. cit. (ch. 3 n. 12).

7 Chadwick, J. 'The Mycenaean Dorians', *Institute of Classical Studies, Mycenaean Seminar*, London 1975.

8 Souvinou-Inwood, C. 'The Problem of the Dorians in Tradition and Archaeology', in Crossland (forthcoming).

9 Bietti-Sestieri, A. M. op. cit. (ch. 4 n. 12); Harding, A. 'The extent and effects of contact between Mycenaean Greece and the rest of Europe', Cambridge 1974, unpubl. dissertation; Macnamara, E. 'A group of bronzes from Surbo', *PPS*, 36 (1970), 241–60.

10 Tritsch, F. ' "The Sackers of Cities" and the "Movement of Populations" ', in Crossland and Birchall 1973, 215–31.

11 Iakovides 1975; many Levantine and Cypriot trinkets, beads, seals and ivories occur in the tombs, e.g. op. cit. vol. III, pls. 23, 47, 48, 61, 65 etc.

12 Wainright, G. A. 'The Teresh, the Etruscans and Asia Minor', *Anatolian Studies*, 9 (1959), 197–213, espec. 106.

13 Luce 1975, 90–1.

14 Hope-Simpson, R. and Lazenby, H. F. *The Catalogue of Ships in Homer*, Oxford 1970; Page, D. L. *History and the Homeric Iliad*, London and Berkeley 1963; Luce 1975, 87–94.

15 Luce 1975, 90.

16 Rutter, J. 'Ceramic Evidence for Northern Intruders in Southern Greece at the Beginning of the Late Helladic IIIC Period', *AJA*, 79 (1975), 17–32, a very thorough discussion with full references; see also Hood, M. S. F. 'Buckelkeramik at Mycenae?', *Festschrift for Ernst Grumach*, Berlin 1967, 120–31; *idem*, 'Mycenaean settlement in Cyprus and the coming of the Greeks', in *The Mycenaeans in the Eastern Mediterranean*, op. cit. (Intro. n. 4), 40–50. *Kummerkeramik* was used to describe coarse handmade pottery by E. Sprockhoff, 'Niedersachsens Bedeutung für die Bronzezeit Westeuropas', *BRGK*, 31 (1941),

1–128. Catling, H. 'Barbarian pottery from the Mycenaean settlement at the Menelaion, Sparta', *BSA*, 76 (1981), 71–82; Popham, M. and Sackett, L. *Excavations at Lefkandi, Euboea, 1964–66*, 18.

17 Souvinou-Inwood, C. op. cit. (n. 8 above). A tentative but attractive suggestion has been made by Dr E. French to account for the 'hand-made burnished wares' of Troy and the mainland as being the work of foreign slave-women, perhaps the 'women from Asia' referred to in the Pylos texts as female workers there: French, E. Paper given to the Fourth International Colloquium on Aegean Prehistory, Sheffield 1977. The subject of the colloquium was Troy; this book was already in the press when it took place, but though much could be added I do not think anything need be removed in consequence. For the Adriatic source see Hallager, B. 'Italians in Late Bronze Age Khania, *Atti XXII Convegno di Studi sulla Magna Grecia e Mondo Micene*, Taranto 1983; Kilian, K. 'Civilta micenea in Grecia: nuovi aspetti storici ed interculturali', *Atti Convegno Magna Grecia*, Taranto 1983.

18 The Trojan chronology is much debated, see discussion in Sandars, N. K. 'From Bronze Age to Iron Age', in Boardman, J., Brown, M. and Powell, T. (eds.) op. cit. (ch. 4 n. 4), 17f. and n. 47. Nylander, C. 'The Fall of Troy', *Antiquity*, xxxvi (1963), 6–11; Luce 1975, 135 ff.; Stubbings, F. in *Cambridge Ancient History*, vol. I, 3rd edn, Cambridge 1975, ch. VI section III, Chronology, The Aegean Bronze Age.

19 N. 17 above, Sheffield Colloquium. For Babadag, see Morintz, S. 'Quelques problèmes, concernant la période ancienne du Hallstatt en bas Danube à la lumière des fouilles de Babadag', *Dacia*, n.s. 8 (1964), 101. For the Maritsa see Čičikova, M. 'Nouvelles données sur la culture Thrace de l'Époque du Hallstatt en Bulgarie du Sud', *Thracia*, 1 (1972), 79–100, with references. Kančev, M. 'Matériaux du site préhistorique de l'âge du Bronze recent . . . près d'Asenovec', *Thracia*, 3 (1974), 65–76; Stafanovich, M. *Thracia*, 3 (1974), 101–5; this volume contains papers given at the First International Congress of Thracology, Sofia 1972, many concerned with Troy and the Balkan Late Bronze Age, by, among others, B. Hänsel, S. Morintz, A. Alexandrescu.

20 Snodgrass, A. 1971, op. cit. (ch. 7 n. 22); Sandars, N. K. 'Thracians, Phrygians and Iron', *Thracia*, 3 (1974), 195–202.

Select bibliography

For abbreviations see p. 208

Acts of the International Archaeological Symposium 'The Mycenaeans in the Eastern Mediterranean', Nicosia 1972, Nicosia 1973

Atzeni, E. et al. Ichnussa: La Sardegna dalle Origini all'età classica, Milan 1984

Balmuth, M. and Rowlands, R. Jr (eds.) Studies in Sardinian Archaeology, Michigan 1984

Bittel, K. et al. Boğazköy, 4 vols., Berlin 1935–69

Blegen, C. and Rawson, M. The Palace of Nestor at Pylos in Western Messenia, Princeton 1966; see also Lang, M.

Blegen, C. (ed.) et al. Troy: Excavations conducted by the University of Cincinnati 1932–38, 4 vols., Princeton 1950–8

Borchhardt, J. Homerische Helme, Mainz 1972

Bouzek, J. Homerisches Griechenland, Prague 1969

Braudel, F. The Mediterranean and the Mediterranean World in the Age of Philip II, Paris 1949, transl. London 1972

Breasted, J. H. Ancient Records of Egypt, vols. III and IV, Chicago 1906

Cambridge Ancient History, vol. II, 3rd edn, Cambridge 1975

Chadwick, J. The Mycenaean World, Cambridge 1976

Christopoulos, G. A. (ed.) A History of the Hellenic World: I Prehistory and Protohistory, Athens and London 1974

Crossland, R. A. and Birchall, A. (eds.) Bronze Age Migrations in the Aegean, Proceedings of the First International Colloquium on Aegean Prehistory (Sheffield 1970), London and Park Ridge 1973

Crossland, R. A. (ed.) The Sea Peoples, Proceedings of the Third International Colloquium on Aegean Prehistory (Sheffield 1973), forthcoming

Desborough, V. R. d'A. The Last Mycenaeans and their successors, Oxford 1964.

— The Greek Dark Ages, London 1972

Dikaios, P. Enkomi Excavations 1948–58, vols. I–III, Mainz 1969

Dothan, M. and Freedman, D. N. Ashdod I–III, 'Atiqot English Series, Tel Aviv 1967–71

Dothan, T. The Philistines and their Material Culture, Yale, London, Jerusalem 1982

Edgerton, W. F. and Wilson, J. A. Historical Records of Ramesses III, The Texts of Medinet Habu, vols. I and II, Chicago 1936

French, E. B. 'A Group of Late Helladic IIIB1 pottery from Mycenae', BSA, 61 (1966)

— 'A Group of Late Helladic IIIB2 Pottery', BSA, 64 (1969)

— 'The First Phase of LH IIIC1', Arch. Anz. (1969/2)

— 'A reassessment of the Mycenaean Pottery at Tarsus', AS, 25 (1975)

Furumark, A. Mycenaean Pottery 1, Analysis and Classification; 2, The Chronology of Mycenaean Pottery, Stockholm 1941, reprinted 1972

Garstang, J. and Gurney, O. The Geography of the Hittite Empire, London 1959

Gray, J. The Legacy of Canaan, The Ras Shamra Texts and their relevance to The Old Testament, 2nd edn, Leiden 1965

Guido, M. Sardinia, London and New York 1963

Gurney, O. The Hittites, Harmondsworth 1969

Hencken, H. Tarquinia, Villanovans and Early Etruscans, Cambridge, Mass. 1968

Huxley, G. L. Achaeans and Hittites, Oxford 1960

Iakovides, Sp. Perati: The cemetery, Athens 1970

Karageorghis, V. Excavations at Kition I, The Tombs, Nicosia 1974

— Kition, London and New York 1976

Kilian, K. and Podzuweit, C. 'Ausgrabungen in Tiryns', Archäologische Anzeiger, Berlin 1978–1981

Lang, M. The Palace of Nestor at Pylos, 2, The Frescoes, Princeton 1969

Luce, J. V. Homer and the Heroic Age, London and New York 1975

McDonald, W. and Rapp, G. Jnr (eds.) The University of Minnesota Messenia Expedition, Minneapolis 1972

Macqueen, J. G. The Hittites and their contemporaries in Asia Minor, London and Boulder, Colorado 1976

Malamat, A. 'The Egyptian Decline in Canaan' and 'The Period of the Judges', in Mazar 1971

Mazar, B. (ed.) The World History of the Jewish People, first series, Ancient Times, III, Tel Aviv 1971

Mozsolics, A. Bronze- und Goldfunde des Karpatenbeckens, Depotfund Horizont von Forrø und Opalyi, Budapest 1973

Müller-Karpe, H. (ed.) Geschichte des 13 und 12 Jahrhundert v. Christ, Frankfurt Colloquium, February 1976, Munich 1977

Nelson, H. H. The Earliest Historical Records of Ramses III, Medinet Habu, vol. I, Chicago 1930; vol. II, Chicago 1932

Otten, H. 'Neue Quellen zum Ausklang des hethitischen Reiches', *MDOG*, 94 (1963), 1–23

Piggott, S. *Ancient Europe*, Edinburgh 1965, Chicago
1966

Pritchard, J. B. (ed.) *Ancient Near Eastern Texts
Relating to the Old Testament*, 3rd edn, Princeton
1969

Schachermeyr, F. *Die Mykenische Zeit und die
Gesittung von Thera, 2, Die Ägaische Frühzeit*,
Vienna 1976

— *Griechenland im Zeitalter der Wanderungen vom
Ende der Mykenischen Ära bis auf die Dorier*, Vienna
1980

— *Die Levante im Zeitalter der Wanderungen vom 13.
bis zum 11. Jahrhundert v. Chr*, Vienna 1982

Schaeffer, C. F. A. *Mission de Ras Shamra, Ugaritica*,
vols I–VI, Paris 1939–69

— *Enkomi-Alasia*, Nouvelles missions en Chypre
1945–50, Paris 1952

— *Alasia I*, Mission archéologique d'Alasia IV, Paris
1971

Smith, G. A. *The Historical Geography of the Holy
Land*, London 1894

Snodgrass, A. M. *The Dark Age of Greece*, Edinburgh
1971

de Vaux, R. *Histoire Ancienne d'Israël des origines à
l'installation en Canaan, 2, la période des Juges*, Paris
1971–3

Vermeule, E. *Greece in the Bronze Age*, Chicago 1964

Wainright, G. A. 'The Teresh, The Etruscans and
Asia Minor', *AS*, 9 (1959), 197–213

— 'Some Sea-Peoples', *JEA*, 47 (1961)

— 'The Meshwesh', *JEA*, 48 (1962)

— 'A Teucrian at Salamis in Cyprus', *The Journal of
Hellenic Studies*, 83 (1963)

Wardle, K. 'Excavations at Assiros 1975–9', *BSA*
(1980)

Winton Thomas, D. *Documents from Old Testament
Times*, Oxford 1967

Wiseman, D. J. (ed.) *Peoples of Old Testament Times*,
Oxford 1973

Wreszinski, W. *Atlas zur Altaegyptischen Kultur-
geschichte*, Leipzig 1935

Yadin, Y. *The Art of War*, London 1963

Acknowledgments

The task of giving as fair as possible an account of the many topics touched on in this history was from the first a really daunting one; but it has been immeasurably lightened by the many friends and scholars whose guidance and advice I have sought, even if I have not invariably followed it. I am greatly in their debt for the prevention of error and invention of solutions to illuminate dark places. Among those who have been generous with their time and all kinds of help, I am especially grateful to Dr Mervyn Popham, Professor Sp. Iakovides, Drs Oliver Gurney, Kenneth Kitchen, and Vassos Karageorghis, Mrs K. R. Maxwell-Hyslop, Mr Sinclair Hood, the Hon.

Mrs Vronwy Hankey, Dr E. B. French, Professor Moshe and Dr Trude Dothan, also Professor Anthony Snodgrass, Professor A. Malamat, Drs A. Mazar, E. Oren, G. Edelstein, Mr Vincent Desborough and Mr Ralph Hoddinott, Professor A. Fasani, Dr K. Nicolaou, Dr H. Catling, Dr K. Kilian, Dr Th. Papadopoulos, and Dr S. Sherratt.

I must also thank especially Mrs Marian Cox for her scrupulous line-drawings, Miss Hebe Jerrold who made the index and the staff of Thames and Hudson for their help and encouragement throughout. I also thank Mrs C. M. Walker and Mrs W. Burnett who typed the text.

List of illustrations

For abbreviations see p. 208

129 Ingot-god, Enkomi. Published by permission of the Director of Antiquities and the Cyprus Museum.

130 Bronze warrior, Sulcis, Sardinia. Museo Preistorico Luigi Pigorini, Rome. Photo Fototeca Unione.

131 Detail of the ivory box from Enkomi (ill. 18), showing a Shekelesh (?).

132 Seal with warrior, Enkomi. Published by permission of the Director of Antiquities and the Cyprus Museum.

Index